Adobe® InDesign® CS2

CLASSROOM
IN A BOOK®

www.adobepress.com

Adobe

Lesson files . . . and so much more

The *Adobe InDesign CS2 Classroom in a Book* CD includes the lesson files that you'll need to complete the exercises in this book, as well as other content to help you learn more about Adobe InDesign and use it with greater efficiency and ease. The diagram below represents the contents of the CD, which should help you locate the files you need.

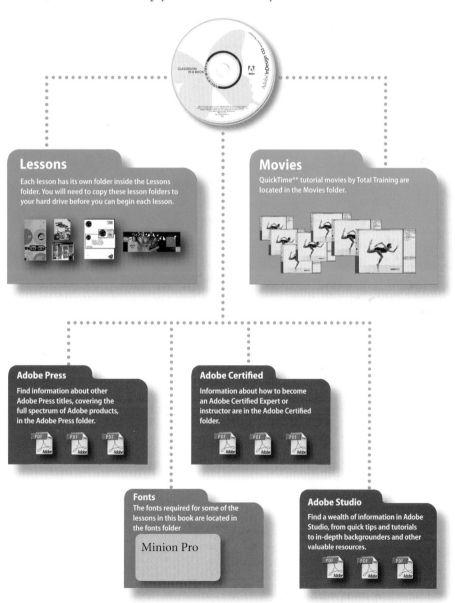

Lessons
Each lesson has its own folder inside the Lessons folder. You will need to copy these lesson folders to your hard drive before you can begin each lesson.

Movies
QuickTime** tutorial movies by Total Training are located in the Movies folder.

Adobe Press
Find information about other Adobe Press titles, covering the full spectrum of Adobe products, in the Adobe Press folder.

Adobe Certified
Information about how to become an Adobe Certified Expert or instructor are in the Adobe Certified folder.

Fonts
The fonts required for some of the lessons in this book are located in the fonts folder

Minion Pro

Adobe Studio
Find a wealth of information in Adobe Studio, from quick tips and tutorials to in-depth backgrounders and other valuable resources.

*** The latest version of Apple QuickTime can be downloaded from www.apple.com/support/downloads/quicktime652.html.*

Contents

Getting Started

What's New in Adobe InDesign CS2

A Quick Tour of Adobe InDesign CS2

1   Getting to Know the Work Area

2   Setting Up Your Document

3   Working with Frames

4   Importing and Editing Text

7	**Working with Styles**

8	**Importing and Linking Graphics**

9 Creating Tables

10   Working with Transparency

11   Working with Long Documents

12   Printing and PDF Exporting

13   Using XML

14 **Working with Adobe Bridge and Version Cue**

Getting Started

Welcome to Adobe InDesign CS2. InDesign is a powerful design and production tool that offers precision, control, and seamless integration with other Adobe professional graphics software. Using InDesign, you can produce professional-quality, full-color documents on high-volume color printing presses, or print to a wide range of output devices and formats, including desktop printers and high-resolution imaging devices. Also, you can create PDF files, and convert your documents for use on the Internet by exporting layouts to Adobe GoLive or XML.

Writers, artists, designers, and publishers can communicate to a broader audience than ever before and through an unprecedented variety of media. InDesign supports this with its seamless integration with Creative Suite 2 applications: *Adobe Photoshop*, *Adobe Illustrator*, *Adobe Acrobat*, and *Adobe GoLive*. The *Adobe InDesign CS2 Classroom in a Book* introduces and describes new features, workflows, and techniques that support this new wave of publishing.

About Classroom in a Book

Adobe InDesign CS2 Classroom in a Book is part of the official training series for Adobe graphics and publishing software from Adobe Systems, Inc.

The lessons are designed so that you can learn at your own pace. If you're new to Adobe InDesign CS2, you'll learn the fundamentals you'll need to master to put the program to work. If you've already been using Adobe InDesign CS2, you'll find that Classroom in a Book teaches many advanced features, including tips and techniques for using this exciting design tool.

Each lesson provides step-by-step instructions for creating a specific project. You can follow the book from start to finish, or do only the lessons that meet your interests and needs. Each lesson concludes with a review section summarizing what you've covered.

Prerequisites

Before beginning to use *Adobe InDesign CS2 Classroom in a Book*, you should have a working knowledge of your computer and its operating system. Make sure you know how to use the mouse and standard menus and commands, and also how to open, save, and close files. If you need to review these techniques, see the printed or online documentation included with your Windows or Mac OS documentation.

Installing the program

You must purchase the Adobe InDesign CS2 software separately. For complete instructions on installing the software, see the "How to Install" Readme file in the application CD.

The Classroom in a Book lesson files use the fonts that installed with Adobe InDesign CS2. If it is necessary to reinstall these font files, you can perform a custom installation from your Adobe InDesign software CD to reinstall only the fonts. See the "How to Install" Readme file in the application CD.

Restoring default preferences

To ensure that the tools and palettes function exactly as described in the lessons, you must delete or deactivate (by renaming) the InDesign Defaults file and the InDesign SavedData file.

The InDesign Defaults file and the InDesign SavedData file control how palettes and command settings appear on your screen when you open the Adobe InDesign program. Each time you exit Adobe InDesign, the position of the palettes and certain command settings are recorded in these files. To ensure that the tools and palettes function exactly as described in this book, you can delete the current InDesign Defaults and InDesign SavedData files at the beginning of each lesson. If they don't already exist, Adobe InDesign creates new versions of these files the next time you start the program.

To delete your preferences to reset to their original default values

1   Start Adobe InDesign CS2.

2   Immediately select Ctrl+Alt+Shift (Windows) or Ctrl+Option+Command+Shift (Mac OS) as the program is starting.

3   Click Yes to delete the InDesign preference files.

Important: If you want to save your current InDesign CS2 settings, rename the defaults files rather than deleting them. When you are ready to restore the settings, change the names back and make sure that the files are located in the InDesign CS2 folder (Windows) or the Preferences folder (Mac OS). If you rename the default files, you will be able to revert to your own default settings after completing your InDesign CS2 Classroom in a Book exercises.

To save your preferences

1 If InDesign is running, choose File > Exit (Windows) or InDesign > Quit InDesign (Mac OS).

2 To locate the InDesign defaults files, do one of the following:

• (Windows) Double-click to open your hard drive containing your operating system folder. Open the Documents and Settings folder and locate the folder for the user name that you created when you installed your computer. Open this folder and locate the Application Data folder and open the Adobe Folder. Inside the Adobe folder, locate the InDesign folder and open the Version 4.0 folder. The InDesign Defaults and InDesign SavedData files are stored in this folder. You may need to set your operating system to show hidden files to make them visible. To do this, Choose Tools > Folder Options and click the View tab then select the Show hidden files and folders radio button. The complete path to locate these files is typically: c\\Documents and Setttings\user name\ Application Data\Adobe\Indesign\Version 4.0. Rename these files by adding the word "backup" to their names. Do not delete or change the name of any other InDesign files in this folder.

• (Mac OS) Open the hard drive containing your operating system and locate your user folder that was created when you installed your operating system. Open this user folder and locate the Library folder. Inside the Library folder, open the Preferences folder and then locate and open the Adobe InDesign folder. Within the InDesign folder is the Version 4.0 folder. The InDesign Defaults and InDesign SavedData files are stored in this folder. Rename these files by adding the word "backup" to their names. Do not delete or change the name of any other InDesign files in this folder. The complete path to locate these files is typically:
\\Users\user name\Library\Preferences\Adobe InDesign\Version 4.0.

If you renamed the defaults files to preserve them, you can return to your previous settings by first deleting the newest copies of the InDesign Defaults and InDesign SavedData files. Then restore the original names of the files you renamed in the steps above.

Copying the Classroom in a Book files

The *Adobe InDesign CS2 Classroom in a Book* CD includes folders containing all the electronic files for the lessons in the book. Each lesson has its own folder; you must copy the folders to your hard disk to complete the lessons. To save room on your disk, you can install only the folder necessary for each lesson as you need it, and remove it when you're done. To install the Classroom in a Book lesson files, do the following:

1   Insert the *Adobe InDesign CS2 Classroom in a Book* CD into your CD-ROM drive.

2   Browse the contents and locate the Lessons folder.

3   Do one of the following:

- To copy all the lesson files, drag the Lessons folder from the CD onto your hard disk.

- To copy only individual lesson files, first create a new folder on your hard disk and name it InDesignCIB. Then, drag the lesson folder or folders that you want to copy from the CD into the InDesignCIB folder on your hard disk.

If you are installing the files in Windows 2000, you may need to unlock the lesson files before you can use them. If you use Windows 2000 and encounter locked files, proceed to Step 4.

4   (Windows 2000 only) Unlock the files you copied:

- Right-click the folder that contains the locked files, such as Lessons, and choose Properties from the contextual menu.

- In the Attributes area of the File Properties dialog box, deselect (uncheck) the Read-only check box, and then click Apply.

- In the Confirm Attributes Changes dialog box, select the option "Apply changes to this folder, subfolders, and files."

- Click OK to close the Confirm Attributes Changes dialog box, and click OK again to close the File Properties dialog box.

This final step is not necessary for Windows XP or Mac OS users.

Note: As you complete each lesson, you will overwrite the start files. If you want to restore the original files, recopy the corresponding Lesson folder from the Adobe InDesign CS2 Classroom in a Book *CD to the Lessons folder on your hard drive.*

Installing the Classroom in a Book fonts

To ensure that the lesson files appear on your system with the correct fonts, you may need to install the Classroom in a Book font files. The fonts are in the Fonts folder on the *Adobe InDesign CS2 Classroom in a Book* CD. If you already have these fonts on your system, you do not need to install them.

Use the following procedure to install the fonts on your computer.

1	Insert the *Adobe InDesign CS2 Classroom in a Book* CD into your CD-ROM drive.

2	Select all of the fonts in the Fonts folder on the CD and drag them into the Fonts folder located in the InDesign CS2 program folder on your hard disk. You can select and drag multiple fonts to install them, but you cannot drag the entire folder to install the fonts.

For more information see Installing Fonts in InDesign Help.

Color Profiles

As you open individual lesson files, you may receive an Embedded Profile Mismatch warning. These warnings are normal, and you should click OK to dismiss the warning if one appears while opening a Classroom in a Book exercise document.

InDesign CS2 supports a variety of settings to accommodate your color management needs. If the settings on your computer do not match those used in creating the document, InDesign uses these messages to alert you when the document is opened. For more information, see About missing and mismatched color profiles in InDesign Help.

Additional resources

Adobe InDesign CS2 Classroom in a Book is not meant to replace documentation that comes with the program. Only the commands and options used in the lessons are explained in this book. For comprehensive information about program features, refer to these resources:

•	InDesign Help, which you can view by choosing Help > InDesign Help. For more information, see Lesson 1, "Getting to Know the Work Area."

•	Training and support resources on the Adobe web site at Adobe.com, which you can view by choosing Help > Online Support if you have a connection to the Internet.

Adobe Certification

The Adobe Training and Certification Programs are designed to help Adobe customers improve and promote their product-proficiency skills. The Adobe Certified Expert (ACE) program is designed to recognize the high-level skills of expert users. Adobe Certified Training Providers (ACTP) use only Adobe Certified Experts to teach Adobe software classes. Available in either ACTP classrooms or on site, these programs are the best way to master Adobe products. For Adobe Certified Training Programs information, visit the Partnering with Adobe web site at Partners.Adobe.com.

What's New in Adobe InDesign CS2

Welcome to Adobe InDesign CS2. This is a significant upgrade to an extremely powerful page layout application. This book provides you with details you need to effectively create layouts using Adobe InDesign CS2. The *Adobe InDesign CS2 Classroom in a Book* has been revised and updated to incorporate new capabilities and features that have been added to the software. If you're already familiar with previous versions of Adobe InDesign, you'll find a wealth of new features to make you more productive.

Here we've assembled an overview of our favorite additions to InDesign CS2. The complete list of new features is much more extensive, and you can find it at Adobe.com.

Object Styles

If you use paragraph and character styles, which are sometimes called style sheets in other applications, you'll appreciate the new capability of object styles. With object styles, you can quickly apply multiple attributes to objects used in your InDesign CS2 layouts, including text frames and picture frames. This provides for one-click application of multiple attributes to a frame, such as a colored background, border, type style, and even drop shadows.

Adobe Bridge and Creative Suite integration

Adobe InDesign CS2 provides improved integration with the other applications in the Creative Suite2: Photoshop, Illustrator, GoLive, and Acrobat. You can now share color swatches and color management settings among these applications, use the improved Version Cue to manage your documents, and take advantage of the new Adobe Bridge to view and organize your documents. The Adobe Bridge is used throughout this Classroom in a Book and is covered in more detail in Lesson 14, "Working with Adobe Bridge and Version Cue."

Improved text handling

Significant enhancements have been made to text importing and handling capabilities. You'll find that InDesign CS2 imports most common file formats, including .xls, .doc, and .txt. Many of these files now import faster and have improved options that allow you to retain or remove text formatting at the time it is imported. With styled .doc files, you can choose to map styles applied in Microsoft Word to the styles used in your InDesign CS2 layout. Similar enhancements have been made for text that is copied and pasted into InDesign, as you can now choose to remove or retain the text formatting at the time text is pasted into your layout. Lessons 4 and 5 cover InDesign's text handling capabilities.

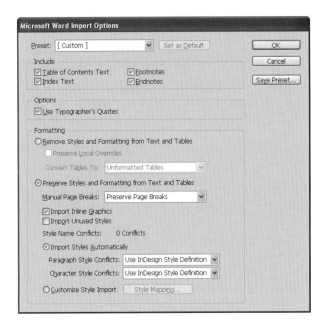

Other text handling improvements include the addition of an automatic bullet and numbering feature, making it easier to build and edit lists. The new data merge capability makes it easy to create customized letters and documents. Additionally, InDesign CS2 adds robust support for anchored objects that are part of a text frame. Learn more about anchored text frames in Lesson 3, "Working with Frames."

Enhanced graphics handling

The enhancements extend to graphic handling and support. InDesign now provides options for enabling or disabling the viewing and printing of individual layers, and layer comps, created in Photoshop. Layers can be enabled or disabled at the time an image is imported, or at any time after it is placed in the layout. Improved link management features make it easier to locate and work with dependent files that have been placed into your layouts. Lesson 8 also covers these important new features.

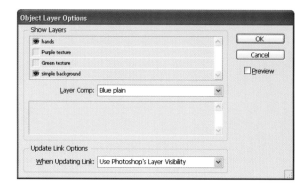

XML features

More advanced users will appreciate the XML enhancements. Imported XML files can be linked, providing notification if the XML foundation for a document has been modified. InDesign CS2 now provides more robust support of InDesign's table capabilities in the XML structure, and objects and groups can be saved as XML snippets. Discover the XML capabilities in Lesson 13, "Using XML."

While this list is by no means a complete description of the new features of InDesign CS2, it exemplifies Adobe's commitment to providing the best tools possible for your publishing needs. We hope you enjoy working with InDesign CS2 as much as we do.

—The *InDesign CS2 Classroom in a Book* Team

This interactive demonstration of Adobe InDesign CS2 provides an overview of key features of the program. It should take you approximately 45 minutes to complete.

A Quick Tour of Adobe InDesign CS2

Getting started

You'll start the tour by opening a partially completed document. You'll add the finishing touches to this six-page article on Mexican folk art, written for an imaginary travel magazine. If you have not already done so in this session, you should restore the default preferences for InDesign CS2. Restoring default preferences ensures that the tools and palettes function exactly as described in this lesson. After you learn how to use InDesign CS2, this step is no longer necessary.

Note: If you are new to InDesign, you might want to begin with Lesson 1, "Getting to Know the Work Area."

1   Delete or reset the InDesign CS2 Defaults file and the InDesign CS2 SavedData file, following the procedure in "Restoring default preferences" on page 2.

2   Start Adobe InDesign CS2. When the Welcome Screen appears, choose Close.

3   Click the Go to Bridge button (📑) in the Control palette. As a default, the Control palette is located at the top of the InDesign work area. Using the Folders tab, in the upper left of the Bridge window, locate the Lesson_00 folder in the InDesignCIB folder you copied from the InDesign CS2 Classroom in a Book CD to your hard disk.

Note: If you did not purchase InDesign CS2 as a part of the Creative Suite 2 package, see the note on page 15.

4   In the Lesson_00 folder, click once on the Tour_done.indd file in the right side of the Bridge window. On the left side of the Bridge window in the Metadata tab, information about the Tour_done.indd file is displayed.

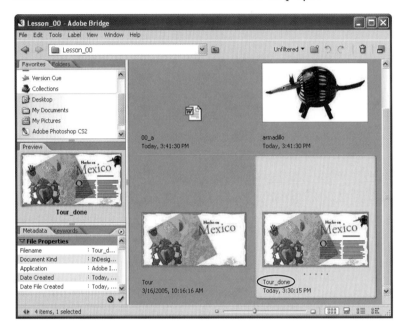

You can view information about the document including colors, fonts, version of InDesign used to create it, and more, by scrolling through the panes on the left side of the Bridge window. You can scale the preview thumbnails by using the scrollbar at the bottom of the Bridge window.

5   Double-click on the Tour_done.indd file to open it.

The finished tour document.

Note: While the Bridge provides a convenient way to access your files and see more information about each file without needing to open it, you can also open files by choosing File > Open at any time. It is not necessary to use Bridge to access your InDesign files, although we recommend using it to work with your files. Read more about Adobe Bridge in Lesson 14, "Working with Adobe Bridge and Version Cue."

Press Alt+Ctrl+0 (zero) (Windows) or Option+Command+0 (Mac OS) to make the first page spread fit in the InDesign window. This is the 6-page tour file that you will complete in this lesson. You can leave it open for reference, or choose File > Close.

Viewing the lesson document

1   Adobe Bridge remains open until you Exit from the application. Return to the Adobe Bridge application and double-click on Tour.indd file. The Tour file opens.

2   Choose View > Fit Spread in Window. The Fit Spread in Window option displays all the adjoining pages in a spread.

The first spread (pages 2 and 3) appears on your screen. You'll now look at the rest of the 6-page article using several navigation methods. First, you'll use the Navigator palette, which is useful for changing the view magnification.

3   Choose File > Save As. Choose Lesson_00 in the Save As window and enter the name **Tour_lesson**. Leave the file type as InDesign CS2 document, and choose Save.

4   Choose Window > Object & Layout > Navigator to open the Navigator palette.

5 Position the pointer, click on the Palette-menu button (⦿) on the right side of the palette and choose View All Spreads.

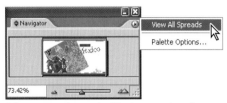

Like many palettes, the Navigator palette has a menu that displays additional options.

6 Drag the lower right corner of the palette down and to the right. Expanding the size of the palette provides a better view of the spreads.

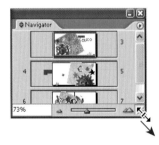

7 In the Navigator palette, click the center of the middle spread to view pages 4 and 5. Notice the red view box in the Navigator palette. This box shows which area of the document is displayed. By rolling over the red view box, the cursor changes to a hand icon, allowing you to reposition the view.

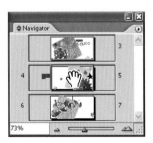

The slider at the bottom of the palette controls the magnification of the document being displayed. Moving the slider to the right increases the magnification, while moving to the left decreases the magnification. The red view box changes size as you move the slider left or right. The red view box appears smaller at greater magnification levels.

8　Choose View > Fit Page in Window. You can see that the magnification displayed in the Navigator palette is automatically updated. You can use the Navigator palette to easily move between pages in your documents, or to move to specific sections of a page.

Now we'll look at the Pages palette, which is another useful tool for navigating in your documents. You'll use the Pages palette throughout this tour, so you'll separate the Pages palette from the docking area.

9　Click the Pages palette tab and drag it to the left, away from the other palettes. Release the palette when it is separated from the docking area. This causes the palette to detach from the docking area on the right. Now it can be positioned in a different location.

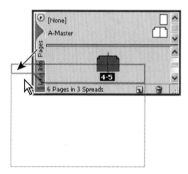

💡 *Feel free to move and rearrange palettes in this Quick Tour as needed. You can move a palette by dragging its title bar. You can place a palette in the docking area on the right side of the document window by dragging a palette by its tab to this portion of the window. You can also minimize the palette by clicking on the Minimize button, or close the palette by clicking on the Close button on the top bar of a palette that has been separated from the docking area.*

10 In the Pages palette, double-click the numbers 6-7 below the page icons to view the last spread in the document.

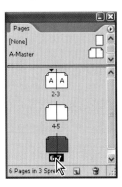

Double-clicking the numbers below the page icons centers the full spread in the document window. Double-clicking an individual page icon centers that page in the document window.

Now that you've seen all three spreads, let's go back to page 3 and start working.

11 In the Pages palette, double-click the page 3 icon to view page 3.

Changing the viewing mode

You can change the viewing mode of a document window using the Mode buttons at the bottom of the toolbox. Use Preview to easily hide nonprinting elements such as guides, grids, and frame edges. You can also preview the document with the bleed or slug areas included.

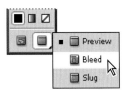

The Preview Mode button.

Click and hold on the Preview Mode button (▣) at the bottom of the toolbox to choose a Preview mode. Preview Mode displays artwork in a standard window, hiding nonprinting elements such as guides, grids, and frame edges.

Choose the Bleed mode button (▣) to preview the document along with its predefined bleed area that extends beyond the page boundaries.

Choose the Slug mode button (▣) to preview the document along with the predefined slug area. The slug area is an area outside the page and bleed that contains printer instructions or job sign-off information.

Choose the Normal mode button (▣) at the bottom of the toolbox to return to the normal view.

💡 *You can also choose View > Screen Mode and then select one of the four viewing modes. A checkmark indicates the selected view mode.*

Viewing guides

In this document, the guides are hidden. You'll turn on the guides to make it easy to see your layout grid and snap objects into place. The guides do not print and do not limit the print area. Guides are for your reference only and can be helpful when aligning objects and text on your page.

• Choose View > Grids & Guides > Show Guides.

Before and after turning on guides.

Adding text

You can import text created in separate word processing programs, or create text using InDesign CS2. In this exercise, you will add a secondary headline to page 3.

1 Using the Type tool (T), click and drag to create a box for this headline between the two guides below the word Mexico, in the right column of the page.

If the text box is not aligned exactly to the size of the guides, use the Selection tool (⬉) to click on the corners of the box and enlarge or reduce them as necessary and then re-select the Type tool.

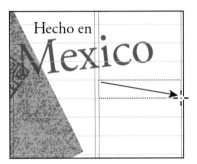

2 Enter the text **Exploring Mexican Folk Art** in the text box.

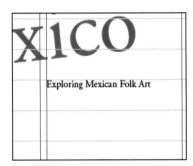

InDesign CS2 placed the text insertion point in the frame after it was created because it was built using the Type tool. For text frames created with other tools, you will first need to click within the text frame using the Type tool before entering text.

3 Use the Type tool to select the text just entered by placing the cursor into the text frame and choosing Edit > Select All to select the text.

4   Use the Control palette to change text attributes. Click on the arrow (▾) to the right of the Font Name drop-down menu and select Adobe Garamond Pro Regular. (Adobe Garamond Pro is alphabetized on the list under "G," not "A.")

5   Click on the arrow (▾) to the right of the Font Size drop-down menu and select "18 points."

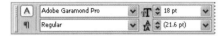

💡 *You can select individual words and characters using the Type tool to format text, as you would with traditional word-processing software.*

Threading text in frames

As a general rule, text is placed inside frames with InDesign CS2. You can either add text to a frame that has already been created, or you can create the frame while you import text.

Placing and flowing text

An article describing Judith and Clyde's trip to Oaxaca has been saved in a word-processor file. You'll place this file on page 3 and then thread it throughout your document.

1   Make sure that no objects are selected by choosing Edit > Deselect All, and then choose File > Place. In the Place dialog box, navigate to the Lesson_00 folder in the Lessons folder and double-click the 00_a.doc file.

The cursor changes to a loaded text icon (▤). With a loaded text icon, you have several choices. You can drag to create a new text frame, click inside an existing frame, or click to create a new text frame within a column. You'll add this text to a column in the lower half of page 3.

2   Position the loaded text icon just below the fourth guide from the bottom margin and just to the right of the left margin, and click.

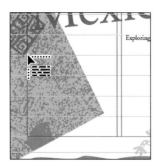 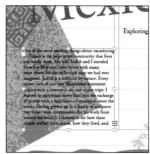

3   The text flows into a new frame in the lower half of the first column on page 3. When a text frame has more text than can fit, the frame is said to have overset text. Overset text is indicated by a red plus symbol in the out port of the frame, which is the small square just above the lower right corner of the frame. You can link overset text to another frame, create a new frame into which the overset text will flow, or expand the size of the frame so that the text is no longer overset.

Note: If the text box is not placed in the left column, click the Selection tool and drag the sizing handles to move it to the proper location.

4   Choose the Selection tool (↖), then click the out port in the selected frame. The cursor becomes a loaded text icon. Now you'll add a column of text to the lower half of the second column.

5   Position the loaded text icon immediately below the fourth guide from the bottom margin and just to the right of the second column guide (be sure not to click on the previously created text frame above), and click. Text now fills the lower portion of the right column.

💡 *You can also divide a single text box into multiple columns by selecting the box and setting the number of columns in the Control palette. This allows you to create multiple columns of type without flowing text.*

Threading text

Clicking the out port and then linking to a text frame is called manual threading.

1   Using the Selection tool (⬉), click the out port in the second column on page 3. This prepares InDesign CS2 to flow the overset text from this text frame to another frame.

2   In the Pages palette, double-click the page 4 icon to center page 4 in the document window.

3   Press and hold the Alt (Windows) or Option (Mac OS) key and position the loaded text icon in the upper left corner of the first column. Click, and then release the Alt/Option key.

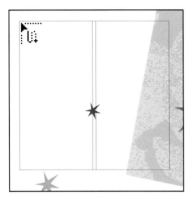

The text flows into the left column. Because you held down Alt/Option, the cursor remains a loaded text icon and you do not need to click in the out port before flowing text from this frame.

Note: After clicking the out port of a text frame, you can hold the Shift key to thread text automatically. Automatically flowing text places any overset text onto the pages of a document, adding pages as necessary. Because the design of this document calls for text to appear only on certain pages, the option to automatically flow text is not appropriate in this document.

4   Position the loaded text icon in the upper left corner of the second column on page 4, and click.

Whenever the cursor displays a loaded text icon, you can click any tool in the toolbar to stop flowing text. No text is lost, and any overset text remains.

Now you'll flow the remaining text into the bottom of the two columns on page 7.

5   Click the out port in the second column of page 4, and then in the Pages palette, double-click the page 7 icon, centering page 7 in the document window.

6   Press and hold Alt (Windows) or Option (Mac OS), and position the loaded text icon in the left column, below the guide on page 7, and click. Release the Alt or Option key. The cursor remains as a loaded text icon, as additional text needs to be flowed.

7   Position the loaded text icon in the second column below the guide, and click. The remaining text from the story flows into the second column. Note that the out port in the lower right corner of the text frame is hollow, indicating that there is no additional text to flow from this frame.

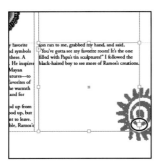

You have finished threading text frames in this document. A threaded set of frames is called a story.

8   Choose File > Save.

Adding a pull-quote

To enhance the design on page 4 of your document, you'll add a pull-quote. We copied text from the article and placed it into a frame on the pasteboard, which is the area outside the page. You will position this pull-quote text frame in the middle of page 4 and finish formatting it.

1 Choose View > Fit Page in Window.

2 In the lower left corner of the document window, click and hold on the arrow ( ) to the right of the page number indicator. Select page 4 from the list of available pages.

If you cannot see the pull-quote text frame to the left of page 4, locate the scroll box on the horizontal scroll bar, and drag it to the left.

3 In the Control palette located just below the menus at the top of the page, click and then enter an X value of **4 in** and a Y value of **3 in,** and then press the Enter or Return key on your keyboard. InDesign moves the selected object to the specified location.

4 If necessary, use the Arrow keys to nudge the location of the frame. The bottom of the frame should pass through the middle of the red star. The pull-quote should now be centered between the columns of text on page 4.

With Adobe InDesign CS2 you can use most forms of measurement throughout the program, including palettes and dialog boxes, as long as you identify them with standard abbreviations, such as in for inch, pt for point or cm for centimeter. InDesign converts the units you enter into the default unit of measurement, which can be changed in Edits > Preferences > Units & Increments.

Wrapping text around an object

The text in the pull-quote is difficult to read because the main story text does not wrap around the text frame. You'll wrap the main story text around the edges of the pull-quote text frame, so the text from the main story will not overlap the pull-quote.

1 Make sure the pull-quote frame is selected.

2 Choose Window > Text Wrap.

3 In the Text Wrap palette, click the third button from the left side (⬛). This causes text to wrap around the object's shape.

4 Click the Close box to close the Text Wrap palette. You can always access this palette or other palettes from the Window menu.

5 Choose File > Save.

Adding a stroke to the frame

Now you'll change the color of the text frame so that the stroke, also described as a border, matches the color of the red star. When you apply colors using InDesign, it's a good idea to use the Swatches palette. Using the Swatches palette makes it easy to apply, edit, and update colors efficiently for all objects in a document.

This magazine article is intended for printing at a commercial press, so it uses CMYK process colors. We've already added the set of necessary colors to the Swatches palette.

1   Choose Window > Swatches.

2   With the text frame still selected, click the Stroke box ( ) in the top of the Swatches palette and then select PANTONE Warm Red CVC in the Swatches palette. You may need to scroll down to select. Selecting the Stroke box causes the frame of the image to be affected by the color you selected.

3   To change the weight of the stroke, right-click (Windows) or Ctrl+click (Mac OS) on the frame, and select Stroke Weight > 0.5 pt from the context menu that appears. The context menus are an easy way to change many attributes of a selected object, including the stroke weight.

4   Choose Edit > Deselect All.

The text frame now has a thin red stroke.

5   Choose File > Save.

Changing the frame and text position

The text in the pull-quote frame is too close to the edge, making it unattractive and difficult to read. You'll now change the position of the text within the frame and change the style of the border.

1   Using the Selection tool (➤), click the pull-quote text frame to select it, and then choose the Align Center (▤) option from the Control palette.

2   With the frame still selected, choose the Thick-Thin stroke type from the Control palette.

3   Use the Control palette to increase the stroke weight to 4 pt, by using the option immediately above the stroke style selection you used in the previous step.

You can also use the Control palette to easily adjust other important attributes for objects on a page, such as size and position.

Adjusting the size of an image

Next you will adjust the size of the picture of the crescent moon on the adjacent page.

1   If necessary, choose page 5 from the drop-down menu in the lower left-hand corner of the document window to move to this page.

2   Choose the Selection tool (↖) and click to select the picture of the crescent moon.

3   Using the Control palette, choose 50% from the X Scale %, which is the top of the two scaling values in the Control palette.

Both the vertical and horizontal sizes adjust proportionally. This is because the Constrain Proportions for Scaling button (▤) is selected to the right of the scaling percentages. You can deselect this button, if you wish, to adjust one value independent of the other. As a general rule, bitmap images, such as those scanned or taken with a digital camera, should not be scaled disproportionately and should not be scaled beyond 120% of their original size, due to the possible loss of quality. In this case, we were proportionally reducing the size of the image, which generally has no adverse impact on its quality.

4   Choose File > Save.

Working with styles

InDesign CS2 includes three kinds of styles: paragraph, character, and object. A paragraph style includes formatting attributes that apply to all text within a paragraph. You do not need to select text to apply a paragraph style, as it applies to all text in the paragraph where your cursor is located. A character style includes only character attributes, making it useful for formatting words and phrases within a paragraph. Text must be selected to apply a character style. An object style allows you to create and apply formatting to selected objects. Using an object style, you can set fill and stroke color, stroke and corner effects, transparency, drop shadows, feathering, text frame options, and even text wrap on a selected object.

Applying paragraph styles

You'll start by applying styles to text, and then move on to object styles. To save time, we created paragraph styles that you'll apply to the text. These styles will help you format the body text in the article.

1   In the Pages palette, double-click the page 3 icon to center page 3 in the document window.

2   Select the Type tool (T), and then click anywhere in the columns of text that you previously placed on this page.

3   Choose Edit > Select All to select the text in all the frames of the story.

4   Choose Type > Paragraph Styles to display the Paragraph Styles palette.

5   In the Paragraph Styles palette, click Body Text to format the entire story with the Body Text style.

> *You can also apply styles from the Character and Paragraph Formatting Control palettes by selecting the style name from the drop-down menu.*

6   Choose Edit > Deselect All to deselect the text.

Now you'll apply a different paragraph style to the first paragraph of the story.

7   Using the Type tool, click anywhere in the first paragraph on page 3.

8   In the Paragraph Styles palette, select Body Text/Drop Cap. Paragraph styles can include a variety of text formatting options, including drop caps.

9   Choose File > Save.

Formatting text for the character style

Now you'll create and apply a character style to emphasize page references within the paragraphs. Before you create this character style, you'll use the Character palette to italicize the text and make it one point smaller. You'll then base the character style on this formatted text, allowing you to easily apply this same style to other text throughout the document.

1   In the Pages palette, double-click the page 7 icon to center page 7 in the document window. To make sure that you can read the text at the bottom of this page, press Ctrl and + (the plus sign) (Windows) or Command and + (Mac OS) to zoom in.

Within the text, there are three references to other pages: (page 7), (page 2), and (page 5). If necessary, use the scroll bars to display this portion of the document window.

2   Using the Type tool (T), select the "(page 7)" reference.

3   Select Italic from the Type Style menu in the Control palette. For font size (T), select 11 pt. The page reference is now formatted.

4   Choose File > Save.

Creating and applying a character style

Now that you have formatted the text, you are ready to create a character style.

1   Make sure that the text you formatted is still selected, and choose Type > Character Styles to display the Character Styles palette.

2   Press the Alt key (Windows) or Option key (Mac OS) and click the New Style button (🗗) at the bottom of the Character Styles palette.

The New Character Style window appears and a new character style named Character Style 1 is created. This new style includes the characteristics of the selected text.

3   For Style Name, type **Emphasis** and click OK.

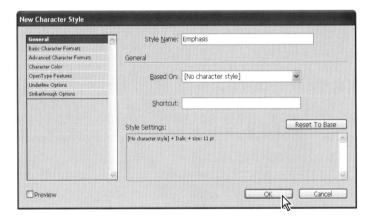

4   Using the Type tool (T), select the text (page 2) in the next paragraph, and then click Emphasis in the Character Styles palette to apply the style.

5   Apply the character style Emphasis to the text "(page 5)" in the same paragraph. Because you used a character style instead of a paragraph style, the style affected only the selected text, not the entire paragraph.

6   Return the previous paragraph to select the text "(page 7)," click Emphasis in the Character Styles palette to apply the style.

Even though you established the style using this text, it never had the style applied. This tags the text to update automatically if the character style attributes are updated.

7   Choose File > Save.

Applying object styles

To save time, we created an object style that you'll apply to the pull-quote on page 4. Use object styles to apply multiple formatting attributes to an object, including text and picture frames.

1   In the Pages palette, double-click the page 4 icon to center page 4 in the document window.

2   Choose the Selection tool (➤) and click the pull-quote, selecting the text frame.

3   Choose Window > Object Styles to display the Object Styles palette.

4   In the Object Styles palette, hold the Alt (Windows) or Option (Mac OS) key and click Pull-Quote to format the selected object with the Pull-Quote object style.

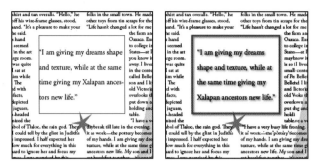

Note: Holding the Alt (Windows) or Option (Mac OS) key clears any existing formatting when applying a style to an object or text.

5   Choose File > Save.

Working with graphics

Graphics used in an InDesign CS2 document are placed inside of frames. When working with placed graphics, you should become familiar with the three Selection tools.

The Selection tool (▸) is used for general layout tasks, such as positioning and moving objects on a page. The Direct Selection tool (▹) is used for tasks involving the content of the frame, or drawing and editing paths; for example, to select frame contents or to move an anchor point on a path. The Direct Selection tool is also used for selecting objects within groups. The Position tool (⬌), hidden in the Direct Selection tool, works in conjunction with the Selection tool to help control the placement of content within a frame, as well as to change the size of the frame. You can use this tool to move a graphic within its frame, or change the visible area of a graphic by adjusting its crop. The Position tool is grouped with the Direct Selection tool in the Tool palette. You may need to click and hold on the Direct Selection tool to select the Position tool.

Note: While learning about the difference between frames and their content, you may want to make frame edges visible by selecting View > Show Frame edges.

Positioning graphics within a frame

Two of the pictures on the first spread need to have their frames resized or the pictures within them repositioned.

1 Select page 2 in the lower left corner of the document window to navigate to page 2. Press Ctrl+0 (zero) (Windows) or Command+0 (Mac OS) to fit the page in the window.

2 Using the Direct Selection tool (↖), position your cursor over the picture of the red sun, which is half-visible. Notice that the cursor changes to a Hand tool, indicating that you can select and manipulate the content of the frame. Click and drag the picture to the right, making the entire sun visible. With the Direct Selection tool, you can reposition graphics within their frame.

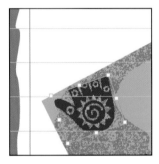

3 Using the Selection tool (↖), click on the picture of the blue hand on the top left side of the page.

4 Click and drag the top center handle upward to expand the size of the frame. By making the frame larger, more of its contents become visible.

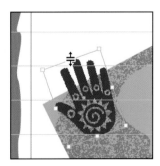

💡 *You can preview the picture as you move or resize the frame if you pause briefly after you first click the frame or picture, and then resize or move the picture or frame.*

5 Choose File > Save.

About the Position tool

The Position tool (⚒) works in conjunction with the Selection tool (▸) to help control the placement of content within a frame. It can also be used to change the size of the frame.

The Position tool is dynamic, and it can be used with either text or graphics. When it's placed over a graphic, it changes to a hand icon (☜), indicating that you can manipulate the content within a frame. When it's positioned over a text frame, the cursor changes to an I-beam, indicating it can be used to add or edit text.

1 Select the Position tool from the toolbox, by clicking and holding on the Direct Selection tool.

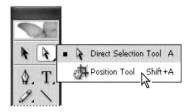

2 Press Ctrl+J (Windows) or Command+J (Mac OS) and type **3**, press Enter. This keyboard shortcut takes you to page 3. Roll over the text "Exploring Mexican Folk. Notice that your cursor changes into the text I-beam.

3 Triple-click on the text to select it. Click and drag over the value in the Font size text field in the Control palette. Type **20** and press Return to change the font size to 20 pt.

Targeting layers when placing

Like both Illustrator CS2 and Photoshop CS2, InDesign CS2 lets you place objects on different layers. Think of layers as sheets of transparent film that are stacked on top of each other. By using layers, you can create and edit objects on one layer without affecting—or being affected by—objects on other layers. Layers also determine the stacking position of objects.

Before you import a photograph of an armadillo into your design, you'll make sure that you add the frame to the appropriate layer.

1 In the Pages palette, double-click the page 3 icon to center page 3 in the document window.

2 Choose Window > Layers to display the Layers palette.

3 Click the word "Photos" in the Layers palette to target the Photos layer. Do not click the boxes to the left of the Photos layer, or you'll hide or lock the layer.

4 Select the Selection tool (￫).

5 Choose Edit > Deselect All. If this option is grayed out, everything is already deselected.

6 Choose File > Place. If necessary, navigate to the Lesson_00 folder and double-click the armadillo.tif. InDesign lets you import images using a variety of file types, including native Photoshop and Illustrator files.

7 With the loaded graphics icon (), click in the white area above the top margin to place the armadillo at the top of the page. You'll move the graphic later, after you rotate and crop it.

Notice that the armadillo frame is the same color as the Photos layer in the Layers palette. An object's frame color describes the layer on which it resides.

8 In the Layers palette, click the box next to the Text layer name so that the layer lock icon ( ) appears.

Locking this layer prevents you from selecting or making any changes to the Text layer or any objects on that layer. With the Text layer locked, you can edit the frame containing the armadillo without accidentally selecting the frame containing "Hecho en Mexico."

Cropping and moving the photograph

You'll now use the Selection tool to crop and move the photograph.

1   Choose Edit > Deselect All.

2   Select the Selection tool (↖) in the toolbox, and then click the armadillo.

3   Position the pointer over the middle handle on the right side of the armadillo frame and hold down the mouse button. Drag the frame toward the center of the armadillo to crop it.

4   Using the Selection tool, position the pointer over the center of the armadillo frame and drag the object so that it snaps to the right edge of the page.

Notice that the edge of the armadillo is behind the decorative border. This is because the Photos layer is below the Graphics layer in the Layers palette.

5   Choose File > Save.

Exploring on your own

Congratulations! You've completed the InDesign CS2 tour. You're now ready to create your own InDesign CS2 documents. To learn more about InDesign CS2, you may want to try the following:

• Continue experimenting with the travel document. Add new pages, edit the master pages, move items among the layers, create text frames, and adjust the graphics using the tools in the toolbox.

• Choose Help > InDesign Help to use Adobe InDesign CS2 Help.

• Go through the lessons in the rest of this book.

It is important to understand the
InDesign CS2 work area in order to
make the most of its powerful layout
and design capabilities. The work area
consists of the document window,
pasteboard, toolbox, and the floating
palettes.

1 Getting to Know the Work Area

In this lesson, you'll learn how to do the following:

- Work with tools, document windows, the pasteboard, and palettes.
- Change the magnification of the document.
- Navigate through a document.
- Work with layers.
- Manage palettes and save your workspace.
- Use context menus and InDesign Help.

Note: This lesson covers tasks that are common to Adobe products such as Photoshop, Illustrator, and Acrobat. If you are familiar with these Adobe products, you may want to skim through this lesson and move ahead to the next lesson.

Getting started

In this lesson, you'll practice using the work area and navigating through pages of the *Exploring The Library* booklet. This is the final version of the document—you won't be changing or adding text or graphics, only checking to make sure everything is ready for print. Before you begin, you'll need to restore the default preferences for Adobe InDesign.

1 To ensure that the tools and palettes function exactly as described in this lesson, delete or deactivate (by renaming) the InDesign Defaults file and the InDesign SavedData file. See "Restoring default preferences" on page 2.

2 Start Adobe InDesign.

To begin working, open an existing InDesign document.

Note: If you have not already copied the resource files for this lesson onto your hard disk from the Lesson_01 folder from the Adobe InDesign CS2 Classroom in a Book CD, do so now. See "Copying the Classroom in a Book files" on page 4.

3 Choose File > Open, and open the 01_a.indd file in the Lesson_01 folder, on your hard disk.

4 Choose File > Save As, rename the file **01_Library.indd**, and save it in the Lesson_01 folder.

Note: This document was saved with the frame edges hidden. You can choose to display the frame edges by choosing View > Show Frame Edges.

Looking at the work area

The InDesign work area encompasses everything you see when you first open or create a document: the toolbox, document window, pasteboard, and palettes. You can customize and save the work area to suit your work style. For example, you can choose to display only those palettes you frequently use, minimize and rearrange palette groups, resize windows, add additional document windows, and so on.

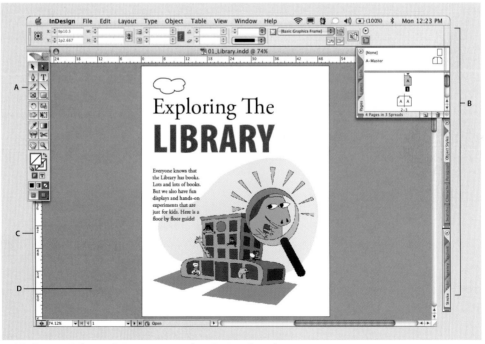

A. Toolbox. B. Palettes. C. Document window. D. Pasteboard.

About the Toolbox

The InDesign toolbox contains tools for selecting objects, working with type, drawing, and viewing, as well as controls for applying and changing color fills, strokes, and gradients.

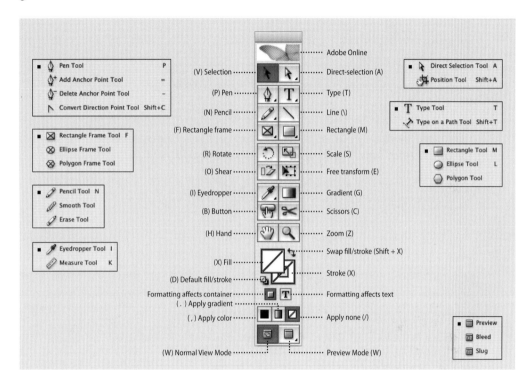

As you work through the lessons, you'll learn about each tool's specific function. Here you'll familiarize yourself with the toolbox and the tools.

1 Position the cursor over the Selection tool (↖) in the toolbox. Notice the name and shortcut are displayed.

💡 *You can select a tool by either clicking the tool in the toolbar or pressing the tool's keyboard shortcut. Because the default keyboard shortcuts work only when you do not have a text insertion point, you can also add other key commands to select tools, even when you are editing text. To do this, use the Edit > Keyboard Shortcuts command. For more information, select Keyboard Shortcuts in InDesign Help.*

2 Position the cursor over the Pen tool (✒) and hold down the mouse button—additional Pen tools appear. Drag down and to the right, and release the mouse button over one of the additional tools to select it. Any tool in the tool palette that displays a small black triangle at the bottom right corner contains additional tools that can be selected by clicking and holding down on the tool.

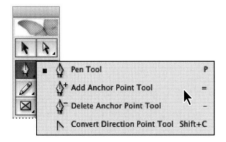

3 Choose the Selection tool again; then click the edge of the little cloud in the top left corner of page 1 to select it.

Now you'll use the color controls, which are located on the bottom half of the toolbox.

4 Select the Fill box to make sure that any changes you make affect the center portion of the object and not its stroke.

5 Click the Color box in the toolbox. The object becomes filled with solid black. Click the Gradient box. The object becomes filled with a white-to-black gradient. Click the None box to return the object to its original unfilled state.

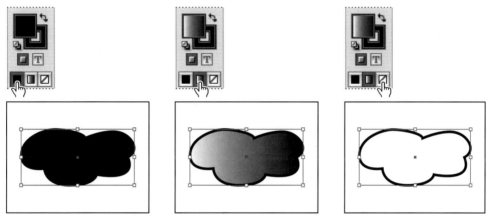

Object filled with black (left), filled with a gradient (center), and reset to no fill (right).

Note: *If you accidentally double-click a Fill or Gradient box, the Color or Gradient palette opens. Close the palette to continue with the lesson.*

6 Now select the Stroke box so that any changes you make affect the object's stroke.

7 Click the Gradient box in the toolbox. The solid stroke becomes a gradient stroke. Click the Color box to return the object to its original stroke. Then click a blank area of the page or pasteboard to deselect the cloud.

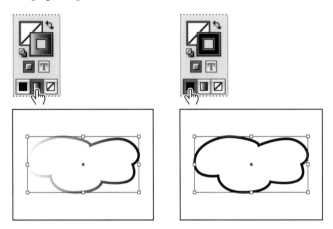

To learn how to change the color of a fill, stroke, or gradient, see Lesson 6, "Working with Color."

Document window

The document window contains your document pages. You can have more than one document window open at a time. Here, you'll open a second window so that, as you work, you can see two different views of the document at the same time.

1 Choose Window > Arrange > New Window. A new window titled 01_Library. indd:2 opens. Notice that the original window is now titled 01_Library.indd:1.

2 To view both windows simultaneously, choose Window > Arrange > Tile.

3   Now select the Zoom tool (🔍) in the toolbox and click twice on the dinosaur in the rightmost document window. Notice that the original document window remains at the original magnification. This arrangement lets you work closely on details and see the overall results on the rest of the page.

4   Close the 01_Library.indd:2 document window by clicking the close window button at the top of the document window. Windows users, be careful not to close the program, as the close window and close program buttons are located adjacent to each other. The original document window remains open. Resize and reposition the remaining window by clicking the Maximize button on the top of your document window.

The Maximize (Windows) button is in the middle box in the upper right corner of any window. In Mac OS, this is the green button in the upper left corner of the window.

Using the Pasteboard

Each page or spread in your document has its own pasteboard surrounding it, where you can store objects relating to your document as you create your layout. The pasteboard also provides additional space along the edges of the document for extending objects past the page's edge. Extending objects past the edge of a page is called a bleed, and is used when an object must print entirely to the edge of a page.

1   To see the full size of the pasteboard for the pages in this document, choose View > Entire Pasteboard.

Note: If you cannot see the graphic of a book on the pasteboard, it may be hidden behind one of the palettes. If necessary, move the palettes so that you can see objects on the pasteboard.

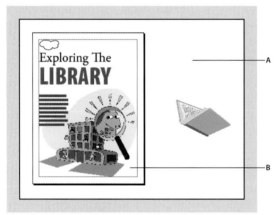

A. *Pasteboard.* **B.** *Document.*

Notice the book graphic on the pasteboard for page 1. This graphic was originally placed in the document, but was then moved to the pasteboard in anticipation that it would be used somewhere else in the document. It is no longer necessary to keep this image with the document, as it will not be used in the final document.

2   Using the Selection tool (↖), select the book image on the pasteboard and press Delete.

3   Choose View > Fit Page in Window to restore the window to its previous size.

4   Choose File > Save.

💡 *Use the pasteboard as an extension of the work area. You can import multiple placed images or text files and hold them on the pasteboard until you are ready to use them.*

Viewing and arranging palettes

Palettes provide quick access to commonly used tools and features in InDesign. By default, palettes appear in stacked groups, which you can reorganize in various ways. Here you'll experiment with hiding, closing, and opening palettes.

1   Choose Window > Workspace > [Default] to reset the palettes to their original location.

2   Click the Layers palette tab to make this palette appear, or choose Window > Layers.

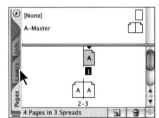 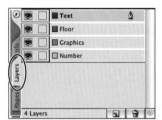

To find a hidden palette, choose the palette name on the Window menu. If the palette name already has a check mark, then the palette is already open and in front of any other palettes in its palette group. If you choose a checked palette name on the Window menu, the palette will close.

When you start InDesign, several groups of palettes are collapsed into tabs at the side of the application window (Windows) or screen (Mac OS). You can move collapsed palettes into windows of their own or collapse other palettes into side tabs. Palettes collapsed into side tabs can be grouped and rearranged.

• To display a collapsed palette: Click the palette's tab to display or hide it.

• To convert a collapsed palette to a floating palette: Drag a palette's tab away from the side of the application window (Windows) or of the screen (Mac OS).

• To collapse a palette into a side tab: Select the palette's tab and drag it to the left or right side of the application window (Windows) or screen (Mac OS).

—From InDesign Help

Now you'll reorganize the palette group.

3 Drag the Layers palette tab outside the group to create a new palette window.

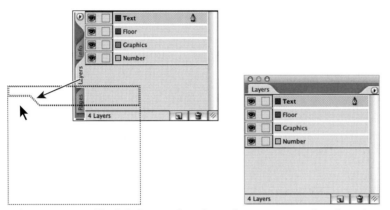

Palettes are grouped by default. Drag the palette tab to separate a palette from the group.

You can also move palettes from one palette group to another to create custom palette groups of the palettes you use most often.

💡 *Press Tab to hide all open palettes and the toolbox. Press Tab again to display them all again. You can hide or display just the palettes (not the toolbox) by pressing Shift+Tab.*

Now you'll practice creating custom palette groups by combining different palettes.

4 If the Paragraph palette is not visible, open it by selecting Type > Paragraph. Then drag the Layers palette tab into the center of the Paragraph palette group and then drag the tab back to the Pages palette group.

Note: To add a palette to a group, make sure you drag its tab into the middle of the palette. If you drag a palette tab to the bottom of another palette, you will dock the palette instead of adding it. See the "Docking palettes" sidebar on the following page.

Docking palettes

Dock palettes by connecting the lower edge of one palette to the top edge of another palette, so that both palettes move together and are shown and hidden together. When you dock palettes, both palettes remain fully visible. In contrast, when you group palettes, only the frontmost palette is visible.

You can dock one palette to another single palette or to a group of palettes. However, you can't dock a group of palettes unless you dock each of them individually, because docking involves dragging an individual palette's tab and not the title bar.

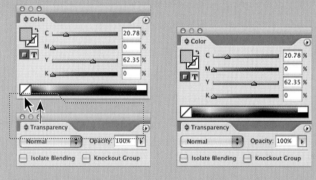

To dock palettes, drag a palette's tab to the bottom edge of another palette. When the bottom edge of the other palette is highlighted, release the mouse.

—From InDesign Help

Now you'll organize the palettes to create more space in your work area.

5   After dragging a palette from the docking area, you can double-click the tab containing the name of the palette to reduce the size of the palette. Double-click the tab again to minimize the palette.

Note: You can double-click a third time to return to the full-size view of the palette. These clicking options work only after the palette has been pulled out from the docking area.

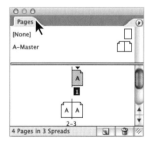

Customizing your workspace

You can save the position of palettes and easily access them at any time by creating a workspace. Next you will create a workspace to access a group of commonly used palettes.

1 Choose Window > Pages, then choose Window > Object & Layout > Navigator, and also choose Window > Object & Layout > Transform.

Note: When a palette has a check mark to the left of the palette name, under the Window menu, it is already visible. Selecting it again will hide the palette.

2 Position the three palettes so they are all visible on the side of the screen.

3 Choose Window > Workspace > Save Workspace. The Save Workspace window opens. Enter the name **Navigation** and then click OK.

4 Return to the default palette layout by choosing Window > Workspace > Default. Note that the palettes return to their default positions. Toggle between the two workspaces using the Window > Workspace command and selecting the workspace you wish to use; return to the Default Workspace before going on to the next exercise.

Using palette menus

Most palettes have a Palette-menu button in the upper corner of the palette window. This menu generally appears in the upper left corner of a docked palette or the upper right corner of a palette that is floating, or not docked. Clicking this arrow-shaped button opens a menu with additional commands and options for the selected palette. You can use this to change options for the palette display or to access additional commands relating to the palette.

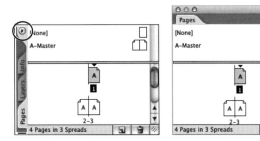

Next you will change the display of one of the palettes, called the Swatches palette, which is used to create and save color.

1   Click the Swatches palette tab in the docking area on the right side of the window. You can also choose Window > Swatches to display this palette.

2   Position the cursor on the Palette-menu button in the upper left corner of the Swatches palette, and click to display the palette menu.

3   Choose Small Name. This command affects the Swatches palette rows but not the other palettes visible on the screen. The commands in the palette menu apply only to the active palette. The size of the color swatches is reduced, allowing more swatches to be displayed in the same area.

4   Click the Swatches palette menu, and choose Name to return the swatches names to their original size.

Changing the magnification of your document

You can view the document at any level from 5% to 4000%. When you are viewing a document, InDesign displays the percentage of the document's actual size in the lower left corner of the document window and also at the top of the document in the title bar of the window, next to the file name.

Using the view commands and magnification menu

You can easily enlarge or reduce the view of a document by doing one of the following:

• Choose a percentage from the magnification menu at the lower left corner of the document window to enlarge or reduce the display by any preset increment.

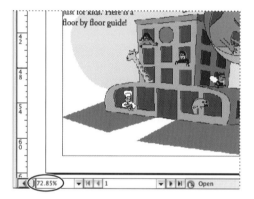

• Type a percentage in the magnification menu by positioning your cursor over this area and clicking to obtain an insertion point, entering the desired viewing percent and then using the return key to enter the value.

• Choose View > Zoom In to enlarge the display by one preset increment.

• Choose View > Zoom Out to reduce the display by one preset increment.

Note: *Preset sizes are those listed in the magnification menu.*

• Choose View > Actual Size to display the document at 100%. (Depending on the dimensions of your document and your screen resolution, you may or may not see the entire document on-screen.)

• Choose View > Fit Page in Window to display the targeted page in the window.

• Choose View > Fit Spread in Window to display the targeted spread in the window.

Using the Zoom tool

In addition to the view commands, you can use the Zoom tool to magnify and reduce the view of a document.

1   Select the Zoom tool (🔍) in the toolbox and position it over the dinosaur on page 1. Notice that a plus sign appears in the center of the Zoom tool (🔍).

2   Click once. The view changes to the next preset magnification, centered on the point where you clicked. Now you'll reduce the view.

3   Position the Zoom tool cursor over the dinosaur and hold down Alt (Windows) or Option (Mac OS). A minus sign appears in the center of the Zoom tool (🔍).

4   With Alt/Option still held down, click once over the dinosaur; the view is reduced.

You can also use the Zoom tool to drag a marquee around a portion of a document to magnify a specific area.

5   With the Zoom tool still selected, hold down the mouse button and drag a marquee around the dinosaur; then release the mouse.

The percentage by which the area is magnified depends upon the size of the marquee: the smaller the marquee, the larger the degree of magnification.

Drag a marquee with   *Resulting view.*
the Zoom tool.

6   In the toolbox, double-click the icon for the Zoom tool to return to a 100% view.

Because the Zoom tool is used frequently during the editing process to enlarge and reduce the view of your document, you can temporarily select it from the keyboard at any time without deselecting any other tool you may be using. You'll do that now.

7 Click the Selection tool (▶) in the toolbox and position it in the document window.

8 Hold down Ctrl+spacebar (Windows) or Command+spacebar (Mac OS) so that the Selection tool icon becomes the Zoom tool icon, and then click on the dinosaur to magnify the view. When you release the keys, the cursor returns to the Selection tool.

9 Hold down Ctrl+Alt+spacebar (Windows) or Command+Option+spacebar (Mac OS) and click to zoom out, returning to a 100% view.

10 Choose View > Fit Spread in Window to center the page.

💡 *You can also change your magnification using key commands. Use Ctrl+= (Windows) or Command+= (Mac OS) to increase the magnification and Ctrl+- (Windows) or Command+- (Mac OS) to decrease the magnification.*

Navigating through your document

InDesign provides several options for viewing and navigating through a document, including the Pages and Navigator palettes, and the scroll bars.

Turning pages

You can turn pages using the Pages palette, the page buttons at the bottom of the document window, the scroll bars, or by using a variety of other commands.

The Pages palette provides page icons for all the pages in your document. Double-clicking on any page icon or page number brings that page or spread into view.

To target or select a page or spread

You either select or target pages or spreads, depending on the task you are performing. Some commands affect the currently selected page or spread, while others affect the target page or spread. For example, you can drag ruler guides only to the selected page or spread, but page-related commands, such as Duplicate Spread or Delete Page, affect the page or spread targeted in the Pages palette. Targeting makes a page or spread active and is helpful when, for example, several spreads are visible in the document window and you want to paste an object onto a specific spread.

Do one of the following:

• To select a page, click a page in the Pages palette. Don't double-click unless you want to target it and move it into view.

• To select a spread, in the Pages palette click the page numbers under the spread, or press Shift as you click the first and last page icons in a spread.

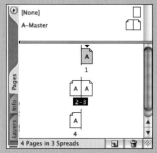

Page 1 is targeted and pages 2 and 3 are selected.

Note: Some spread options, such as those in the Pages palette menu, are available only when an entire spread is selected.

• To target a page or spread, in the document window click a page, any object on the page, or its pasteboard. The vertical ruler is dimmed alongside all but the targeted page or spread.

• To both target and select a page or spread, double-click its page numbers in the Pages palette. If the page or spread is not visible in the document window, it shifts into view.

Note: When you click an object in the document, you target the page or spread, as well as select the page or spread in the Pages palette.

—From InDesign Help

1   Make sure that the Selection tool (↖) is still selected and select Window > Pages if the Pages palette is not already open.

2   In the Pages palette, double-click the 2-3 page numbers below the page icons to target and view the spread on pages 2 and 3. You may need to scroll in the Pages palette to see pages 2 and 3. Choose View > Fit Spread in Window to view both pages of the spread.

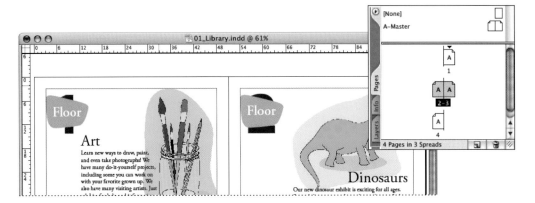

3   Double-click the page 3 icon to select and center it in the document window.

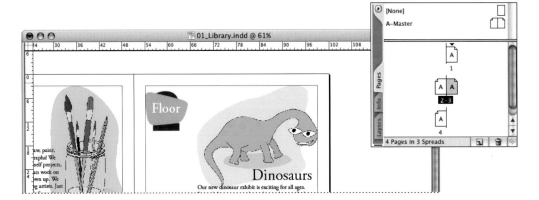

Now you'll use the page buttons at the bottom of the document window to change pages.

4   Click the next-page button (▶) at the lower left corner of the document window to go to page 4. This is located to the right of the magnification percentage.

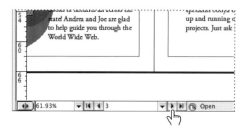

You can also turn to a specific page number by typing the number in the page box. Use the Enter or Return key after entering the page number.

5   Click and drag to select the page number 4 in the page box at the lower left of the document window, type **1**, and press Enter or Return.

Now you'll change pages using a menu command.

6   Choose Layout > Go Back to return to page 4.

7   Choose Layout > Previous Page to turn to page 3.

You can also turn to a specific page number by selecting the page number from the Page drop-down menu in the bottom of the document window. You'll use this procedure to switch pages in the next step.

8   Click the downward facing arrow (▼) to the right of the page box, and select 2 from the Page drop-down menu that appears.

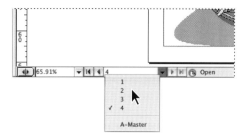

You can experiment with all the different methods for navigating through a document. For a full list of commands used for turning pages, see "Keys for viewing documents and document workspaces" in the InDesign Help.

Scrolling through a document

You can also use the Hand tool from the Tools palette, or the scroll bars along the side of the document window, to move to different areas or pages of a document. Here you'll use both methods to navigate through the document.

1 Drag the scrollbar along the right side of the document window all the way to the top to view page 1. If necessary, drag the horizontal scroll bar across the bottom of the window until you can see page 1.

2 With the Selection tool (✹) selected in the toolbox and the cursor positioned over the document, hold down the spacebar on the keyboard. Notice that the Selection tool icon changes to the Hand tool (✹). You can use this shortcut when you don't want to change tools while moving through the document. You can also select the Hand tool in the toolbox.

3 While holding down the spacebar, click and drag upward in the document window until the page 2-3 spread appears on-screen. As you drag, the document moves with the hand. The Hand tool lets you scroll both vertically and horizontally within your documents without using the scroll bars.

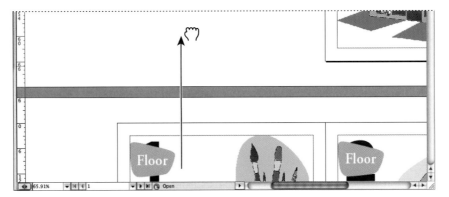

You can also use the Hand tool as a shortcut to fit the page or spread in the window.

4 In the toolbox, double-click the icon for the Hand tool to fit the spread in the window.

5 Using the Hand tool, click on or near the bug in the lower right corner and drag to center it in the window.

Using the Navigator palette

The Navigator palette provides several navigation and view tools in one location, so you can quickly and easily magnify and scroll to a desired location.

1 Choose Window > Object & Layout > Navigator to access the Navigator palette.

2 In the bottom of the Navigator palette, drag the slider to the right to increase the magnification of the document on your monitor. As you drag the slider to increase the level of magnification, the red outline in the Navigator window decreases in size, showing you the area that is visible on your monitor.

 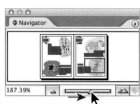 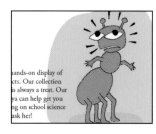

Increasing the magnification using the Navigator palette.

3 In the Navigator palette, position the cursor inside the red outline. The cursor becomes a hand, which you can use to scroll to different areas of the page or spread.

4 From within the red box, drag the hand to scroll to the upper left corner of page 2 to change the page that is visible within the document window.

5 Close the Navigator palette and save the file.

 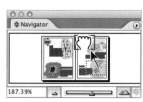 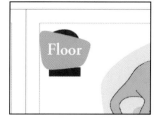

Scrolling to a different area using the Navigator palette.

Working with layers

By default, a new document contains just one layer (named Layer 1). You can rename the layer and add more layers at any time as you create your document. Placing objects on different layers lets you organize them for easy selection and editing. Using the Layers palette, you can select, display, edit, and print different layers individually, in groups, or all together.

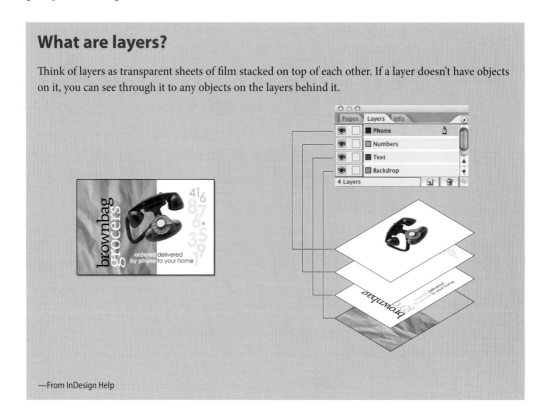

What are layers?

Think of layers as transparent sheets of film stacked on top of each other. If a layer doesn't have objects on it, you can see through it to any objects on the layers behind it.

—From InDesign Help

The 01_Library.indd document has four layers. You'll experiment with these layers to learn how the order of the layers and the placement of objects on layers can greatly affect the design of your document.

1   Double-click on the page 2 thumbnail in the Pages palette to move to page 2 of the document. Then, click the Layers palette tab to activate the palette, or choose Window > Layers.

2　In the Layers palette, click the Number layer. Notice that a pen icon (✏) appears to the right of the layer name. This icon indicates that this layer is the target layer, and anything you import or create will be placed on this layer. The highlight indicates that the layer is selected.

3　Position the cursor in the Layers palette, then click and drag the Number layer between the Floor layer and the Graphics layer. When you see a black line appearing where you would like to move the layer, release the mouse. Notice how the objects now appear in a different stacking order in your document, as some objects are now positioned on top of others.

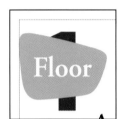
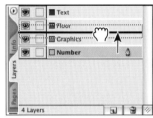

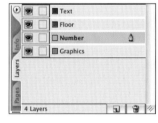

4　Click the empty square to the left of the Number layer name. This square lets you lock a layer so objects on the layer cannot be edited. When you lock a layer, the palette displays a crossed-out pencil icon (✗) in the square.

5   Using the Selection tool (▶), click the word "Floor" in the document window.

Notice in the Layers palette that the Graphics layer is selected and a dot appears to the right of the layer name. This indicates that the selected object belongs to this layer. You can move objects from one layer to another by dragging this dot between the layers in the palette.

6   In the Layers palette, drag the dot from the Graphics layer to the Floor layer. The word "Floor" now belongs to the Floor layer and appears in the stacking order in the document accordingly.

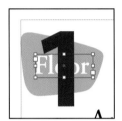 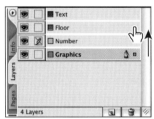

 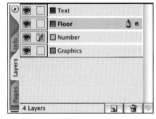

7   Now that you're done editing the layers, you can click on the crossed-out pencil icon for the Number layer to unlock this layer.

8   Choose File > Save to save the file.

Using context menus

In addition to the menus at the top of your screen, you can use context-sensitive menus to display commands relevant to the active tool or selection.

To display context-sensitive menus, position the cursor over an object or anywhere in the document window, and click with the right mouse button (Windows) or press Ctrl and hold down the mouse button (Mac OS).

1   Make sure that the word "Floor" is still selected.

2 With the Selection tool (↖), right-click (Windows) or Ctrl+click (Mac OS) the word "Floor." Options for the text under the tool are displayed in the context-sensitive menu. These same options are also in the Object menu. Being careful not to select any of the commands on the context menu, click a blank area of the page to close the menu.

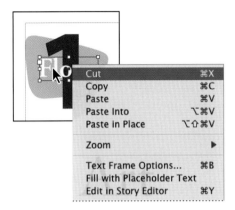

3 Choose Edit > Deselect all to make sure that all objects are deselected, then right-click (Windows) or Ctrl+click (Mac OS) the pasteboard outside the page area. Notice that the options listed on the context menu have changed so that they relate to the area of the page where you right-click or Ctrl+click.

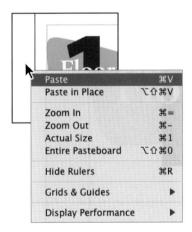

Selecting Objects

InDesign lets you know which objects will be selected when you move your Selection tool over an object by highlighting the object frame. You can then use commands to help select objects that are placed behind other items on your page.

1   Choose the Selection tool (![arrow]). If necessary, navigate to page 2.

2   Move the cursor over various blocks of text and graphics on the page and notice how the cursor changes to include a point (![arrow]) as the cursor passes over them. This signals that an object will be selected if you click.

3   Click between the two o's in the word "Floor," where it overlaps the number 1. The text box containing the word "Floor" is selected.

4   Right-click (Windows) or Ctrl+click (Mac OS) and choose Select > Next object below. Repeat this process until you have cycled through the three separate objects. You can also hold down your Ctrl key (Windows) or Command key (Mac OS) and click to cycle through stacked objects.

Using InDesign Help

You can use Help to find in-depth information about Adobe InDesign CS2. InDesign Help appears in the Adobe Help Center window.

1   Choose Help > InDesign Help. The Adobe Help Center opens.

InDesign Help includes its own complete set of instructions on how to use the Help system, which may be slightly different from other Help systems you may have used.

You can click any interactive text links to jump to a specific topic. Your cursor turns into a pointing-finger icon (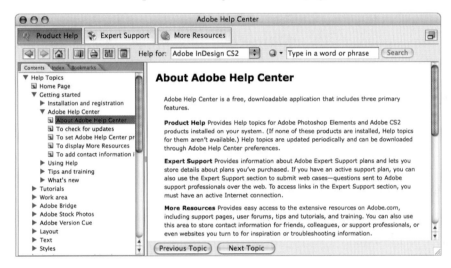) when you move it over any link or hotspot in the main document window on the right side of the display.

2 Click Getting started under the Help Topics listed down the left side. Click the triangle to the left of Adobe Help Center. Then click the topic "About Adobe Help Center." Information opens on the right side of the page.

3 When you finish reading the "About Adobe Help Center" page, click the Next Topic button at the bottom of the page.

4 Continue exploring each of the "Adobe Help Center" topics until you are comfortable using InDesign Help.

5 When you are finished using Help, you can close or minimize the Help window, or you can leave it open and switch back to InDesign.

Exploring on your own

Now that you have explored the work area, try some of the following tasks using either the Library_01.indd document or your own document.

1   Choose Window > Info to display the Info palette. Notice the information provided about the document, or click to select individual items and see how it changes as you select them.

2   Learn more about existing key commands and how you can change key commands by exploring the Keyboard Shortcuts window (Edit > Keyboard Shortcuts...).

3   After you've been working on a document and using multiple palettes, choose Window > Workspace > Default to reset your palettes to their default location. Try organizing your palettes to meet your needs, and creating your own workspace by choosing Window > Workspace > Save Workspace.

Review

▶ **Review questions**

1 Describe two ways to change your view of a document.

2 How do you select tools in InDesign?

3 Describe three ways to change the palette display.

4 Describe two ways to get more information about the InDesign program.

▶ **Review answers**

1 You can select commands from the View menu to zoom in or out of a document, or fit it to your screen; you can also use the Zoom tools in the toolbox, and click or drag over a document to enlarge or reduce the view. In addition, you can use keyboard shortcuts to magnify or reduce the display. You can also use the Navigator palette to scroll through a document or change its magnification without using the document window.

2 To select a tool, you can either click the tool in the toolbox or you can press the tool's keyboard shortcut. For example, you can press V to select the Selection tool from the keyboard. You select hidden tools by clicking the triangle on a tool in the toolbox and dragging to select from the additional tools that appear.

3 To make a palette appear, you can click its tab or choose its name on either the Window menu or the Type menu, for example, Window > Object Layout > Align. You can drag a palette's tab to separate the palette from its group and create a new group, or drag the palette into another group. You can drag a palette group's title bar to move the entire group. Double-click a palette's tab to display palette titles only. You can also press Shift+Tab to hide or display all palettes, but keep the toolbox open.

4 Adobe InDesign contains interactive Help, which includes keyboard shortcuts and full-color illustrations. You can also find links to training and support resources on the Adobe Systems web site, Adobe.com.

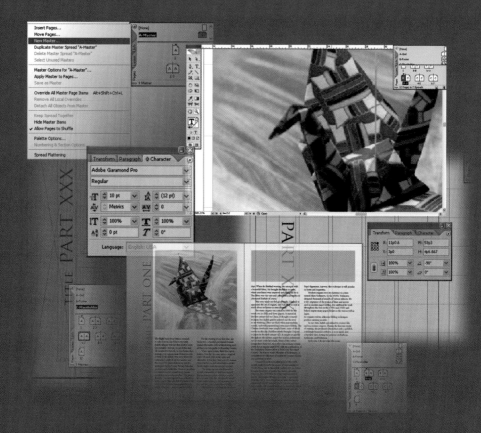

By taking advantage of the tools that help you set up your document, you can ensure a consistent page layout and simplify your work. In this lesson, you'll learn how to set up a new document, create master pages, and set columns and guides.

2 | Setting Up Your Document

In this introduction to setting up your document, you'll learn how to do the following:

- Start a new document.
- Create, edit, and apply master pages.
- Set document defaults.
- Adjust pasteboard size and bleed area.
- Add sections to change page numbering.
- Override master page items on document pages.
- Add graphics and text to document pages.

Getting started

In this lesson, you'll set up a 12-page magazine article about origami, the Japanese art of folding paper, and then you will place text and graphics on one of the spreads. Before you begin, you'll need to restore the default preferences for Adobe InDesign to ensure that the tools and palettes function exactly as described in this lesson. Then you'll open the finished document for this lesson to see what you'll be creating.

Note: If you have not already copied the resource files for this lesson onto your hard disk from the Lesson_02 folder from the Adobe InDesign CS2 Classroom in a Book CD, do so now. See "Copying the Classroom in a Book files" on page 4.

1   Delete or deactivate (by renaming) the InDesign Defaults file and the InDesign SavedData file. See "Restoring default preferences" on page 2.

2   Start Adobe InDesign CS2.

3   To see what the finished document will look like, open the 02_b.indd file in the Lesson_02 folder, located inside the Lessons folder within the InDesignCIB folder on your hard disk. If you receive Profile or Policy Mismatch warnings for the RGB and CMYK color profiles, click OK. This will convert to your color settings. Read more about color in Lesson 6, "Working with Color." You can leave this document open to act as a guide as you work.

The document window shows several spreads, including pages 2-3, which is the only spread that you'll complete in this lesson. You can refer to this document throughout this lesson.

4   Close the 02_b.indd file after you have completed examining it, or you can leave this document open for reference.

Note: As you work, feel free to move palettes or change the magnification to meet your needs.

Creating and saving a custom page size

InDesign lets you save your common page defaults, including page size, number of pages and margins. This lets you quickly build new documents using these saved document parameters, called presets.

1   Choose File > Document Presets and click Define.

2   Click New in the Document Presets dialog window that opens.

3   In the New Document Preset dialog window, set the following:

• For Document Preset Name, type **Magazine**.

• For Number of Pages, type **12**.

• Make sure that the Facing Pages option is selected.

• For Width, type **50p3** (the abbreviation for 50 picas and 3 points).

• For Height, type **65p3**.

• Under Columns, type **5** for Number, leaving the gutter at 1p0.

• Under Margins, type **4** for Bottom and leave the Top, Inside, and Outside margins at 3 picas (3p0).

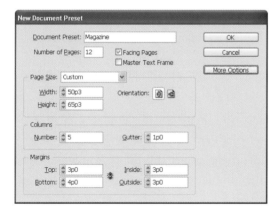

4 Click More Options, which expands the dialog window and enter **.25 in** for the Bleed on the Top text field. Then select the Make all settings the same chain button to enter that same amount into the Bottom, Inside and Outside text fields. InDesign automatically converts the measurements to the point equivalent.

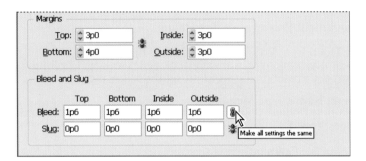

This creates an area outside the page that will print and is used when you have items that extend off the page area, such as a picture or a colored background on a page.

*You can use any form of measurement in any dialog window or palette. If you are using a value other than the default form of measurement, simply type the indicator for the unit you want to use, such as **p** for picas, **pt** for points, and either **in** or ˝ (quotation marks) for inches. You can change the default units by choosing Edit > Preferences > Units & Increments (Windows) or InDesign > Preferences > Units & Increments (Mac OS).*

5 Click OK in both dialog windows to save the Document Preset.

Starting a new document

When you start a new document, the Document Setup dialog window appears. You can use a document preset to build the document, or use this dialog window to specify the number of pages, the page size, and the number of columns. In this section you'll use the magazine preset that you just created.

1 Choose File > New > Document.

2 In the New Document dialog window, the Magazine document preset is selected. If Magazine is not the default preset, click and hold on the Document Preset drop-down menu to select it.

3   Click OK.

InDesign creates a new document using all the specifications from the Document Preset, including the page size, margins and number of pages.

4   Open the Pages palette by selecting Window > Pages, if it is not already open.

In the Pages palette, the page which is currently visible, page 1, is highlighted in the palette. The Pages palette is divided into two sections. The top section displays icons for the master pages. The bottom half displays icons for document pages. In this document, the master page consists of a two-page spread of facing pages.

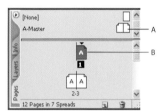

A. Master pages icon.
B. Document page icon.

5   Choose File > Save As, name the file **02_Setup.indd** in the Lesson_02 folder, and then click Save.

Editing master pages

Before you add graphics and text frames to the document, you'll set up the master pages. A master page is like a template that you can apply to many pages in your document. Any object that you add to a master page will appear on document pages to which the master page is applied.

In this document, you'll use three sets of master pages. One contains a grid, another contains footer information, and a third contains placeholder frames. By creating several types of master pages, you allow for variation of pages in a document while ensuring a consistent design.

Adding guides to the master

You'll start by adding guides to the document. Guides are non-printing lines that help you lay out your design precisely. Guides that you place on master pages appear on any document pages to which the master is applied. For this document, you'll add a series of guides that, along with the column guides, act as a grid to which you can snap graphics and text frames into place.

1 In the upper section of the Pages palette, double-click A-Master.

The left and right master pages appear centered in the document window.

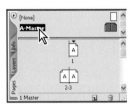

Double-clicking the name of the master page displays both pages of the A-Master.

2 Choose Layout > Create Guides.

3 Select the Preview checkbox.

4 Under Rows, type **8** for Number, and type **0** for Gutter.

5 For Fit Guides to, select Margins to see how the horizontal guides will appear on your master pages.

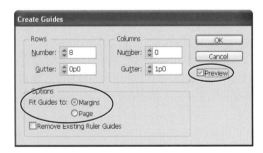

Selecting Margins instead of Page causes the guides to fit within the margin boundaries rather than the page boundaries. You won't add column guides because column lines already appear in your document.

6   Click OK.

Grids can also be added to individual document pages using the same command when working on a document page rather than a master page.

Renaming the master page

You will rename this first master page "Grid." When documents contain several master pages, you may want to rename each master page to give them more descriptive names.

1   Confirm that the A-Master page is still selected. Click the Palette Menu button (▶) in the upper corner of the Pages palette, and choose Master Options for "A-Master."

2   For Name, type **Grid,** and then click OK.

Note: In addition to changing the name of master pages, you can also use the Master Options dialog window to change other properties of existing master pages.

Creating a master page for footers

The grid you added to the master is necessary for most of the pages in the document. In addition to the common grid, most document pages will require consistent text along their top (a header), or consistent text along their bottom (a footer). Some document pages will also require consistent placement of text and graphics. To accommodate these different designs, you'll create a separate master for pages that require footers, and another master that contains placeholder frames for text and graphics.

You can build each master page independently, or you can base master pages on other master pages. In this document, the Footer master will be based on the Grids master, and the Placeholder master will be based on the Footer master. By basing master pages on other masters, any change to the parent master will appear on the child masters.

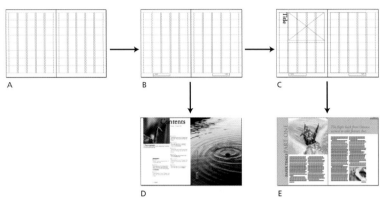

A. *A-Grid master.* **B.** *B-Footer master.* **C.** *C-Placeholder master.*
D. *Document pages based on B-Footer.* **E.** *Document pages based on C-Placeholder.*

1 In the Pages palette, choose New Master from the Pages palette menu.

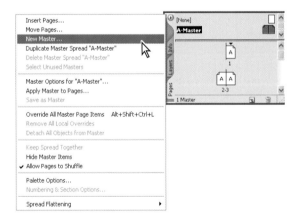

2 For Name, type **Footer**.

3   For Based on Master, choose A-Grid, and then click OK.

You're now working on a separate master page spread, as indicated by the selected B-Footer icons that appear in the upper section of the Pages palette. You can also confirm the current page in the lower left corner of the document window. The grid you added to the A-Grid master appears on the new master spread.

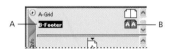

A. Name of Master.
B. The A's indicate that the B-Master
is based on the A-Master.

Dragging guides from rulers

Footers are often placed below the lower margin of the page where there are no column guides. To position the footers accurately, you will add a horizontal ruler guide and two vertical ruler guides.

1   Make sure that the B-Footer master pages are still selected in the Pages palette and visible in your document window. If necessary, double-click the B-footer master in the Pages palette to select it.

2   Without clicking in your document, move the cursor around the document window and watch the horizontal and vertical rulers as the cursor moves. Notice how the hairline indicators in the rulers correspond to the cursor's position. Also notice that the dimmed X and Y values in the Control palette indicate the position of the cursor.

3 Holding down Ctrl (Windows) or Command (Mac OS), position the cursor in the horizontal ruler, click and drag down to the 62 pica marker to create a ruler guide. Don't worry about placing the guide exactly at 62 picas—you'll do that in the next step. (You can look in the Transform palette to see the current position.)

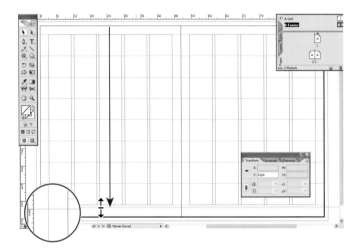

Holding down Ctrl (Windows) or Command (Mac OS), while dragging a guide applies the guide to the spread instead of the individual page.

💡 *You can also drag the ruler guide without the Ctrl or Command keys and release the guide over the pasteboard to have a guide appear across all pages in a spread as well as the pasteboard.*

4 To make sure the guide is at the 62 pica location, select the Selection tool (▶) and click the guide to select it. When selected, the guide changes color. In the Control palette, the Y value is no longer dimmed, because the guide is selected. If the guide is not at the 62p location, select the Y value in the Control palette. In the Y text field, type **62p** to replace the current value, and then press Return or Enter.

5 Click and drag a ruler guide from the vertical ruler to the 12p0.6 marker. The ruler guide snaps to the column guide at that location. Refer to the X value in the Control palette as you drag.

6   Drag another guide from the vertical ruler to the 88p5.4 marker.

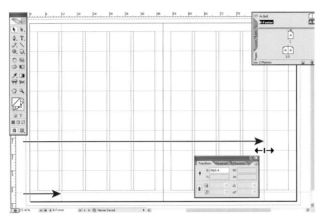

7   Choose File > Save.

Note: You can create page ruler guides which apply only to the page on which you drag, or a spread ruler guide which applies across all pages in the spread and across the pasteboard.

Creating a footer text frame in the master page

Any text or graphics that you place on the master page will appear on pages to which the master is applied. To create a footer, you'll add a publication title ("Origami") and a page-number marker to the bottom of both master pages.

1   Make sure that you can see the bottom of the left master page. If necessary, zoom in and use the scroll bars or Hand tool (🖑).

2   Select the Type tool (T) in the toolbox. On the left master page, drag to create a text frame below the second column where the guides intersect, as shown. Don't worry about drawing the frame in exactly the right location—you'll snap it into place later.

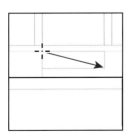

Note: When drawing a frame with the Type tool, the frame starts where the horizontal baseline intersects the I beam in the cursor—not the upper corner of cursor.

3   With the text insertion point blinking in the new text frame, choose Type > Insert Special Character > Auto Page Number.

The letter B, which represents the B-Footer master, appears in your text frame. This character reflects the current page number in your document pages, such as "2" on page 2.

4   To add an em space after the page number, right-click (Windows) or Ctrl+click (Mac OS) with your cursor blinking in the text frame to display a context menu, and then choose Insert White Space > Em Space. You can also choose this same command under the Type menu if you prefer.

5   Type **Origami** after the em space.

Next, you'll change the font and size of the text in the frame.

6   In the toolbox, select the Selection tool (⬆) and click on the text frame containing the footer.

7   Choose Type > Character to view the Character palette.

8   In the Character palette, click and hold the font family drop-down menu, scroll to the g's on the alphabetical list and select Adobe Garamond Pro.

9   Using the font size drop-down menu, select 10 pt.

Note: *You can edit the attributes of all text in a frame by selecting the frame with the Selection tool. To change the attributes of a portion of text, select the Type tool.*

Note: *It's easy to confuse the Font Size menu (T) with the Leading menu (A). Make sure that you change the font size, not the leading.*

💡 *When no items are selected, changes made in the Character palette or other palettes become your default settings. To avoid modifying your defaults, be certain an object is selected before making changes in a palette.*

10 In the toolbox, select the Selection tool. If necessary, drag the footer frame so that it snaps to the horizontal and vertical guides, as shown.

11 Check coordinates by clicking on the upper left corner of the Reference Point indicator (▦), in the upper left of the Control palette. The Control palette should display an X value of 12p06 and a Y value of 62p.

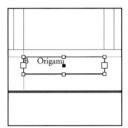

12 Click a blank area of your document window or choose Edit > Deselect All to deselect the text frame.

Duplicating to create a second footer

You have created a footer text frame on the left master page. Unless you insert a similar footer on the right master page, only the left-facing pages in your document will have page numbers. You'll copy the text frame to the right master page, and edit it from there.

1 Choose View > Fit Spread in Window to show both master pages.

2 Using the Selection tool (▶), select the footer frame on the left page. Hold down the Alt key (Windows) or Option key (Mac OS), and click and drag the text frame to the right master page so that it snaps to the guides, mirroring the right master page as shown.

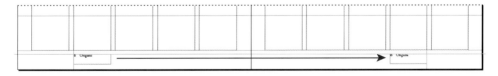

3 Make sure that you can see the bottom of the right master page. If necessary, increase the magnification and scroll as needed to view the text on the bottom of the right master page.

4   Select the Type tool (T), and then click anywhere inside the text frame on the right master page, creating an insertion point.

5   Click the Paragraph Formatting Controls button (¶) in the Control palette, and then click Align Right.

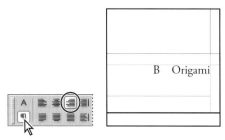

Click on the Paragraph Formatting Controls button in the upper left of the Control palette to see alignment options.

The text is now right-aligned within the footer frame on the right master page. Now you will modify the right master page, placing the page number on the right side of the word "Origami."

6   Delete the em space and page number at the beginning of the footer.

7   Click to place the insertion point at the end of the word "Origami," and then choose Type > Insert Special Character > Auto Page Number.

8   Place the insertion point between "Origami" and the page number; right-click (Windows) or Ctrl+click (Mac OS), and then choose Insert White Space > Em Space.

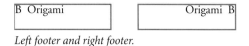

Left footer and right footer.

9   Choose Edit > Deselect All and then choose File > Save.

Creating a placeholder master

Next, you'll create a third master page for placeholders for the text and graphics that will appear in your articles. By creating placeholders on the master pages, you can ensure a consistent layout among articles, and you won't need to create text frames for each page in your document.

1   In the Pages palette, choose New Master from the Pages palette menu.

2   For Name, type **Placeholder**.

3   For Based on Master, choose B-Footer, and then click OK.

Notice that the C-Placeholder icons display the letter B in each page in the Pages palette. This letter indicates that the B-Footer master serves as the foundation for the C-Placeholder master. If you were to change either the A-Grid master or the B-Footer master, the changes would also be reflected in the C-Placeholder master. You may also notice that you cannot easily select objects, such as the footers, from other master pages. You'll learn about selecting and overriding master page objects later in this lesson.

Adding a title placeholder frame

The first placeholder will contain the title of the article in a rotated text box.

1   To center the left page in the document window, double-click the left page icon of the C-Placeholder master in the Pages palette.

2   Select the Type tool (T). Position your cursor to the left of the edge of the page, in the pasteboard area. Click and drag to create a text frame that is slightly wider than the page, and approximately as tall as one of the grid blocks. You'll position and resize this text frame later.

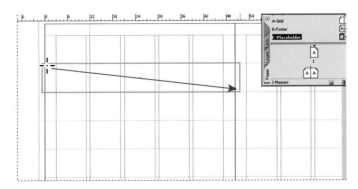

3   With the text insertion point inside of the new text frame, type **title part xxx**.

4   Triple-click the text you typed in the previous step to select all the characters in the frame.

5   Click the Character Formatting Controls button (Ⓐ) in the Control palette to view the Character formatting options. Select the font family drop-down menu and choose Trajan Pro.

The Trajan font family has only capital letters, so now the text you typed appears in all capitals.

6   Double-click to select the word "TITLE." Using the font size drop-down menu in the Control palette, select 36 pt. Next select the words "PART XXX" and select 60 pt for the type size.

7   In the Control palette, select the Paragraph Formatting Controls button and click the Align Center option.

8   Select the Selection tool (↖); the text frame is selected. Click and drag the lower center handle of the text frame until the frame is just large enough to contain the text. If the text disappears, drag the handle down again to make it larger. When you finish, choose View > Fit Spread in Window to zoom out.

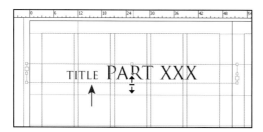

9 In the Control palette, select the upper left point of the Reference Point indicator (⬛). Choose the Rotation Angle drop-down menu on the right of the Control palette and select -90 degrees.

10 Drag the rotated text frame down so that it snaps to the top of the right column guide in the far left column. Then drag the center handle on the bottom of the frame to stretch the frame to the lower margin of the page.

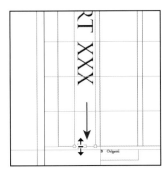

11 Click a blank area of the page or pasteboard to deselect, and then save the document.

Adding a placeholder frame for graphics

You have now created the placeholder text frame for the title of your article. Next, you'll add two graphics frames to the master pages. Similar to the text frames, these graphics frames act as placeholders for the document pages, helping you to maintain a consistent design.

Note: While you are creating placeholder frames for text and graphics in this exercise, it is not necessary to build placeholder frames on every document you create. For some smaller documents, you may not need to create master pages and placeholder frames.

Two tools can create rectangles: the Rectangle tool (▢) and the Rectangle Frame tool (⊠). Although they are more or less interchangeable, the Rectangle Frame tool—which includes a non-printing X—is commonly used for creating placeholders for graphics.

Creating a guide before you draw makes it easy to position the graphics frames.

1 Choose View > Grids & Guides and confirm there is a check mark next to the Snap to Guides option.

2 Drag a ruler guide from the horizontal ruler to the 36 picas position on the left master page. Remember that you can use the Control palette to identify the location of the guide as you position it.

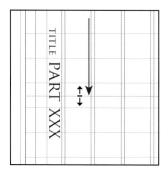

To make sure that the guide is at the 36-pica location, select the Selection tool (➤) in the toolbox and click the guide to select it (the guide changes color). Then type **36p** in the Y text field of the Control palette, and press Enter or Return.

3 Select the Rectangle Frame tool (⊠) in the toolbox.

4 Position the cursor in the upper left corner of the left page, at the position X 12p0.6 and Y 3p0. Click and drag to create a frame, so that the frame covers the area from the top edge of the page down to the horizontal guide you set at the 36 pica mark and spreads across the page to the guide at the 47p3 position.

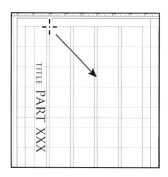 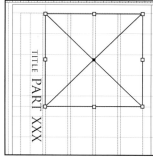

5 Choose File > Save.

Drawing a colored shape

You'll now add a background for the title bar and another background across the top of the right master. These elements will then appear on any pages that you assign to the C-Placeholder master. This time, you'll use the Rectangle tool instead of the Rectangle Frame tool because you'll fill the frames with a color swatch.

1   Choose Edit > Deselect All.

2   In the Pages palette, double-click the right page of the C-Placeholder master page or scroll horizontally so that the right page is centered in the document window.

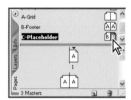

3   In the toolbox, select the Selection tool (✸) and drag from the horizontal ruler to the 16 pica mark to create a new ruler guide. Then click a blank area to deselect the guide.

Hold down the Shift key while creating ruler guides to have them positioned at the increments shown on the ruler.

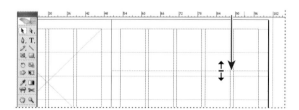

When you are selecting and dragging frames, it's common to accidentally move guides. To prevent guides from accidentally moving, you'll lock the guides.

4   Choose View > Grids & Guides > Lock Guides.

The Lock Guides command is also available from the context menu when right-clicking (Windows) or Ctrl+clicking (Mac OS) on a blank area of the page or pasteboard.

5   Choose Window > Swatches to open the Swatches palette.

6   In the upper left corner of the palette, click the Stroke box (⌷) to activate it, and then click None in the list of Swatches. This eliminates the outline around the edge of the shape you are going to draw.

Notice that the Stroke box is also in front of the Fill box in the toolbox.

7   In the same area of the Stroke palette, click the Fill box (■) to make it active. Then click [Paper] in the list of swatches, to set Paper as a placeholder color for the objects you draw next.

8   Select the Rectangle Frame tool (⊠) in the toolbox. Position your cursor approximately at 50pX and 0pY location on the page. Click and drag, drawing a frame from the top edge of the paper to the horizontal guide at 16 picas, and stretching from one edge of the page to the other.

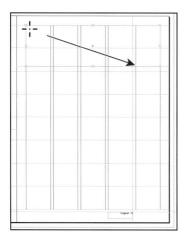

9   In the Pages palette, double-click the left page icon for C-Placeholder, to center the left master page in the document window.

10   Still using the Rectangle tool, draw a frame covering the left margin of the page along with the first column and extending from the top to the bottom of the page.

Notice that the new frame blocks the title placeholder text from view.

11 With the new rectangle frame still selected, choose Object > Arrange > Send to Back.

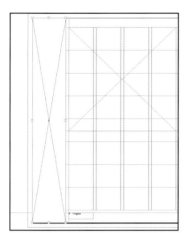 

12 Choose File > Save to save your file.

Creating text frames with columns

You have added placeholders for the title, graphic, and two background blocks for the C-Placeholder master pages. To finish the C-Placeholder master, you'll create the text frames for the story text.

1 Select the Type tool (T), and on the left master page, approximately position your cursor at the X position of 12p and Y position of 39p. Click and drag down and to the right, creating a text frame. As you create the frame, snap it to the guides so that it is three rows tall and four columns wide. This text frame occupies the area at the bottom of the left master page.

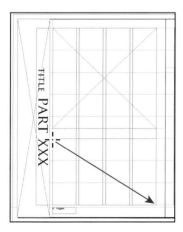

2   Choose View > Fit Spread in Window. Close or hide any palettes, as necessary, to view the spread.

3   On the right master page, position your cursor at approximately the X position of 53p3 and Y position of 17p6, then click and drag to create a text frame six rows tall and five columns wide, snapping to the guides as shown.

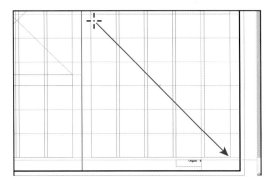

Next, you'll make sure that each of the main-story text frames has two columns.

4   Select the Selection tool (⭠). Shift+click to select both text frames.

5   In the Control palette, click the up arrow in the Number of Columns field to increase the number of columns to 2.

Each of the main-story text frames will include two columns of text. To make the text flow from one text frame to the next, you will thread the frames.

6   Click the out port in the lower right corner of the text frame on the left master page. Position the cursor over the text frame on the right master page so that it changes from a loaded text icon (⬛) to a link icon (🔗), and then click. The text frames are now linked.

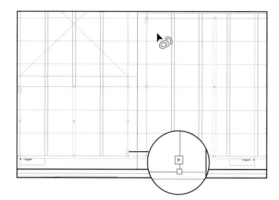

7   Save the document.

Note: Choose View > Show Text Threads to see visual representatives of threaded frames. You can thread text frames whether or not they contain text.

Applying the masters to document pages

Now that you have created all the master pages, it's time to apply them to the pages in your layout. By default, all the document pages are formatted with the A-Grid master. You will apply the B-Footer master and the C-Placeholder master to the appropriate pages. You can apply master pages by dragging the master page icons onto the document-page icons or by using a palette-menu option.

In large documents, you may find it easier to display the page icons horizontally in the Pages palette.

1   In the Pages palette, click the palette menu and choose Palette Options.

Note: Palette menus may be located in either the upper left or upper right corner of a palette, depending upon whether it is docked.

2   In the Pages section, deselect the Show Vertically option, and then click OK.

3   Position your cursor over the horizontal bar, located beneath the master pages. Click and drag down, so that you can see all the master pages. Then position the cursor in the lower right corner of the Pages palette, click and drag the lower right corner of the Pages palette down, until you can see all the spreads.

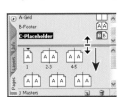 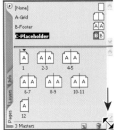

Now that you can see all the pages in the document, you'll apply the C-Placeholder master to pages in the document that will contain articles.

4   Click the C-Placeholder name, drag the name down and position it immediately to the left of the number 6 or immediately to the right of the number 7, below the page icons. Do not position the cursor over the page icons. When a box appears around both page icons representing the spread, release the mouse button.

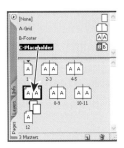 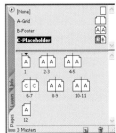

The C-Placeholder master pages are applied to pages 6 and 7, as indicated by the letter C in the page icons. Instead of dragging the C-Placeholder master to the remaining spreads, you'll use a different method to apply master pages.

5   In the Pages palette menu, located in the upper corner of the pages palette, choose Apply Master to Pages. For Apply Master, choose C-Placeholder. For To Pages, type **8-11**. Click OK.

Notice that pages 6-11 in the Pages palette are now formatted with the C-Placeholder master. Now you'll format pages 2-5 with the B-Footer master. Pages 2-5 will contain introductory material that requires a footer without placeholder frames.

6   Choose Apply Master to Pages from the Pages palette menu. For Apply Master, choose B-Footer. For To Pages, type **2-5**. Click OK.

Page 12 requires individual formatting without page numbering, so no master page formatting is required for this page.

7   In the Pages palette, click and drag the None master page down onto the page 12 icon. Release the cursor when the icon is highlighted.

Make sure that the A-Grid master is assigned to page 1, the B-Footer master is assigned to pages 2-5, and the C-Placeholder master is assigned to pages 6-11; page 12 should have no master page assigned to it.

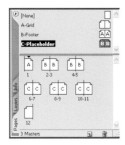

8   Choose File > Save.

Adding sections to change page numbering

The magazine you're working on requires introductory material that is numbered with lowercase Roman numerals (i, ii, iii, and so on). You can use different kinds of page numbering by adding a section. You'll start a new section on page 2 to create Roman-numeral page numbering, and then you'll start another section on page 6 to revert to Arabic numerals and restart numbering sequence.

1   In the Pages palette, double-click the page 2 icon to select it within the palette and view page 2 in the document window.

Notice that because the B-Footer master is assigned to page 2, the page includes the guides and footer information, but it does not include any of the placeholder frames that you added to the C-Placeholder master.

2   In the Pages palette menu, choose Numbering & Section Options. In the New Section dialog window, make sure that Start Section and Automatic Page Numbering are selected, or select them now.

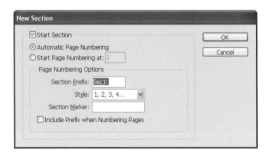

3   For Style, choose i, ii, iii, iv from the drop-down menu. Click OK and examine the page icons in the Pages palette. Starting with page 2, the numbers now appear as Roman numerals in the footers of the pages.

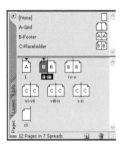

The triangle above page ii indicates the start of a section.

Now you'll specify that the document uses Arabic numbers for the pages from 6 through the end of the document.

4   Click page 6 (vi) in the Pages palette to select it.

Note: Single-clicking a page targets the page for editing purposes. If you want to navigate to a page, double-click the page in the Pages palette.

5   Click the Pages palette menu in the upper corner of the Pages palette and choose Numbering & Section Options.

6   In the New Section dialog window, make sure that the Start Section is selected or select it now.

7   Select Start Page Numbering At, press Tab and type **2** to start the section numbering with page 2.

8   For Style, select 1, 2, 3, 4 and then click OK.

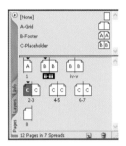

Now your pages are properly renumbered. Notice that a black triangle appears above pages 1, ii, and 2 in the Pages palette. These triangles indicate the start of a new section.

9   Choose File > Save.

Adding new pages

You can also add new pages to your existing document. We are going to add two additional pages.

1   In the Pages palette menu, choose Insert Pages.

2   Enter **2** for the number of pages, choose At End of Document from the drop-down menu and then select C-Placeholder for the Master page that will be applied to the new pages.

3   Click OK. The document now has two additional pages.

Deleting and arranging pages

With the pages palette, you can also arrange the sequence of pages, and delete extra pages.

1　In the Pages palette, double-click the page 9 icon, then click and drag it to the left of the page 8 icon. When you see a black bar to the left of page 8, let go. Page 9 is moved to the position of page 8, and page 8 is moved to the position previously held by page 9.

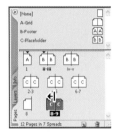

2　Double-click the hyphen beneath the spread containing the icons for pages 8 and 9 to select both pages.

3　Click the Trash button at the bottom of the palette. Pages 8 and 9 are deleted from the document.

Placing text and graphics on the document pages

Now that the framework of the 12-page publication is in place, you're ready to format the individual articles. To see how the changes you made to the master pages affect document pages, you'll add text and graphics to the spread on pages 2 and 3.

1　In the Pages palette, double-click the page 2 icon (not page ii) to center the page in the document window.

Notice that because the C-Placeholder master is assigned to page 2, the page includes the grid, the footers, and the placeholder frames.

To import text and graphics from other applications, such as images from Adobe Photoshop or text from Microsoft Word, you'll use the Place command.

2 To be certain sure that nothing is selected, choose Edit > Deselect All. Then choose File > Place. Open the Lesson_02 folder in your InDesignCIB folder, and double-click 02_c.doc, a text file created using Microsoft Word.

The cursor changes to a loaded text icon (⬚), indicating that it can be used to place the text you are importing. With a loaded text icon, you can drag to create a text frame, or click inside an existing text frame. When you hold the loaded text icon over an existing text frame, the icon appears in parentheses (⬚). You can click to insert the text into the individual frame, or you can Shift+click to autoflow the text into the threaded frames. You'll use several of these methods to better understand how to import and flow text.

3 As you hold down the Shift key, the loaded text icon changes to the automatic flow icon (⬚). Click anywhere inside the text frame on the bottom of page 2. Release the Shift key.

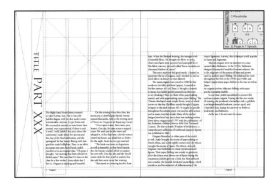

The text flowed into the text frames on pages 2 and 3. The text followed the link you created between the text frames when you set up the master page because you held down the Shift key and auto-flowed the text. Now you'll add a native Photoshop file, saved with layers to the placeholder frame.

Note: If your text did not flow as indicated, Edit > Undo and reposition the cursor so that it is in the 2-column text frame.

4 Choose Edit > Deselect All to make sure that no frames are selected.

💡 *If a frame is selected when you place a file, the contents of the file will be added to the selected frame. You can avoid this by either deselecting objects prior to importing, or by deselecting "Replace Selected Item" in the Place dialog window when importing text or graphics.*

5   Choose File > Place and check the Show Import Options checkbox. Select the 02_d.psd file in the Lesson_02 folder.

6   The Image Import Options window appears. Since this .psd file was saved with layers, you can turn the visibility on or off, right in InDesign. Turn the visibility off of the layer named second bird by clicking on the eye icon (👁) to the left of the named layer. Click OK.

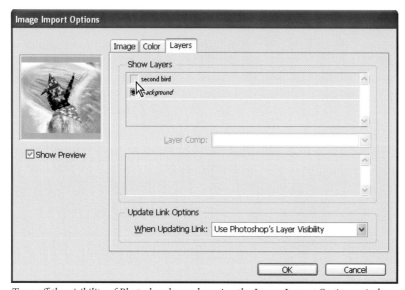

Turn off the visibility of Photoshop layers by using the Image Import Options window.

7   The cursor takes the shape of a loaded graphics icon (🖌). Position the loaded graphics icon over the graphics-frame placeholder on page 2 so that the cursor appears in parentheses (🖌), and click.

💡 *Parentheses appear when InDesign recognizes a pre-existing frame beneath the cursor when importing text or graphics into your layout. InDesign uses the existing frame rather than creating a new text or graphic frame.*

8   To position the image correctly, choose Object > Fitting > Center Content. Then click on an empty portion of the page to deselect all objects or choose Edit > Deselect All.

9   Choose File > Save, to save your artwork.

Overriding master page items on document pages

The placeholders you added to the master pages appear on the document pages. InDesign prevents you from accidentally moving or deleting these objects by requiring you to use special modifier keys when selecting them on your document pages. You'll now replace the word "Title" with "History of Origami." Editing this text requires you to select the master page frame that contains the text "Title."

1   To make sure you're on page 2, select Sec2:2 from the Pages pop-up list in the status bar at the bottom left corner of the document window.

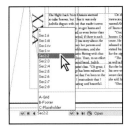

2   If necessary, adjust your view so that you can see the "TITLE PART XXX" text on page 2. Choose the Selection tool (↖) and try to select this text frame by clicking on it.

You cannot select master page items on the document pages simply by clicking. However, by holding down a modifier key on your keyboard, you can then select a master page object such as this text frame.

3   Holding down Shift+Ctrl (Windows) or Shift+Command (Mac OS), click the title placeholder frame on the left side of page 2 to select it.

4   Using the Type tool (T), double-click the word "TITLE" to select it, and then type **paper trails**. Then select the "XXX," and type **one**. The text is now replaced on the document page.

5   Using the Type tool, triple-click in the text "PAPER TRAILS PART ONE" to select all the text.

6   In the toolbox, select the Zoom tool (⌕) and then drag a marquee around the image of the origami crane to magnify the image, so that the area you drag fills the window.

7   In the toolbox, make sure that the Text Fill box (⊤) is selected, and then select the Eyedropper tool (✎). Move the tip of the Eyedropper tool over one of the deep red stripes on the crane and click to select it. The color you click becomes the fill color that is applied to the text you selected.

Dragging a zoom marquee.   Selecting color with the
Eyedropper tool.

8   Choose View > Fit Spread in Window. Notice that even though you've used other tools, the text is still selected. Choose Edit > Deselect All to see the text now filled with the red color you selected.

9   Using the Selection tool (▸), hold down Ctrl+Shift (Windows) or Command+Shift (Mac OS) and click to select the two rectangles you created on the placeholder master pages.

Note: *While you created these rectangles on a master page, they appear on the document page you are currently formatting, because the master page is applied to this document page.*

10 Repeat steps 6 and 7, but this time select a mustard yellow color from the origami crane to fill the rectangles. Keep the rectangle frames selected.

The document with the rectangle frames selected.   *Color is applied to the rectangle frames.*

11 Choose View > Fit Spread in Window, and choose Object > Arrange > Send to Back so that the yellow rectangles do not hide the title text, then choose Edit > Deselect All.

12 Choose File > Save to save your work.

Editing master pages

You can make changes to master pages even after you have applied them. You'll change the master page, reversing the direction of the vertical text.

1 In the Pages palette, double-click the C-Placeholder to display these pages.

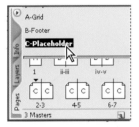

2 Select the Selection tool (), and then click the "TITLE PART XXX" text frame.

The Reference Point indicator (⊞) in both the Control and Transform palettes determines the anchor point that is used for measurements and transformations, such as rotation.

3 In the Transform palette, select the center point in the Reference Point indicator (⊞) so the object will rotate on that point.

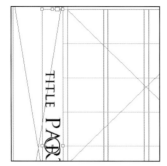

4 In the Control palette menu, select Rotate 90° from the Rotation Angle drop-down menu. The text block now reads up from the bottom of the column. Choose Edit > Deselect All.

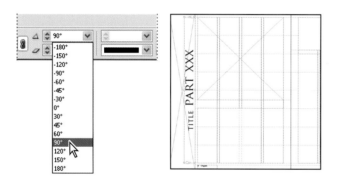

5 In the Pages palette, double-click page 2 (not page ii) to switch views from the master pages to the page with the origami story.

Notice that the settings you applied (local overrides) to the title text on the document page remain in effect—that is, the text is still red and still says "PAPER TRAILS" instead of "TITLE," and "PART ONE" instead of "XXX."

Rotating the frame on the master page affected all the pages to which the master was applied, including the page containing the text you changed, which is called a local override. When you change a master page item on a document page, you override only the set of attributes that you modify. In this case, you changed the text and the color of text on the document page. If you were to change the text or color of text on the master page, those changes would not affect this overridden object.

Viewing the completed spread

Now you'll hide guides and frames to see what the completed spread looks like.

1 Choose View > Fit Spread in Window and hide any palettes, if necessary.

2 In the toolbox, click the Preview Mode button (⬛) to hide all guides, grids, frame edges, and the pasteboard.

You have formatted enough of the 12-page document to see how adding objects to the master pages helps you maintain a consistent design throughout your document.

3 Choose File > Save.

Congratulations. You have finished the lesson.

Exploring on your own

A good way to reinforce the skills you've learned in this lesson is to experiment with them. Try some of the following exercises that give you more practice with InDesign techniques.

1   Place another photograph at the bottom of the second column of text on page 3. Use the 02_e.jpg image that is inside the Extras folder within the Lesson_02 folder.

2   Add a read-in pull-quote: Using the Type tool (T), select the opening phrase of the story, from "The flight..." through "...take forever." Choose Edit > Cut. Then use the Type tool to drag a frame in the yellow panel across the top of page 3, and choose Edit > Paste. Triple-click the text you pasted, and use the Character palette to format it using the font, size, style, and color of your choice.

3   Try rotating the "title" text block using different corners or edges of the Reference Point indicator (⌗) in the Control or Transform palette, and notice the difference in the results.

4   Create a new pair of master pages for a spread that you could use for the continuation of this story. Name the new master page **D-Next** and select B-Footer for the Based On option. Then create placeholder frames for the text and graphics, giving the spread a different arrangement from C-Placeholder master pages. When you finish, apply the D-Next master pages to pages 4-5 of your document.

Review

▶ **Review questions**

1   What are the advantages of adding objects to master pages?

2   How do you change the page-numbering scheme?

3   How do you select a master page item on a document page?

▶ **Review answers**

1   By adding objects such as guides, footers, and placeholder frames to master pages, you can maintain a consistent layout on the pages to which the master is applied.

2   In the Pages palette, select the page icon where you want new page numbering to begin. Then choose Section Options from the Pages palette menu and specify the new page-numbering scheme.

3   Hold down Shift+Ctrl (Windows) or Shift+Command (Mac OS), and then click the object to select it. You can then edit, delete, or otherwise manipulate the object.

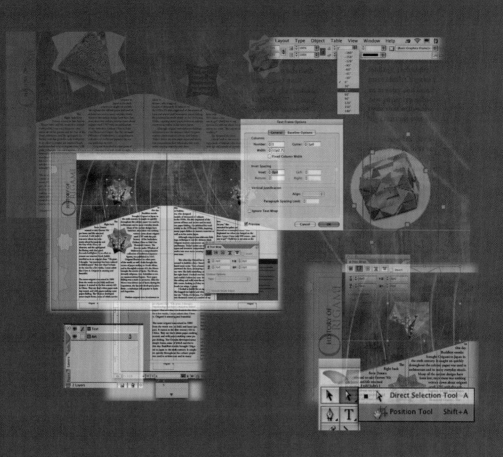

InDesign frames may contain either text or graphics. As you work with frames, you'll notice that InDesign provides a great amount of flexibility and control over your design.

3 | Working with Frames

In this introduction to working with frames, you'll learn how to do the following:

- Use the Selection and Direct Selection tools to modify frames.
- Resize and reshape text and graphics frames.
- Distinguish between bounding boxes and their frames.
- Crop a graphic.
- Scale an image contained in a graphics frame.
- Move a graphic within its frame.
- Convert a graphics frame to a text frame.
- Wrap text around an object.
- Create and rotate a polygon frame.
- Align graphic objects to each other.
- Center and scale an object within a frame.

Getting started

In this lesson, you'll work on a two-page article for a magazine about origami, the Japanese art of paper folding. Before you begin, you'll need to restore the default preferences for Adobe InDesign to ensure that the tools and palettes function exactly as described in this lesson. Then you'll open the finished document for this lesson to see what you'll be creating.

1   Delete or deactivate (by renaming) the InDesign Defaults file and the InDesign SavedData file, as described in "Restoring default preferences" on page 2.

2   Start Adobe InDesign. To begin working, you'll open an InDesign document that is already partially completed.

3   Choose File > Open, and open the 03_a.indd file in the Lesson_03 folder, located inside the Lessons folder within the InDesignCIB folder on your hard disk. If you receive Profile or Policy Mismatch warnings for the RGB and CMYK color profiles, click OK. This will convert to your color settings. Read more about color in Lesson 6, "Working with Color."

Note: If you have not already copied the resource files for this lesson onto your hard disk from the Lesson_03 folder from the Adobe InDesign CS2 Classroom in a Book CD, do so now. See "Copying the Classroom in a Book files" on page 4.

4   Choose File > Save As, rename the file **03_frames.indd**, and save it in the Lesson_03 folder.

5   To see what the finished document will look like, open the 03_b.indd file in the same folder. You can leave this document open to act as a guide as you work. When you're ready to resume working on the lesson document, choose Window > 03_frames.indd.

Note: As you work through the lesson, feel free to move palettes around or change the magnification to a level that works best for you.

Modifying text frames

In most cases, text must be placed inside of a frame. The size and location of a frame determine how the text appears on a page.

Resizing text frames

You'll resize a text frame using the Selection tool. The size of the text characters inside the frame remains unchanged, but when you resize a frame, the text flow will wrap differently or may display more or less text after you change the frame size.

This document includes two layers: Art and Text. You'll lock the Art layer so that you won't accidentally select the shapes while you resize the text frames.

1   Click the Layers palette tab (or choose Window > Layers if you do not see the Layers palette), and do the following:

*   Click the layer lock box ( ) to the left of the Art layer to lock the layer.

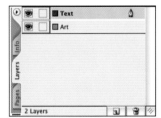 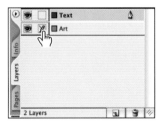

*   Using the Selection tool ( ), click to select the text frame on the left page. Notice that the text frame has eight hollow handles and a solid center point.

2   Drag the center top handle upward to resize the height of the frame until it snaps to the horizontal guide immediately above the frame (near 22 picas on the vertical ruler). When you release the mouse, text reflows throughout the entire frame.

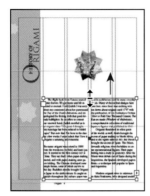 

Click and drag center point   Result.
of frame to resize.

When you want to simultaneously resize a text frame and the text characters inside it, use the Scale tool (⊞).

About frames, paths, and selections

When you select an object on an InDesign page, various color-coded lines and small squares appear around the object. These items represent the bounding box, handles, path, anchor points, and center point. The colors defined in the Layer palette determine how these attributes appear on screen.

• The frame is a container for text, graphics, or colored fills, or it can be empty. The frame is independent of its contents, so the edges of the frame may hide part of its graphic contents, or the contents may not entirely fill the frame. A frame with no content can serve as a placeholder for text, images, or fills that you add later.

• A bounding box is always rectangular, enclosing the maximum horizontal and vertical extensions of the selected item. The bounding boxes for a frame and for the graphic inside it can be different sizes.

• The path and the shape of a frame are identical and do not have to be rectangular. A path is a vector graphic. You can use InDesign drawing tools to create paths and then do all the things you can do to any closed paths, such as add fills, specify stroke attributes, and edit the paths with the Pen tool (✒).

• There are eight handles and a center point for a bounding box, appearing as small squares in the corners, at the midpoints of top, bottom, and sides, and in the center. Dragging a handle modifies the bounding box.

• The path is defined by anchor points, which look like smaller handles. You drag anchor points to alter the shape of the path. When the anchor points are visible, you can also see the center point for the frame. When the path is visible, you can click the center point to select all anchor points in the path.

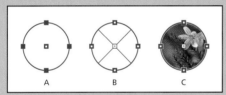

A. Path. *B.* Frame as a graphic container.
C. Frame with a placed graphic.

The tool you use to select an object determines how you can change it.

• Use the Type tool (T) to type text and to select and edit text within a text frame.

• Use the Selection tool (▶) to move or resize a frame.

• Use the Direct Selection tool (▷) to reshape the path by selecting and working with anchor points. Also use this tool to set path characteristics and to resize, reshape, and move the graphic within a graphics frame without altering the frame itself.

Using anchor points to reshape a text frame

So far, you've dragged a handle to resize the text frame, using the Selection tool. Now, you'll use an anchor point to reshape the frame, using the Direct Selection tool.

1   If the text frame on the left page is not selected, use the Selection tool (▶) to select it now.

2   In the toolbox, click the Direct Selection tool (▷). Four very small anchor points now appear at the corners of the selected text frame. The anchor points are hollow, indicating that none of them are selected.

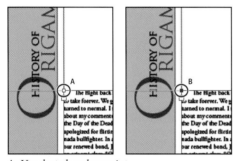

A. Unselected anchor point.
B. Selected anchor point.

3   Select the anchor point in the upper left corner of the text frame and drag it downward until it snaps to the horizontal guide below it. (After you start dragging, you can hold down the Shift key to restrict any horizontal movement.)

Make sure you drag only the anchor point—if you drag just below the anchor point, you'll move the text frame.

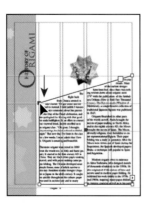

4   Press V on your keyboard to switch to the Selection tool.

To see both the bounding box and the path, choose View > Show Frame Edges. To turn frame edges off again, choose View > Hide Frame Edges.

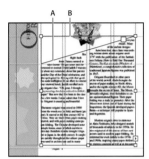

A. *Bounding box.* B. *Frame.*

Next, you'll change the text frame on the right page of the spread so that it mirrors the text frame on the left page.

5   Click a blank area of your document to deselect the text frame, or choose Edit > Deselect All.

6   Press A on your keyboard to switch back to the Direct Selection tool and click the large text block on page 5. Select the upper left anchor point of the text frame and drag it up to the same horizontal guide you used to reshape text on the left page. You can hold down the Shift key as you drag to ensure that the change is only vertical.

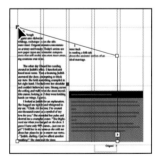

7   Deselect all objects and then choose File > Save.

Pressing the A and V keys to toggle between the Selection and Direct Selection tools are just two of many keyboard shortcuts available in InDesign. For more shortcuts, refer to "Keyboard shortcuts" in InDesign Help.

Modifying graphics frames

In this section, you'll focus on different techniques for modifying frames and frame contents. To start, you'll import an image and place it in your document spread. Because you'll be working on graphics rather than text, your first step is to make sure that the graphics appear on the Art layer rather than on the Text layer. Isolating items on different layers helps your work process so that it's easier to find and edit elements of your design.

1   In the Layers palette, click the second-column box to unlock the Art layer. Lock the Text layer by clicking in the second column box. Then select the Art layer by clicking on the name of the layer so that new elements will be assigned to this layer.

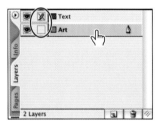

2   To center page 4 in the document window, choose 4 from the Pages pop-up menu at the bottom of the document window.

3   Choose File > Place and in the Place dialog box deselect "Replace Selected Item" and then double-click 03_c.tif in the Lesson_03 folder.

The cursor changes to a loaded graphics icon (🏊).

Note: If the cursor appears with a line through it (🏊), the current layer is selected but still locked. You cannot add objects to a locked layer. Make sure that the Art layer in the Layers palette is both unlocked and selected. The cursor should then appear as a loaded graphics icon so that you can proceed with this step.

4   Click near the top left corner of page 4, but not on the yellow bar, to place the graphic. It doesn't matter exactly where you place it, nor that the purple image may cover some of the story text. You'll fix that later.

Note: If you accidently click on a frame, your graphic will replace the current content. Use Edit > Undo, or the keyboard shortcut Ctrl+Z (Windows)/Command+Z (Mac OS) to undo and see the loaded graphic icon again.

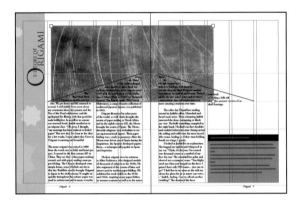

5   Press V to select the Selection tool (↖). Then drag the image so that it snaps into place at the top of the page and on the left side of the column gutter. The left edge of the graphic should fit snugly against the yellow bar of the title column, with no gap between them.

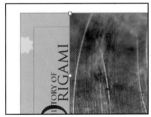

Resizing a graphics frame

The design for this page calls for the purple background image to extend across the page from the title panel to the right edge of the page. Although this image is not yet the right size or shape to do that, you'll start making those adjustments now.

First, you'll stretch the frame to fit the width of your spread.

1 Choose View > Fit Spread in Window so that you can see all of pages 4 and 5 in the document window. If necessary, scroll horizontally so that you can see the right edge of page 5 and hide the Layers palette by clicking on the Layers tab.

2 Using the Selection tool (▸), click the purple-texture graphic. Drag the lower right handle until the right side of the bounding box snaps into place against the horizontal guide at the 32-pica mark on the vertical ruler and to the last column of page 5.

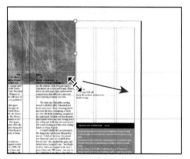 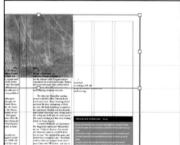

Notice that only the frame bounding box changes, not the purple image itself.

Resizing and moving an image within a frame

You have just finished resizing a graphics frame, but the content image remains unchanged. You'll now resize just the image so that it fills the designated area.

> 💡 *In addition to the methods we use here, you can also use the context menus to resize pictures to fit within their frame. Do this by right-clicking (Windows) or Ctrl+clicking (Mac OS) and selecting Fitting > Fit Content Proportionally.*

The content and frame for any placed graphics are separate elements. Unlike text objects, the frame and content for a graphic each has its own bounding box. Resizing the graphic contents is exactly like resizing the frame, except that you work with the bounding box for the contents using the Direct Selection tool (▸).

1   Press A to switch to the Direct Selection tool (↖), then position the cursor over the purple background image until the cursor appears as a hand icon (✋), then click to select the frame contents (the image itself). The bounding box changes to a brown color, indicating that the frame is no longer selected, but the contents are.

2   Select the handle in the lower right corner of the graphic bounding box, and then hold down the Shift key and drag to enlarge the image. Continue dragging until the image dimensions are even larger than the frame, so that the handle is off the page and onto the pasteboard.

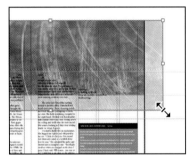 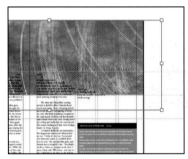

Dragging bounding box of contents, and view after dragging.

3   Move the Direct Selection tool over the purple image so that you see the hand icon. Click and drag the image with the hand icon, and notice how the area of the image that is visible within the frame changes as you drag. If you drag too far to the right, notice that the image no longer covers the left side of the frame area.

💡 *Before you start dragging, click and hold down the mouse button until the hand icon turns into a solid arrow (▶). The arrow is white on Windows, black on Mac OS. Then, after you start dragging, you'll see a ghosted image of the hidden areas of the graphic contents, a feature called Dynamic Preview. If you don't wait for the cursor icon to change, you'll still see the bounding box of the graphic as you drag.*

4   Make sure that the image entirely fills the frame, and then click a blank area of the page to deselect the purple image. Save your work.

💡 *Images expanded beyond 120% of their original size may not contain enough pixel information for high-resolution offset printing. Check with your printer or service provider if you are uncertain as to the resolution and scaling requirements needed for any documents you are having printed.*

Changing the shape of the frame

When you resized the frame using the Selection tool, the frame maintained its rectangular shape. Now you will use the Pen tool and the Direct Selection tool to reshape the frame.

1 Press A for the Direct Selection tool (⟨↖⟩). Then move the tip of the cursor over the edge of the purple-image frame, and click when the cursor appears with a small diagonal line (⟨↖⟩). This selects the path and reveals the anchor points and center point for the frame. Leave the path selected.

2 Press P to switch to the Pen tool. Carefully position the cursor over the lower edge of the frame path where it intersects with the right margin of page 4. When you see the Add Anchor Point Pen tool (⟨✎⁺⟩), click. A new anchor point is added. The Pen tool automatically changes to the Add Anchor Point tool when it is crossed over an existing path.

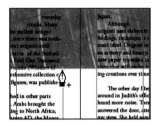

3 Move to page 5, where the lower side of the path intersects with the left margin, and using the Add Anchor Point Pen tool, click again to add another new anchor point.

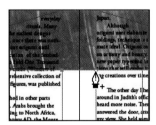

Both anchor points are solid, indicating they are selected.

4   Switch to the Direct Selection tool and drag upwards, holding down the Shift key as you drag from either one of the new anchor points or the path segment between them. When both anchor points snap into place on the next guide (at 22p on the vertical ruler), release the mouse button and the Shift key.

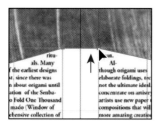

The graphic is now properly shaped and sized for the design.

5   Press V to switch to the Selection tool (↖), and select the purple graphic. Then choose Object > Arrange > Send to Back, so that the graphic appears to be behind other elements in the Art layer.

6   While the graphic is still selected, choose Object > Lock Position. This will help avoid accidental repositioning of the graphic.

💡 *You can simultaneously resize both a graphic image and its frame by using the Selection tool and holding down Ctrl+Shift (Windows) or Command+Shift (Mac OS) as you drag a handle of the frame. In this case, the Shift key maintains the proportions of the bounding boxes, so that the graphic image is not distorted. Using the Shift key is optional if distorting the image doesn't matter to your design.*

Modifying a frame within grouped objects

You can select individual elements of a grouped object using the Direct Selection tool. The black and gray rectangles behind the sidebar story in the lower right corner of page 5 are grouped, so that you can select and modify them as a unit. You'll now change the fill color of just one of the rectangles without ungrouping or changing the other elements of the group.

1   In the Layers palette, make sure the Text layer is locked and that the Art layer is selected.

2   Using the Selection tool (➤), click either the gray or the black background behind the sidebar story. The entire sidebar background is selected, showing the usual eight handles in the bounding box. Notice that a question mark appears in the toolbox Fill box (▣), indicating that the grouped items do not all have the same fill color.

3   Press Ctrl+Shift+A (Windows) or Command+Shift+A (Mac OS) to deselect the group.

4   Press A to switch to the Direct Selection tool (▷), and click the black fill in the upper part of the sidebar background. Now the four anchor points and center point for the black rectangle appear. Notice that the Fill box in the toolbox is black and that Black is highlighted in the Swatches palette.

5   Make sure that the Fill box is still selected in the toolbox. Select Window > Swatches to open the Swatches palette. Then scroll down the Swatches palette and select the Black 80% tint. Now the upper rectangle behind the text block has a dark gray fill but the lower one remains filled with light gray.

6   Save your file.

When you have the smaller rectangle selected, notice what happens if you switch back to the Selection tool: The handles appear, but only for the upper rectangle, not for the entire group, as they appeared when you did step 2, above. This can be handy when you have nested objects and want to adjust the frame without ungrouping.

Wrapping text around a graphic

You can wrap text around the frame of an object or around the object itself. In this procedure, you'll see the difference between wrapping text around the bounding box and wrapping text around the graphic.

Your first task is to move the graphic, which couldn't be easier; you just select it and drag. For precise positioning, you can also use the arrow keys to nudge a frame, or you can type exact position coordinates on the Transform palette.

1   Using the Selection tool (➤), select the eight-pointed graphics frame with the image of an origami crane that is on page 4. Being careful not to select one of the handles, move the frame down so that the bottom of the graphic snaps into alignment with the lower guide, at 42 picas on the vertical ruler. Make sure that the center point of the graphic is aligned with the middle of the gutter between the two columns of text. The frame should not have changed size, but it should have moved on the page.

Notice that the text appears on top of the image. You'll change this by applying text wrap.

2 Choose Window > Text Wrap to open the Text Wrap palette, and select the second wrap option so that the text wraps around the bounding box, not around the star-shaped frame.

 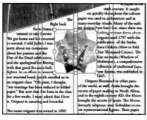

*Text wrapped around
bounding box.*

Result.

3 Next, select the third wrap option so that the text wraps around the contour of the image frame instead of the bounding box. Click a blank area to deselect all, or choose Edit > Deselect All.

 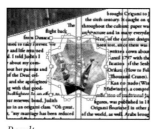

Text wrapped around content.   *Result.*

4 Leave the Text Wrap palette open for now, and choose File > Save.

Creating new frames and adjusting the contents

So far in this lesson, you've changed the size, shape, position, and color of frames and the contents within the frames. In this section, you'll experiment with different ways to create new frames quickly, with a minimum of effort. These include duplicating existing frames, drawing new frames, and replacing the existing contents of a frame. Because frames are independent of their contents, you can replace the contents of any frame with either graphics or text. You'll get experience doing both in these procedures.

Duplicating a frame and its contents

Using the familiar copy-and-paste technique, you can quickly duplicate objects in your design. In this procedure, you'll also use a keyboard shortcut to duplicate and move an object in one action.

1   Using the Selection tool (▶), select the crane graphic, and choose Edit > Copy.

2   Choose Edit > Paste. A duplicate of the crane and its frame appears in the center of the window.

3   Drag the new crane graphic up into the purple background area on page 4 so that the lower edge snaps into position with the guide at 22 picas on the vertical ruler.

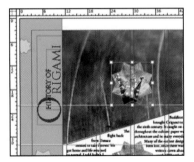

4   Choose View > Fit Spread in Window.

5   Hold down Alt (Windows) or Option (Mac OS) and drag the crane graphic to page 5. When you release the mouse, you'll see that by using the Alt or Option key, you have moved a new copy of the graphic, as the original remains in place.

> 💡 *If you hold down the mouse button for a few seconds before you start to drag, you'll see the ghosted copy of the duplicate graphic frame and contents as you move it.*

6 With the crane graphic selected on page 5, hold down the Shift key and click the crane on page 4. Turn off the text wrap option for both these graphics by selecting the No text wrap button in the Text Wrap palette.

7 Choose Edit > Deselect All.

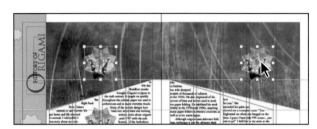

Replacing the contents of graphics frames

After you create the two duplicates, it's easy to replace the contents with other graphics or text. Your next task is to resize the new star-shaped frames and replace the crane images with other images. Because the frame and contents are independent, it's easy to swap out one image for another.

1 Using the Selection tool (⬉), select the new crane graphic you placed in the upper area of page 4. Hold down the Shift key to maintain the symmetry of the frame, drag up from the upper right handle to above the top edge of the spread so that part of the image bleeds off the page. Leave the frame selected.

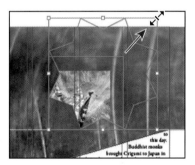

2 Choose File > Place, and browse as needed to find the 03_d.tif file in your Lesson_03 folder. Select "Replace Selected Item" in the Place dialog box.

3   Double-click the 03_d.tif to place the new image directly into the selected frame, replacing the crane image.

4   With the frame still selected, choose Object > Fitting > Fill Frame Proportionally. InDesign resizes the graphic so that it fits into the frame.

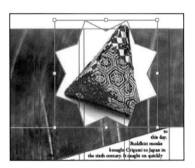

💡 *You can also access the fitting commands from the context menus by either right-clicking (Windows) or Option+clicking (Mac OS).*

5   Select the duplicate crane image on page 5.

6   Choose File > Place, and select the 03_e.jpg file in your Lesson_03 folder. Select Open. The image of an origami box replaces the image of the origami crane.

7   With the box graphic still selected, choose Object > Fitting > Fit Content to Frame. Now you've used a single frame shape three times to hold three different images.

Converting shapes

You can now change the shape of an existing frame by using the Object menu in InDesign. The shape of a frame can also be converted, even if the frame already contains text or graphics.

1   Using the Selection tool (✸), be certain the graphic you placed in the upper area of page 5 is selected.

2 Select Object > Convert Shape > Ellipse. Click and drag the Ellipse to the right of the page. Exact position is not important.

3 Select the graphic on page 4 and select Object > Convert Shape > Triangle.

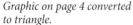

Graphic on page 4 converted to triangle.

Graphic on page 5 converted to circle.

Using the Position tool

The Position tool allows you to manipulate a frame's graphic content and the frame itself using one tool. You would typically use the Direct Selection tool in order to move a graphic within a graphics frame. You could then manipulate the position of the frame by switching to the Selection tool and moving the frame to its new position. The Position tool now allows you to perform either task without switching between two tools. The Direct Selection tool can still be used to select and modify individual points of frames.

1 Choose Edit > Deselect All.

2 Using the Direct Selection tool (⤵), click onto the edge of the triangle-shaped graphics frame on page 4.

3   Click onto the topmost point of the triangle and drag down to match the shape of the graphic.

4   Repeat step 2 with the two remaining points of the triangle frame, cropping the graphic to reveal only the origami shape.

5   Select the Position tool in the toolbox by clicking and holding on the Direct Selection tool.

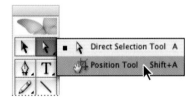

6   Click into the graphic on page 4. Notice that your cursor changes into the Hand tool (🖐) when you put your cursor over the graphic contents of the frame.

7 Position your cursor just over the edge of the origami art, noticing that your cursor changes to a triangle with a dot (▸). This indicates that you will be selecting a frame if clicked. Click on the frame and drag it to the left-hand side of the page so that its center point aligns with the margin of the first column.

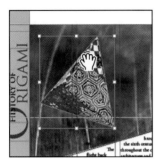

The Position tool can be used to manipulate content or a frame without switching tools.

Drawing a new graphics frame

Until now, you've used only frames prepared for you for this lesson. Now it's time to create a frame on your own, using the Drawing tools in the toolbox.

1 In the toolbox, hold down the mouse on the Rectangle tool (□) until you see other options, and select the Polygon tool (○).

2   Double-click the Polygon tool to open the Polygon Settings dialog box, and specify the following:

- For Number of Sides, type **4**.

- Type **20%** for Star Inset and then click OK.

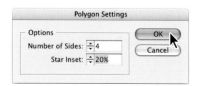

3   Hold down the Shift key and drag to draw a four-pointed star that is 12p x 12p. Use the H and W values in either the Control or Transform palette as a reference as you draw the star. If you have difficulty getting the values exactly at 12 picas, leave the star selected, type the values in the W and H boxes of the Control or Transform palette, and press Enter or Return.

4   Press V to switch to the Selection tool (➤) and then drag the new star into position in the purple background on page 5, so that it is slightly off center and entirely within the purple background image. Leave the star selected.

5   Make sure that the Fill box (◼) is selected in the toolbox.

6   Click the Swatches palette tab (or choose Window > Swatches) and select the color named C=0, M=28, Y=100, K=0 to fill the star with a mustard yellow color.

7   In the toolbox, select the Stroke box (▣) and then click the Apply None button (☑) to remove the black stroke color.

Placing and coloring text in a color-filled frame

You can place text in a frame of any closed shape, and the text will flow in to fill the shape from the top. You can even replace a graphic in a frame with text. In this case, however, the frame does not have a graphic as its contents, just a fill. The fill color simply appears as a background for the imported text.

1 Using the Selection tool (➤), select the four-point star and then hold down Alt (Windows) or Option (Mac OS) and drag a short distance to create a duplicate frame.

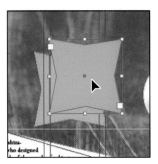

2 In the toolbox, select the Fill box (■), and then in the Swatches palette, select 80% black as the fill color for the new frame.

3 In the Layers palette, click the layer lock icon (✗) to unlock the Text layer.

4 With the 80% gray star selected, drag the dot from the Art layer to the Text layer to move the star to that layer. Leave the star selected.

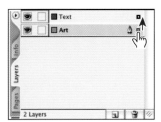

5   Choose File > Place, and then browse to the Lesson_03 folder and double-click the 03_f.doc file. The text appears in the star, with the same text formatting that it had in the original .doc file. The out port on the bounding box is empty, indicating that all the text for the pull-quote fits into the 12-pica star shape.

6   Using the Type tool (T), select the text inside the frame. Center-align the text by selecting Ctrl+Shift+C (Windows) or Cmd+Shift+C (Mac OS).

7   Make sure the Text Fill box (⊞) is selected in the Swatches palette, then click to select C=0, M=28, Y=100, K=0 so that the text is also mustard-colored.

Orienting objects in space

You've already seen how you can move, reshape, and resize elements on your document layout. In this section, you'll use various features that adjust the orientation of objects on the page and in relationship to each other. To begin, you'll adjust the inset between text and the frame that contains it. Then you'll work with rotation techniques and alignment of selected objects.

Adjusting text inset within a frame

Your next task is to finish up the pull-quote items by fitting the text nicely into the star frame. By adjusting the inset between the frame and the text, you make it easier to read.

1   Click to select the Selection tool (➤) in the toolbox, and then select the star with the pull-quote text.

Note: Do not try to use a keyboard shortcut to switch to another tool when the Text tool is active, especially if you have text selected or an insertion point placed in a block of text. Doing so would enter text, so the action would not change the tool selection.

2   Choose Object > Text Frame Options to open the Text Frame Options dialog box. If necessary, drag the dialog box aside so that you can still see the star as you set options.

3   In the dialog box, make sure that the Preview option is selected. Then, under Inset Spacing, change the Inset value to shrink the text area until it fits nicely in the frame. (The sample uses 0p2.) Then click OK to close the dialog box.

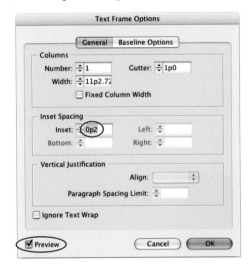

Rotating an object

There are several options within InDesign for rotating objects. In this topic, you'll use the Transform palette.

1   Using the Selection tool (➤), select the four-pointed yellow star.

2   In the Control palette, make sure that the center point is selected on the Reference Point indicator (⊞) so that the object rotates around its center, and then select 45° from the Rotation angle drop-down menu.

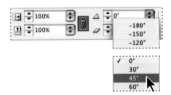

Aligning multiple objects

Now that the two four-pointed stars are set at a 45° angle from each other, you can position one on top of the other so that all eight points radiate from the same center-point position. Precise alignment is easiest when you use the Align palette.

1   Using the Selection tool (▶), select the yellow star and then hold down the Shift key and click the gray star so that both four-pointed stars are selected.

2   Choose Window > Object & Layout > Align to open the Align palette.

3   In the Align palette, select the Align horizontal centers button (♨). The two stars are now lined up exactly side by side.

4   Again, in the Align palette, click the Align vertical centers button (▦). The two stars are now centered on the same location in the layout.

5   Click a blank area to deselect all, and then save your file.

Rotating an image within its frame

You can rotate both the frame and contents in one action by selecting the object with the Selection tool (▶) and then dragging one of the handles with the Rotation tool. However, sometimes you just want to set the image at a jaunty angle. That process is just a slight variation on the procedure.

When you rotated the yellow star, you used the Transform palette to set a precise rotation angle. In this procedure, you'll use the Rotation tool to rotate the graphic freely.

1   Press A to switch to the Direct Selection tool (▷), and then position the cursor over the origami box image in the circle on page 5 and then click.

2 In the Control palette, make sure that the center point in the Reference Point indicator (⬚) is selected.

3 Press R to select the Rotation tool (⟳).

4 Move the crosshair over one of the corner handles and hold down the mouse button and then drag the handle counterclockwise to rotate both the image and the frame, stopping when you like the look of the results. The sample uses a rotation of 25°.

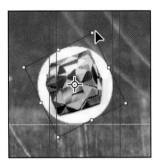

Note: Waiting for the crosshair to become a solid arrow lets you preview the contents on-the-fly as you rotate. If you don't wait for the solid arrow, the bounding box will remain visible as you drag to rotate.

Finishing up

Now it's time to admire your work.

1 Choose Edit > Deselect All.

2 Choose View > Fit Spread in Window.

3 In the toolbox, click the Preview Mode button to hide all guides and frames.

4 Press the Tab key to close all palettes.

5   Save your file one more time, and then choose File > Close to keep InDesign open or File > Exit to end your InDesign session.

Congratulations. You have finished the lesson.

Exploring on your own

One of the best ways to learn about frames is to experiment on your own. In this section, you will learn how to nest an object inside a shape you create. Follow these steps to learn more about selecting and manipulating frames:

1   Using the Direct Selection tool (⬧), select and copy any image on page 4 or 5.

2   To create a new page, choose Insert Pages from the Pages palette menu and then click OK.

3   Use the Polygon tool (◯) to draw a shape on the new page (use any number of sides and any value for the star inset). Select the shape using the Direct Selection tool, and then choose Edit > Paste Into to nest the image inside the frame. (If you choose Edit > Paste, the object will not be pasted inside the selected frame.)

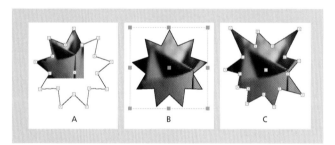

A. *Image pasted into frame.*
B. *Image moved and scaled within the frame.*
C. *Polygon frame reshaped.*

4   Use the Direct Selection tool to move and scale the image within the frame.

5   Use the Direct Selection tool to change the shape of the polygon frame.

6   Use the Selection tool (⬧) to rotate both the frame and the image. Use the Direct Selection tool to rotate only the image within the frame.

7   When you are done experimenting, close the document without saving.

Review

▶ **Review questions**

1   When should you use the Selection tool to select an object, and when should you use the Direct Selection tool to select an object?

2   How do you resize a frame and its contents simultaneously?

3   How do you rotate a graphic within a frame without rotating the frame?

4   Without ungrouping objects, how do you select an object within a group?

▶ **Review answers**

1   Use the Selection tool for general layout tasks, such as positioning and sizing objects. Use the Direct Selection tool for tasks involving drawing and editing paths or frames, for example, to select frame contents or to move an anchor point on a path.

2   To resize a frame and its contents simultaneously, choose the Selection tool, hold down Ctrl (Windows) or Command (Mac OS), and then drag a handle. Hold down the Shift key to maintain the object's proportions.

3   To rotate a graphic within a frame, use the Direct Selection tool to select the graphic within the frame. Select the Rotation tool, and then drag one of the handles to rotate only the graphic, not the frame.

4   To select an object within a group, select it using the Direct Selection tool.

With Adobe InDesign CS2, you can import text, thread it through frames, and edit text within the frames. Once you import text, you can create and apply styles, find and replace text and formatting, and use different language dictionaries to check spelling in any part of your document, and use dynamic tools to correct spelling errors.

4 | Importing and Editing Text

In this introduction to importing and editing text, you'll learn how to do the following:

- Enter text into text frames.
- Flow text manually and automatically.
- Load styles from another document and apply them.
- Thread text.
- Use semi-autoflow to place text frames.
- Find and change text and formatting.
- Find and change a missing font.
- Check Spelling in a document.
- Automatically correct misspelled words.
- Set type to follow a curved path.

Getting started

In this lesson, you'll work on an 8-page newsletter for TravelNE, a fictitious New England tour group. Several pages of the newsletter have already been completed. Now that the final article for the newsletter has been written, you're ready to flow the article into the document and add the finishing touches to the newsletter.

Note: If you have not already copied the resource files for this lesson from the Lesson_04 folder of the Adobe InDesign CS2 Classroom in a Book CD, do so now. See "Copying the Classroom in a Book files" on page 4.

When your preparations are complete, you're ready to start work on the lesson.

1   To ensure that the tools and palettes function exactly as described in this lesson, delete or deactivate (by renaming) the InDesign Defaults file and the InDesign SavedData file. See "Restoring default preferences" on page 2.

2   Start Adobe InDesign.

Managing fonts

To begin working, you'll open an existing InDesign document. We have added a font to this document that you may not have on your system, so you may receive an error message relating to the missing font. You will replace this font later in this lesson.

1   Choose File > Open, and open the 04_a.indd file in the Lesson_04 folder, located inside the Lessons folder within the InDesignCIB folder on your hard disk.

When you open a file that includes fonts not installed on your system, an alert message indicates which font is missing. The text that uses this missing font is also highlighted in pink. You will fix this missing font problem later in this lesson by replacing the missing font with an available font. This is useful because InDesign makes it clear which fonts might cause problems when printing, and provides several opportunities to correct the situation.

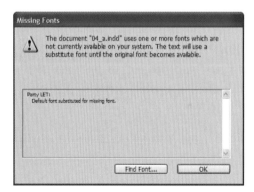

2   Click OK to close the alert message.

Navigate through the pages in the document and you can see that pages 5 through 8 have already been completed. The missing font is located on page 8. In this lesson, you will complete the first four pages of the newsletter and then replace the missing font.

3   Choose File > Save As and name the file **04_News**, and save it in the Lesson_04 folder.

4   To see what the finished document will look like, open the 04_b.indd file in the same folder. If you prefer, you can leave the document open to act as a guide as you work. When you're ready to resume working on the lesson document, choose its name from the Window menu.

Creating and entering text

You can use InDesign to enter text into your documents, or you can import text created in other programs, such as word processing software.

Creating a headline and applying a style

In the area beneath the banner, "TravelNEws," and above the space that will contain the start of the article, you'll create a text frame for the article headline, "Winter Fun in New England." This headline text frame will span the two columns. You'll then apply a headline style to this headline and format the headline.

1   While viewing page 1, double-click the Zoom tool (⊗) to increase the magnification to 100%.

2   To mark the location of the top of your headline frame, you will drag to create a guide, and then create the frame. To help you position the guide, watch the Y value in either the Control or Transform palettes as you drag. Hold down the Shift key and drag a guide from the horizontal ruler to the 18p6 (18 picas, 6 points) location on page 1. Holding down the Shift key constrains the position of the guide to the increments visible on the ruler.

3　Using the Type tool (T), position the type cursor next to the left margin over the 18p6 guide. The horizontal crossbar on the type cursor should be at 18p6.

4　Drag to create a text frame in the blank area below the 18p6 guide and above the 21p guide. The text frame should span the two columns, and the top of the frame should snap to the 18p6 guide, while the bottom snaps to the 21p guide.

💡 *If you need to resize the frame, select the Selection tool, and drag the handles of the frame to snap to the guides. Then select the Type tool and click inside the frame.*

After you draw a text frame using the Type tool, an insertion point appears, ready for you to begin typing.

5　In the text frame you just created, type **Winter Fun in New England**.

To make this headline consistent with other headlines used in the newsletter, you'll apply the Head 1 style. When you apply a paragraph style, you can place the insertion point anywhere in the paragraph or select any part of the paragraph.

6   Choose Window > Type & Tables > Paragraph Styles. With the insertion point anywhere in the headline text you just typed, select Head 1 in the Paragraph Styles palette.

7   Save the file.

Flowing text

The process of taking imported text, such as that from a word processing program, and placing it across several linked text frames is called flowing text. InDesign lets you flow text manually for greater control, or automatically to save time.

Flowing text manually

To flow text manually, you first select a word processing file to import. You can then drag to create a frame, or you can click anywhere on the page to create a text frame in a column. In this exercise you will use both methods to flow the text into the columns on the first page of the newsletter.

1   In the Pages palette, double-click the page 1 icon to center the first page in the document window. Click on a blank part of the page to deselect all items.

2   Choose File > Place. In the place dialog box, make sure that Show Import Options is selected, locate and select 04_c.doc in the Lesson_04 folder, and click Open.

3   Make certain that Remove Styles and Formatting from Text and Tables is not selected in the Import Options dialog box. Deselecting this option causes the text to be imported with the same formatting that was applied in the word-processing application. Selecting this option would remove any formatting that was applied to the text. You want to keep the formatting, so you will keep this option deselected, and click OK.

You will now create a text frame between the light blue guides below the banner on the left side of page 1.

4   Create a text frame in the left column of page 1 by positioning the loaded text icon (▦) next to the left margin at the 21p (21-pica) guide and dragging down to the right side of the first column at the 30p guide.

Dragging to create a text frame.

Notice that the text frame includes an out port in the lower right corner. The red plus sign indicates that there is overset text. There is more text than fits into the existing text frame. You will now flow this text into the second column on page 1.

5   Using the Selection tool (➤), click the out port of the frame you just created.

If you change your mind and decide you don't want to flow overset text, you can click any tool in the toolbox to cancel the loaded text icon. No text will be deleted.

6   Position the loaded text icon in the upper left corner of the second column just below the sidebar frame, and click.

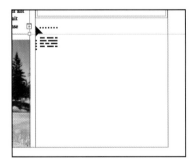

The text flows into a new frame from where you clicked to the bottom of the second column. The out port in the new column contains a red plus sign, again indicating that there is still overset text.

Note: While you can create separate, linked frames for each column, it is also possible to work with one large column that is divided into multiple columns using Object > Text Frame Options. Each method has its advantages in certain types of documents.

Flowing text automatically

You will use autoflow to place the rest of the overset text into the document. When you autoflow text, InDesign creates new text frames within column guides on subsequent pages until all the overset text is flowed. If there are not enough pages in your document when you use autoflow, InDesign adds new pages until all the text is placed.

Note: A connected series of text frames is called a story.

1   Using the Selection tool (↖), click the out port in the lower right corner of the frame you just created in the second column on page 1.

While the loaded text icon is active (⊞), you can still navigate to different document pages, or create new pages. This allows you to continue flowing text onto other pages in your document—even if these pages have not yet been created at the time you click on the out port of a text frame.

2   In the Pages palette, double-click the page 2 icon to center page 2 in the document window. (You may need to scroll down the palette to find the icon for page 2.) Notice that there are no text frames on page 2. Also notice that the text icon is still loaded.

3   Holding down the Shift key, position the loaded text icon in the upper left corner of the left column on page 2, and click. Release the Shift key.

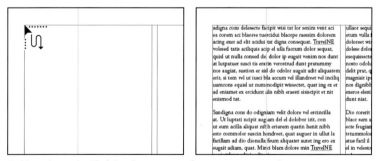

Holding down the Shift key lets you autoflow text into your document.

Notice that two new text frames were added to each page within the column guides. This is because you held down the Shift key to autoflow text. All the text in the story is now placed.

Resizing a text frame

When you create a text frame by clicking the loaded text icon, InDesign creates the new text frame as wide as the column where you click. Although these frames are placed within the column margins, you can move, resize, and reshape any of these text frames if necessary.

1   Navigate to page 4 by clicking the page selector in the lower left corner of the document window.

Notice that the text frame in the left column covers the photograph that was placed on this page. When you autoflow text, the text frames are created within the column settings regardless of whether objects appear in those columns. You can fix this overlap by adding a text wrap to the image or by resizing the text frame. In this exercise you will resize the text frame.

2   Using the Selection tool (↖), click the text frame in the left column on page 4 to select the text frame, and then drag the lower middle handle of the text frame above the photograph to approximately the 31p location (you can look at the vertical ruler as you drag, or in the transform palette).

Before and after resizing text frame.

3   Choose File > Save.

Flowing text into an existing frame

When you place text, you can flow text into a new frame or into an existing frame. To flow text into an existing frame, you can click an insertion point to flow text at that point, or you can click the loaded text icon in an existing frame, which replaces that frame's contents.

The first page of the newsletter includes a placeholder frame for a sidebar. You'll place the text in this frame that announces upcoming cycling events.

1   Turn to the first page of the newsletter.

2   Choose File > Place. In the Place dialog box, turn off the Show Import Options feature. Locate and double-click 04_d.doc in the Lesson_04 folder.

The pointer becomes a loaded text icon (⌷). When you move the loaded text icon over an empty text frame, parentheses enclose the icon (⌷).

3   Position the loaded text icon over the placeholder frame at the top of the second column, and click.

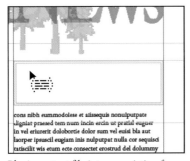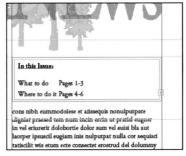

Placing a text file into an existing frame.

You will apply styles to format this text later in this lesson.

4   Choose File > Save.

Note: *You will be changing all the formatting for this text block in the next set of steps.*

Working with styles

Styles make it easy to apply repetitive formatting across an entire document. For example, to keep all headlines formatted consistently through your document, you can create a headline style that contains the necessary formatting attributes. Styles can save time when you apply and revise text formatting and can help provide a consistent look to your documents.

Applying a style

To make the appearance of the article consistent with the other articles in the newsletter, you will apply a paragraph style called Body Copy. We created this style for formatting the body text of the main articles in the newsletter.

1   Click the Paragraph Styles palette (or choose Window > Type & Tables > Paragraph Styles) to make the palette visible, if it is not already open.

The Paragraph Styles palette for this document now includes four styles: Body Copy, Head 1, Head 2, and Normal. The Normal style has a disk icon (🖫) next to it, indicating that the style was imported from a different application. In this case, Normal is a Microsoft Word style that was imported when you placed the article. You'll now apply the InDesign style, Body Copy, to the text.

Note: The Basic Paragraph style is the only paragraph style available when you first create a document with InDesign. You can create new styles or add styles from other InDesign documents. Styles are also added to InDesign documents when you import text with styles from Microsoft Word.

2   Using the Type tool (T), click an insertion point anywhere in the main article you placed. Then choose Edit > Select All to select all the body text in the story. Notice that the sidebar text is not selected; this text belongs to a different story.

3   Once all the text is selected, select Body Copy in the Paragraph Styles palette.

4   Choose Edit > Deselect All. The article is now formatted in a different font, and the first line of each paragraph is now indented.

Before and after style is applied.

Loading styles from another document

Styles appear only in the document in which you create them. However, it's easy to share styles between InDesign documents by loading, or importing, styles from other InDesign documents. In this exercise, you will take styles from another document. This other document includes several styles that will work well for the text in this newsletter. Instead of re-creating these styles, you'll load the styles from the other document and apply them to text in the newsletter.

1   Click the Palette Menu button (⊙) and choose Load All Styles from the Paragraph Styles palette menu.

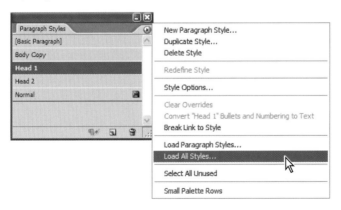

2   In the Open a File dialog box, double-click styles.indd from the Lesson_04 folder. Click OK in the Load Styles dialog box that appears. In the Paragraph Styles palette, notice the new styles called Sidebar Copy and Sidebar Head. You may need to scroll through the list or resize the palette to see these additional styles.

3   In the document window, change the view so that you can see the sidebar heading ("In this Issue:") on page 1.

4   Using the Type tool (T), click an insertion point in the sidebar, and then choose Edit > Select All.

5   In the Paragraph Styles palette, click to select the Sidebar Copy style.

6   Click an insertion point in the sidebar heading, "In this Issue:"

7   In the Paragraph Styles palette, select Sidebar Head.

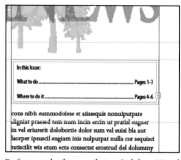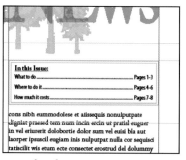

Before and after applying Sidebar Head paragraph style.

Vertically aligning text

To evenly distribute the space on the top and bottom of the text frame, you will center the text vertically using vertical justification.

1   With the insertion point anywhere in the sidebar frame, choose Object > Text Frame Options.

2   Under Vertical Justification, for Align, select Justify, and then click OK.

3   Choose File > Save.

Note: If all the text doesn't fit in the frame, you can select the middle handle at the lower edge of the frame and drag it downward, just as you did in "Resizing a text frame" earlier in this lesson. Because the text is set to be justified vertically, the spacing between lines changes when you release the mouse.

You have finished formatting the first page of the newsletter.

Threading text

When you autoflowed text into the document, InDesign created links between the frames so that text would flow from one frame to another. These links are called threads. You can break the threads between frames, add new frames between the threaded frames, and rearrange how frames are threaded.

1   In the Pages palette, double-click the numbers below the page 2-3 icons. If the entire spread does not automatically appear in the document window, choose View > Fit Spread in Window to view the spread.

2   Choose the Selection tool (↖), and then click the text frame in the right column on page 2 to select it.

3   Choose View > Show Text Threads. Blue lines appear that represent the connections (threads) between text frames in the selected story. Each thread goes from the out port of one frame to the in port of the next frame in the sequence.

4   With the text frame in the right column of page 2 still selected, press Backspace or Delete to delete this text frame. Click to select a different frame in the story so that the text threads become visible.

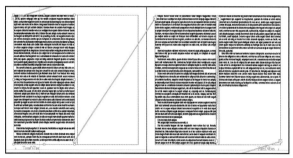

After deleting a threaded frame.

Note: Text threads display only when a frame within the text flow is selected.

Notice that the text flows from the left column on page 2 to the left column on page 3. Although the text frame was deleted, no text in the story was deleted—it flowed into the next frame.

5   Press Ctrl+D (Windows) or Command+D (Mac OS) to open the Place dialog box. If necessary, deselect Replace Selected Item and Show Import Options and then locate and double-click 04_e.tif in the Lesson_04 folder.

6   Click the loaded graphics icon (📰) in the upper left corner of the blank column, just below the guide. If necessary, after placing the graphic, drag the picture so that it snaps to the top margin of the column.

You'll fill the space under the picture by creating a new text frame and threading the placed story through the new frame. To thread a new frame in the middle of a story, you can click the out port of the previous frame or the in port of the subsequent frame.

7   Holding down Ctrl (Windows) or Command (Mac OS), drag a guide from the horizontal ruler to the 28p mark. Holding the modifier key applies the guide across the entire spread rather than the entire page.

*For accuracy, hold down Shift as you drag to move the guide in p6 increments, or you can select the guide with the Selection tool and then type **28p** in the Y box of the Control or Transform palettes.*

8   Click the left text frame on page 2 to select it, and then click the out port in the lower right corner of the frame. The out port appears as a blue arrow, indicating that the story is continued in another frame.

9   Position the loaded text icon (⬚) just below the 28p guide near the bottom of the right column, and click to create a frame that fills the rest of the column.

Threading a new text frame in the middle of a story.

A text frame is created that is the width of the column. You have now completed page 2 of the newsletter.

10   Choose View > Hide Text Threads.

Now you'll use a keyboard shortcut, instead of using a menu, for deselecting.

11   Press Shift+Ctrl+A (Windows) or Shift+Command+A (Mac OS) to deselect everything. Then save the file.

Changing the number of columns on a page

You will now create a full-page sidebar on page 3. To simplify creating the text frames for these columns, you will change the number of columns on page 3.

1   In the Pages palette, double-click the page 3 icon to center the page in the document window. Make sure that only page 3 in the Pages palette is highlighted so that the column change will affect only page 3. If necessary, click another page icon, and then click the page 3 icon.

2   Choose Layout > Margins and Columns. Under Columns, type **3** for Number and click OK.

Even though the number of columns changed, the widths of the existing text frames did not change.

Notice that the text frames are independent of the number of columns. Column margins can determine how text frames are created, but the text frame widths do not change when you redefine columns. One exception to this rule is when Layout Adjustment is turned on—you can learn more about Layout Adjustment in "Exploring on your own" at the end of this lesson.

3 Using the Selection tool (➤), select a text frame on page 3 and press Backspace or Delete.

4 Select the other text frame on page 3 and press Backspace or Delete. Both text frames on page 3 should be deleted.

Once again, you have deleted text frames, but you did not delete any text; the text flowed into the text frames on page 4. Now you'll place an Adobe Photoshop file that has been sized to fit within the newsletter page.

5 Press Ctrl+D (Windows) or Command+D (Mac OS) to open the Place dialog box. Deselect Show Import Options, then locate and double-click 04_f.psd in the Lesson_04 folder.

6 Click the loaded graphics icon (🗶) in the upper left corner of page 3. If necessary, drag the image so that it snaps to the margin guides at the top, left, and right sides of the page.

Using semi-autoflow to place text frames

Now you will use semi-autoflow to place a text file into the three columns. Semi-autoflow lets you create text frames one at a time, without having to reload the text icon.

1 Choose File > Place to open the Place dialog box, and then deselect Replace Selected Items. Locate and double-click 04_g.doc in the Lesson_04 folder.

2 Holding down Alt (Windows) or Option (Mac OS), position the semi-autoflow loaded text icon in the left column at the 28p guide, and click.

Flowing text semi-automatically.

The text flows into the left column. Because you held down Alt or Option, the pointer is still a loaded text icon, ready for you to flow text into another frame.

3 Holding down Alt or Option, position the loaded text icon in the second column at the 28p guide, and click. Release the Alt or Option key.

Now you will create the final column. You won't hold down Alt or Option since there will only be three frames in this story.

4 Position the loaded text icon in the third column at the 28p guide, and click.

The text is overset in the third column, but after you format the text with styles, the text should then fit within the frames, leaving no overset text remaining.

Applying and editing the sidebar styles

To make the text consistent with the rest of the newsletter, you'll apply the sidebar styles to the text you just added. You will also edit the Sidebar Head style so that each heading starts at the top of the next column. You'll start by using the keyboard to select all the text in the story.

1 Using the Type tool (T), click an insertion point in the sidebar. Then press Ctrl+A (Windows) or Command+A (Mac OS) to select all the text in the story.

2 Select the Sidebar Copy style in the Paragraph Styles palette.

3 Click an insertion point inside the "Nordic Skiing" heading, and then select the Sidebar Head style in the Paragraph Styles palette.

4 Apply the Sidebar Head style to the other two headings, "Snowmobiling" and "Tubing."

To ensure that the headings will always appear at the top of each frame, you'll edit the sidebar heading style.

5 Before you edit the style, deselect all text.

6 In the Paragraph Styles palette, double-click Sidebar Head to open the Paragraph Style Options dialog box for that style.

7 In the left panel, select Keep Options and then select In Next Column from the Start Paragraph drop-down menu. Then click OK.

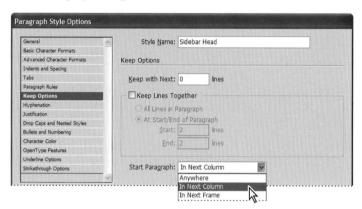

The sidebar headings on page 3 are now forced to start at the top of each column. Now that you've finished placing text and graphics in the newsletter, you'll use some of InDesign's word processing features to add finishing touches to the text throughout the newsletter.

8 Save the file.

The context menu gives you another way to move text to the beginning of the next column. To do this, make sure that the cursor is in the place where you want to create the break, and then right-click (Windows) or Ctrl+click (Mac OS) to open the context menu. Choose Insert Break Character > Column Break. You can also use context menu commands to move text to the next frame, page, odd page, or even page.

Adding a page continuation note

Because the story on page 2 links to another page, you can let readers know where they can resume reading when they get to the bottom of the page. To do this you will add a "(Continued on page x)" frame. You can add an automatic page number that will automatically reflect the number of the next page in the text flow.

1   Center page 2 in the document window by scrolling or using the Pages palette.

2   Drag a guide from the horizontal ruler down to the 46p location. Zoom in so that you can read the text in the columns easily.

3   Select the Selection tool (▶), click the text frame in the right column on page 2, and then drag the lower middle handle up to the 46p guide.

4   Select the Type tool (T), and then drag to create a text frame that fills the space at the bottom of the right-most column on page 2.

5   With a text insertion point active in the new text frame, type (**Continued on page**), including the space and the parentheses. Then use the left arrow key to move the insertion point to the left of the close parenthesis.

6   Right-click (Windows) or Ctrl+click (Mac OS) the text frame, and in the context menu that appears, choose Insert Special Character > Next Page Number. The text now reads "(Continued on page 4)."

Note: The text frame containing the jump line must touch or overlap the frame linked text for the "Next Page Number" character to work properly.

7   If necessary, select the Selection tool, and then drag the top of the new text frame up so that it snaps to the text frame above it.

8   With the Selection tool, click the text frame containing the "Continued on page" text, and then Shift+click to select the text frame immediately above it. Then choose Object > Group. This keeps the story and its jump line together if you move them.

Changing horizontal and vertical text alignment

The jump line text is probably formatted with a different paragraph style than you want to use. Next, you'll reformat that text.

1   Select the Type tool (T), and then triple-click "(Continued on page 4)" to select the text.

2   In the Paragraph Styles palette, click Body Copy.

3   In the Character section of the Control palette, select Italic from the Type Style menu.

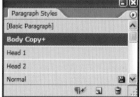

Notice that the Body Copy style has a plus sign next to it in the Paragraph Styles palette. The plus sign next to a style indicates that the current text has formats applied to it in addition to the style.

4   In the Control palette, click the Paragraph Formatting Controls button (¶), then click the Align Right (≣) button.

Now you will align the text at the bottom of the frame.

5   Choose Object > Text Frame Options.

6   In the Align drop-down menu under Vertical Justification, select Bottom. Then click OK.

7   Press Shift+Ctrl+A (Windows) or Shift+Command+A (Mac OS) to deselect the text. Then save the file.

Finding and changing

Like most popular word processors, InDesign lets you find text and replace it. You can also search for and change formatting and special characters.

Finding text and changing formatting

You will search for occurrences of the word "TravelNE" in this document. Make sure that your view-magnification level is set so that you can easily read the text and see the formatting. You do not have to have anything selected for this procedure.

The author of the main article used underline instead of italics to indicate the name of the tour group. You want to remove the underlining and replace it with italics.

1   Choose Edit > Find/Change. For Find What, type **TravelNE**.

2   Press Tab to move to the Change To box, and make certain that the Change To box is empty. For Search, make sure Document is selected.

These settings tell InDesign to search all text frames throughout the document for the word TravelNE and to keep the same word. Next we will tell InDesign to change the format of the words it locates.

3   Click More Options to display additional formatting options in the dialog box.

4   Under Find Format Settings, click Format to open the Find Format Settings dialog box.

5   In the left side of the Find Format Settings dialog box, select Basic Character Formats. Then, in the right side, click the Underline check box to place a check mark, indicating that it is selected.

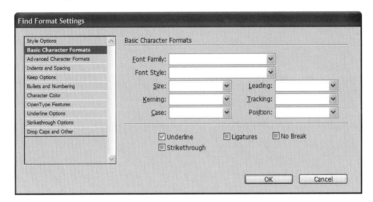

6   Leave the other check boxes as they are: either with green boxes (Windows) or dashes (Mac OS). These marks indicate attributes that are irrelevant to the search—they will not act as criteria for the search. Click OK to return to the Find/Change dialog box.

Notice the alert icon (⚠) above the Find what box. This icon indicates that InDesign will search for text containing the specified formatting. In this case, InDesign will search for underlined occurrences of "TravelNE."

7   Under Change Format Settings, click Format to open the Change Format Settings dialog box, and set all the following options:

- On the left side of the dialog box, choose Basic Character Formats.

- On the right side, use the drop-down menus to select Adobe Garamond Pro for Font Family and Italic for the font style. (Adobe Garamond is alphabetized on the list under "G," not "A.")

- For Size, select 11 pt.

- For Leading, select 12 pt.

- Click the Underline check box twice to clear it.

- Click OK.

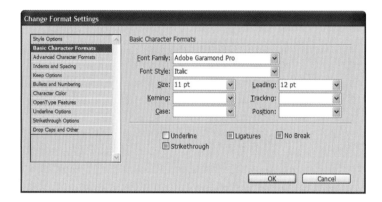

8   Click Change All. A message appears, telling you that InDesign found and changed the three occurrences of the underlined word "TravelNE."

9   Click OK to close the message, and then click Done to close the Find/Change dialog box. Then save the file.

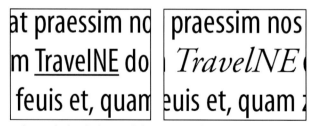

Before and after finding and changing attributes.

Finding and changing special characters

The text in the sidebar on page 1 currently uses hyphens between page numbers (such as Pages 1-3) instead of en dashes. You will replace these hyphens (-) with en dashes (–).

1   Turn to page 1, and use the Zoom tool (🔍) to magnify the "In this Issue:" text frame.

2   Using the Type tool (T), click inside the "In this Issue:" sidebar.

3   Press Ctrl+F (Windows) or Command+F (Mac OS) to open the Find/Change dialog box.

In this case, you want InDesign to replace only the hyphens in the text frame on the first page, so you will limit the search range to only the story, which consists solely of the sidebar frame.

4   For Search, choose Story to narrow the search to only the sidebar.

5   For Find what, delete the word "TravelNE" and type - (a hyphen).

6   Press Tab to shift focus to the Change To box. Click the arrow button (▶) to the right of the Change To box and choose En Dash from the drop-down menu. The Change To field is populated by ^= (a caret and equal sign), a code for the en dash character.

7   Under Find Format Settings, click Clear. Then click Clear under Change Format Settings. This clears the underline attribute you searched for in your last search, so that InDesign will not look for underlines in this step.

8   Click Change All.

The three hyphens are replaced by en dashes in the sidebar.

Note: If you are notified that considerably more than three changes were made, you may have forgotten to choose Story instead of Document for search, or you didn't click an insertion point inside the sidebar frame. Choose Edit > Undo Replace Text and try again.

9 Click OK to close the message, and then click Done to close the Find/Change dialog box. Save the file.

Finding and changing a missing font

When you opened the document based on the template, the Party LET font may have been missing. We include this font in this lesson, as it is not commonly used. If you have this font installed on your computer, you will not receive a warning indicator, but can follow along with the steps. You will now search for text containing the Party LET font and replace it with the Myriad Pro Bold font.

1 In the Pages palette, double-click the page 8 icon (you may need to scroll in the Pages palette). Choose View > Fit Page in Window. The pink highlight indicates that the text is formatted with a missing font.

2 Choose Type > Find Font to open the Find Font dialog box. This dialog box lists all fonts used in the document and the type of font—such as PostScript, True Type, or Open Type. Missing fonts are indicated by an alert icon (⚠).

3 Select Party LET in the list.

4 For Replace With, select Myriad Pro from the Font Family menu, and Bold from the Font Style menu.

5 Click Change All. Click Done to close the dialog box and see the replaced font in the document.

Note: For your own projects, you may need to add the missing font to your system instead of replacing the missing font. You can fix missing fonts by installing the font on your system, by activating the font using font management software, or by adding the font files to the InDesign Fonts folder. For more information, see Installing Fonts in InDesign Help.

Checking Spelling of a story

InDesign includes a utility much like those used in word processing programs for checking spelling. You can check the spelling in selected text, an entire story, all stories in a document, or all stories in several open documents at once. When you Check Spelling, InDesign uses the dictionary for the languages you assigned to the text in your document.

1   On page 1, click the cursor before the word "This" in the first paragraph. Choose Edit > Spelling > Check Spelling to open the Check Spelling dialog box.

2   From the Search menu, choose Document to check the spelling in the entire newsletter document.

3   Click Start to find the first misspelled word in the document. The word "TravelNEws" will appear in the Not In Dictionary field.

4   Note the choices offered in the Suggested Corrections list. If you wanted to replace the word, you'd select an alternate spelling from this list or simply type the corrected spelling into the Change To field. Then you'd decide whether you want to change just this instance of the word (by clicking the Change button), or all instances of the word (by clicking the Change All button).

5   Since "TravelNEws" is the proper title of your newsletter, click the Skip button to ignore this assumed misspelling. However, this will skip only the first instance of the word, and "TravelNEws" will come up again as misspelled, as InDesign continues to check the spelling in the document. To avoid this, click the Ignore All button when the next instance is found.

6   Click Done to close the Check Spelling dialog box.

7   Choose File > Save.

Adding words to a dictionary

If you choose to simply Ignore All instances of a word, it will ignore only the misspelling until InDesign is restarted. Adding the word to an external user dictionary will prevent it from repeatedly being identified as misspelled in other InDesign documents.

1   Close your newsletter document, and then quit and restart InDesign.

2   Choose File > Open, and open 04_News from the Lesson_04 folder.

3   On page 1, click the cursor before the word "This" in the first paragraph. Choose Edit > Spelling > Check Spelling to open the Check Spelling dialog box.

4   From the Search menu, choose Document to check the spelling in the entire newsletter document.

5   Click Start to find the first misspelled word in the document. The word "TravelNEws" will appear in the Not In Dictionary field.

6   Click the Add button to add this word to the external user dictionary file, ENG. UDC. Since this dictionary is application-wide, InDesign will recognize "TravelNEws" as correctly spelled in all future documents.

Adding words to a document-specific dictionary

You may occasionally want to link the specific spelling of a word to a single document only. Storing a word in an open InDesign document's internal dictionary restricts it to that document.

1   Choose Edit > Spelling > Dictionary. Note that the Target dictionary is the default ENG.UDC, and "TravelNEws" is listed under Dictionary List: Added Words. To remove the word from the external user dictionary, select it in the list, and then click on the Remove button.

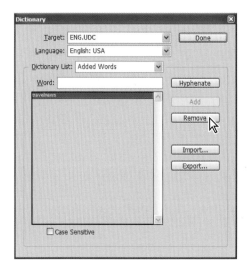

2   From the Target menu, scroll down to select your file's name, 04_News.

3   Type the word **TravelNEws** into the Word field, and click the Add button. The word is added to the Dictionary List for this document only. This spelling of the word will be recognized only within this document, and subsequent InDesign documents will continue to list the word as misspelled. Click Done.

Note: To include the capitalization of the characters, select Case Sensitive when adding words to the dictionary.

Checking Spelling dynamically

It's not necessary for you to wait until a document is finished before checking its spelling. InDesign incorporates a Dynamic Spelling utility that allows you to see misspelled words as they are entered. If you turn on Dynamic Spelling after text has been entered, all misspellings will be highlighted.

1   Before activating this feature, choose Edit > Preferences > Spelling (Windows) or InDesign > Preferences > Spelling (Mac OS). Make sure that the Enable Dynamic Spelling box is checked. Then decide which errors you want highlighted (in the Find section), and how you want them highlighted (in the Underline Color section). Close the Preference dialog box and return to your document. (Misspelled words, according to the default user dictionary, are immediately highlighted with a red underline.)

Note: To disable Dynamic Spelling, choose Edit > Spelling > Dynamic Spelling.

*Words that are not in the dictionary
are underlined when Dynamic Spelling is enabled.*

2   If you add a misspelled word to the document with Dynamic Spelling activated, the word becomes highlighted with an underline as you type it. Try typing the word "snew" into the first column on page 1 to see this feature in action.

Automatically correcting misspelled words

InDesign's Autocorrect utility takes the concept of checking spelling dynamically to the next level. With this function activated, InDesign automatically corrects misspelled words as you type them. Changes made are based on an internal list of commonly misspelled words and their correct spellings. This list can also be changed to include commonly misspelled words in other languages.

1   Before activating this feature, choose Edit > Preferences > Autocorrect (Windows) or InDesign > Preferences > Autocorrect (Mac OS). Make sure that the Enable Autocorrect box is checked. You can also choose to automatically correct capitalization errors by checking this option.

2   Note the list of commonly misspelled words, and the Language listed by default as English: USA. Change the language to French and note the commonly misspelled words in that language. Change the language back to English: USA before proceeding.

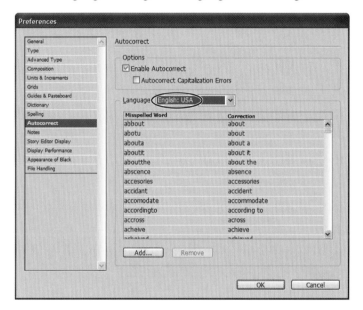

3   Click the Add button to bring up the Add to Autocorrect List dialog box. Type the word **snew** in the Misspelled Word field, and **snow** into the Correction field. Click OK and then click OK on the Preferences dialog box.

4   Now type the word **snew** into the first column on page 1 again to see the Autocorrect feature in action.

Checking Spelling with other languages

The text in the "See it, then SKI it!" story on page 5 includes Spanish and Italian phrases. Before you check the spelling of the story, you will assign the appropriate language to each phrase. InDesign includes the ability to check the spelling and hyphenate text using multiple languages.

1 In the document window, turn to page 5. Change your view so that you can comfortably read the paragraph below the image in the right column.

2 In the paragraph in the right column beginning "William Johnson," use the Type tool (T) to select "¡Yo tengo un cuaderno rojo!"

3 From the Character section of the Control palette, choose Spanish: Castilian from the Language menu on the right.

Assigning languages lets you check the spelling of a document more accurately and efficiently.

Note: *If you do not see the Spanish and other dictionaries on the Language menu, either your dictionaries have been deleted from your hard disk or your installation of InDesign did not include them. To install the dictionaries you need for this task, save your file, quit all programs, and insert the InDesign application CD into your computer's CD-ROM drive. Open the CD and double-click the installation icon. Follow the on-screen instructions for a custom installation, specifying only the dictionaries. You do not need to reinstall the InDesign program; only the dictionaries need to be installed. Then reopen your 04_News. indd file and resume your work.*

4 In the same paragraph, select "Sono il campione delmondo" (this is intentionally misspelled). In the Character palette, choose Italian from the Language menu.

The text may shift when you apply the language attribute. This occurs because hyphenation rules are different for each language.

5 Choose Edit > Spelling > Check Spelling...

6 For Search, choose Selection so you don't have to check the spelling of the entire document.

7   Click Start. When "delmondo" is highlighted, select "del mondo" under Suggested Corrections, and then click Change. When you finish checking the spelling, click Done.

8   Save the file.

Drag and drop text editing

For misplaced words in your document, InDesign offers a Drag and Drop Text feature that allows you to move text within and between frames, layout windows, and documents. You'll now use this utility to move text from one paragraph to another in your newsletter.

1   Before attempting to move this type, choose Edit > Preferences > Type (Windows) or InDesign > Preferences > Type (Mac OS). In the Drag and Drop Text editing section, make sure that the Enable in Layout View box is checked. This allows you to move text into and out of open document windows, and within documents in the Layout View. Click OK.

2   In your document window, turn to page 5. Change your view so that you can comfortably read the paragraphs at the top of the first column.

3   The word "therefore" was mistakenly placed at the end of the first paragraph. Using your Type tool (T), drag to select this word.

4   Without changing tools, rest your cursor on the highlighted word. You should see the cursor change to a new icon (▶T). Click and drag the word to its correct location, to the right of the word "Skiing" in the first line of the second paragraph.

ril ipis nulla augue tisim nulluptatet, quatio iscidunt lor adip ea cor sent iusto od et ute us augait ullum velit wisi therefore.
quipisim dolessequat. Iquam zzriliq uiscinibh d magna feu faci eugait wismodo lenibh et cip et nummy niatem illutpat utatuer irit acin ullam vulla aliqui blaore erostrud tet nim am

by Franz Climber

Lustinci eui tincidunt adipit iril ipis nulla a euguerit wisit alisseq uipiscip euiscidunt lor a eummy nit vulla acidunt nostion us augait ull

Skiing, therefore qui erostrud ea feum zzriliq uiscinibh eros non endreet ver iuerost modo lenibh et praestrud ea feum nos atinit pat utatuer irit acin utat. Deliquis nulpute et,

5   When you release the mouse, "therefore" will have moved to the new location. (If you wanted to copy the word instead of moving it, you would have simply pressed the Opt/Alt key while dragging).

Using the story editor

If you're more comfortable working with an editing interface that focuses solely on the text being edited, InDesign includes a feature called the Story Editor.

1   With page 5 of the newsletter in your document window, select the Type tool (T) and click inside the first column to place a blinking insertion point.

2   Choose Edit > Edit in Story Editor. The Story Editor window opens, showing raw text with no formatting applied. Any graphics and other non-text elements have been omitted to make editing easier.

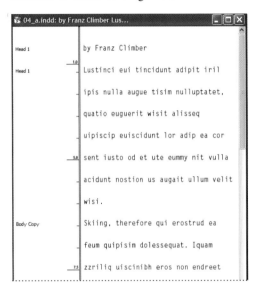

3   In the Story Editor window, select and change the word "therefore" in the second paragraph to "after all." If necessary, move the Story Editor window aside, so you can see that the corresponding text has also been changed in the document window.

4   Note that the Story Editor displays line numbers for reference purposes, and that misspelled words are highlighted by dynamic spelling, just as they are in the document window. If the Enable in Story Editor option is selected in the Type Preferences, you can also drag and drop type in the Story Editor, just as you did in the last lesson.

5   To make viewing and editing type easier, the display characteristics of the Story Editor window can be changed by choosing Edit > Preferences > Story Editor Display (Windows) or InDesign > Preferences > Story Editor Display (Mac OS). Try changing the font size to 14 points and the Line Spacing to Doublespace to see if it facilitates editing.

6 While paragraph styles aren't displayed in the Story Editor window, they are listed in the column on the left, and can be applied (but not seen) in this window. For more information on applying styles in InDesign, see Lesson 7, "Working with Styles."

7 Close Story Editor.

Creating text on a path

You can create type that flows along the edge of an open or closed path of any shape. For this lesson, you will draw a circle around the photograph of the skating girl on page 8, and then flow type around the circle.

1 Choose 8 from the Page pop-up menu at the bottom of the document window to turn to page 8.

2 Using the Selection tool (↖), click the elliptical frame that contains the photograph. Notice the center point of the graphic. You will use this center point to help you draw the circle.

3 Hold down the mouse on the Rectangle tool in the toolbox, and select the Ellipse tool (○).

4 Click the Default Fill and Stroke button (⬚) near the bottom of the toolbox.

5 Holding down Alt+Shift (Windows) or Option+Shift (Mac OS), place the pointer over the center point of the graphic and drag outward to create a circle slightly larger than the photograph (about 20 picas, as shown in the Transform and Control palettes for W and H).

The Shift key constrains the shape to a circle; the Alt or Option key makes the center of the circle the starting point of your drawing so that you draw outward from the center.

6 Click and hold the mouse pointer over the Type tool in the toolbox, and then select the Path Type tool (⤳).

7   Position the pointer over the upper left part of the circle until a small plus sign appears next to the pointer (⤲), click and drag along the arc to the same relative position on the other side of the circle.

If you click an insertion point on a path, the range of type will extend along the entire path. If you drag, type will appear only along the length specified when you dragged.

8   In the Control palette, choose Adobe Caslon Pro as the font and set the size to 11pt. Type the following: **Skating away on the thin ice of a brand new day...**

9   Choose the Selection tool.

Note: If you see a red plus sign (+) in the out port at the end of the text on the path, it indicates overset text. To display all the text on the path, you will adjust the path type's start and end indicators, which are the blue lines that appear before and after the pasted text. Select the Direct Selection tool (⟩) and move it over the blue indicator at the beginning of the text path. When the Direct Selection pointer is properly positioned, it appears as a solid arrowhead with a small vertical line and an arrow (▶ᵥ). Drag the start indicator line (not the in port) along the circle to the left. Then drag the end indicator line (not the out port) along the circle to the right until all the text appears.

Finishing up

To complete the newsletter, you will clean up the design on page 8 by removing the circle's stroke.

1 Choose the Selection tool (↖), and then click the text on the path.

2 Select the Stroke box (⧉) in the toolbox, and then click the None button (⊘).

3 Save the file.

Congratulations. You have finished the lesson.

Exploring on your own

Follow these steps to learn more about layout adjustment and styles.

When you changed the number of columns in this lesson, the size of the text frames remained unchanged. However, if you need to change your document setup after you've begun laying out your document, you can turn on the Layout Adjustment option, which can save you time in reformatting your document. Try this:

1 Go to page 4 and choose Layout > Layout Adjustment. Select Enable Layout Adjustment and click OK. Now change the number of columns to 3 using Layout > Margins and Columns.

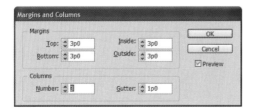

Notice that the photograph is resized and the two text frames shrink to fit the first two columns.

2   Resize the text frames and graphics frame to clean up the page. Add threaded text frames as necessary to finish the redesign.

Before column change (left), after column change with Layout Adjustment turned on (middle), and finished redesign (right).

In this lesson, we covered only the basics of creating and applying styles. If you do a significant amount of writing in InDesign, you'll want to learn how Next Style works and how to apply styles using shortcut keystrokes.

Note: In Windows, Num Lock must be on for the following shortcut keystrokes to work.

3   With no text selected, double-click the Head 2 style in the Paragraph Styles palette. Click an insertion point in the Shortcut text box. Using numbers from only the numeric keypad, press Ctrl+Alt+2 (Windows) or Command+Option+2 (Mac OS). For Next Style, select Body Copy. Click OK to close the dialog box. Now practice applying the Head 2 style using your keyboard shortcut. Notice that when you press Enter or Return at the end of a Head 2 paragraph, the next paragraph automatically has the Body Copy style.

Note: If text does not appear in the Shortcut text box, make sure that you use the numbers from the numeric keypad. In Windows, make sure that Num Lock is on. If you are using a laptop computer that does not include a numeric keypad, choose the style names from the Paragraph Styles menu.

Review

▶ **Review questions**

1   How do you autoflow text? How do you flow text one frame at a time?

2   How can using styles save time?

3   When searching for text using the Find/Change command, you get a "Cannot find match" message. What are some reasons InDesign might have failed to find a match?

4   While checking the spelling of your document, InDesign flags words used in other languages. How can you fix this problem?

▶ **Review answers**

1   When the loaded text icon appears after using the Place command or clicking an out port, hold down the Shift key and click. To flow text one frame at a time, you can hold down Alt (Windows) or Option (Mac OS) to reload the text icon after you click or drag to create a frame.

2   Styles save time by letting you keep a group of formatting attributes together that you can quickly apply to text. If you need to update the text, you don't have to change each paragraph formatted with the style individually. Instead, you can simply modify the style.

3   If you get a "Cannot find match" message, you may not have typed the text properly, you may have selected Whole Word or Case Sensitive, or you may not have cleared formatting used in a previous search. Another possibility is that you selected Story for Search while the text you're looking for is in a different story. Finally, you may be searching for text that does not exist in your document.

4   Before you check the spelling of your document, select any phrase from a different language and use the Character palette to specify the language for that text.

With InDesign you can precisely control the type and formatting of your document. You can easily change font and type styles, modify the alignment, add tabs and indents, and apply colors and strokes to text.

5 Working with Typography

In this lesson, you'll learn how to do the following:

- Prepare and use a baseline grid.

- Change type spacing and appearance.

- Create special characters.

- Create a tabbed table with tab leaders and hanging indents.

- Insert special characters in text using OpenType fonts.

Getting started

In this lesson, you'll create one two-page spread for the annual report of the TravelNE company. Your work in this sample file will involve using one of the Open Type fonts that shipped on the application CD with Adobe InDesign CS2.

Before you begin, you should restore the default preferences for Adobe InDesign.

Note: To ensure that the tools and palettes function exactly as described in this lesson, delete or deactivate (by renaming) the InDesign Defaults file and the InDesign SavedData file. See "Restoring default preferences" on page 2.

1   Start Adobe InDesign.

To begin working, you'll open an existing InDesign document.

2   Choose File > Open, and open the 05_a.indd file in the Lesson_05 folder, located inside the Lessons folder within the InDesignCIB folder on your hard disk.

Note: If you have not already copied the resource files for this lesson onto your hard disk from the Lesson_05 folder from the Adobe InDesign CS2 Classroom in a Book CD, do so now. See "Copying the Classroom in a Book files" on page 4.

3   Choose File > Save As, rename the file **05_report.indd**, and save it in the Lesson_05 folder.

4   If you want to see what the finished document will look like, open the 05_b.indd file in the same folder. You can leave this document open to act as a guide as you work. When you're ready to resume working on the lesson document, choose its name from the Window menu.

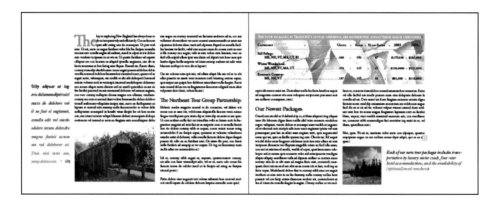

Adjusting vertical spacing

InDesign provides several options for customizing and adjusting the vertical spacing in your document. You can:

- Set the space between all lines of text using a baseline grid.
- Set the space between each line using the Leading option in the Control palette.
- Set the space between each paragraph separately using the Space Before/Space After options in the Control palette.
- Use the Vertical Justification options in the Text Frame Options dialog box to align text within a frame.

In this section of the lesson, you will use the baseline grid to align text.

Using a baseline grid to align text

Once you've decided on the font size and leading for your document's body text, you may want to set up a baseline grid (also called a leading grid) for the entire document. Baseline grids represent the leading for your document's body text and are used to align the baseline of type in one column of text with the baseline of type in neighboring columns.

Before you set the baseline grid, you'll want to check the margin value for the top of your document and the leading value for the body text. These elements work together with the grid to create a cohesive design.

1   To view the top margin value for the page, choose Layout > Margins and Columns. The top margin is set to 6p0 (6 picas, 0 points). Click Cancel to close the dialog box.

2   To determine the leading value, select the Type tool (T) in the toolbox and click in a body-text paragraph. Check the leading value (⌃A) in the Control palette. The leading is set to 14 pt (14 points).

3   Choose Edit > Preferences > Grids (Windows) or InDesign > Preferences > Grids (Mac OS) to set your grid options. In the Baseline Grid section, type **6** for Start to match your top margin setting of 6p0. This option sets the location of the first grid line for the document. If you use InDesign's default value of 3p0, the first grid line would appear above the top margin.

4   For Increment Every, type **14pt** to match your leading. When you select another option, InDesign automatically converts the points value to picas (to 1p2).

5   Choose 100% for View Threshold.

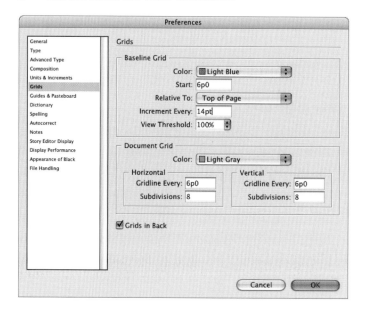

The View Threshold option sets the minimum value at which you can see the grid on-screen. At 100%, the grid appears in the document window only at magnifications of 100% or higher.

6   Click OK to close the dialog box.

Viewing the baseline grid

Now you'll make the grid you just set up visible on-screen.

1   To view the grid in the document window, choose View > Grids & Guides > Show Baseline Grid. The grid does not appear because the document view is lower than the grid's View Threshold value. Choose 100% from the magnification menu at the lower left corner of the document window—the grid now appears on-screen.

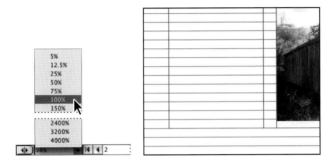

Now you'll use the Control palette to align all the text to the grid. You can align multiple stories independently of one another, or all at once. You'll align all the stories in this spread simultaneously.

2   If the Control palette isn't visible, click Window > Control to make it visible.

3   With the Type tool (T), click an insertion point anywhere in the first paragraph on the spread, and then choose Edit > Select All to select all the text in the main story.

💡 *When applying paragraph attributes, it is not necessary to select an entire paragraph with the Type tool. Just select a portion of the paragraph or paragraphs you want to format. If you are formatting only one paragraph, you can simply click in the paragraph to make an insertion point.*

4 In the Control palette, make sure the Paragraph Formatting Controls button is active (¶), and click the Align to baseline grid button (≣). The text shifts so that the baselines of the characters rest on the grid lines.

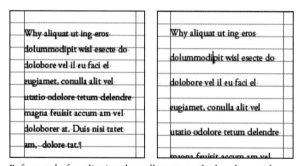

Before and after aligning the text to the baseline grid.

5 If necessary, scroll to the left side of the spread so you can see the pull-quote on the side of the page; then click an insertion point in the pull-quote.

6 In the Control palette, click the Align to Baseline Grid button. Because this text is formatted using 18 point leading, not the baseline grid leading value of 14pt or 1p2, aligning to the grid causes the text to expand to every other grid line (using 28 point leading).

Before and after aligning the pull-quote to the baseline grid.

7 Save the file.

Changing the spacing above and below paragraphs

When you apply a space before or after a paragraph that you have previously aligned to the grid, the space automatically adjusts to the next highest multiple of the grid value. For example, if your grid is set to 14 points (1p2) and you specify Space After of any value under 14, InDesign automatically increases the space value to 14; if you specify a value over 14, such as 16, InDesign increases it to the next higher multiple, or 28. You can use the Space Before or Space After value instead of the Baseline Grid value, by selecting the Do Not Align to Baseline Grid option for the affected paragraph.

No space (left), space adjusted to fit grid at 28 pt (right).

Here you'll increase the space below the second paragraph of the main story. All other paragraphs in the spread have already been formatted with a 1p2 Space After value.

1   Using the Type tool (T), click anywhere in the second paragraph on the page on the left (page 1).

2   In the Control palette, type **1p2** for Space After (⌐≣) and press Enter or Return. The text in the next heading shifts automatically to the next grid line.

Before and after applying a Space After value to the upper paragraph.

Now you'll increase the space before the heading "The Northeast Tour Group Partnership" to give it even more space.

3 Click an insertion point in the heading "The Northeast Tour Group Partnership." In the Control palette, type **0p6** for Space Before (⁺▤) and then press Enter or Return. Because you previously aligned the heading to the baseline grid, the Space Before jumps to 14 points instead of 6 points.

To use the 0p6 value instead of 14, and to add more space between the heading and the following paragraph, you'll unalign the heading from the grid.

4 With an insertion point still in the heading "The Northeast Tour Group Partnership," click the Do not align to baseline grid button (▤) in the Control palette. The heading shifts upward a bit, away from the body text below.

Before and after unaligning the heading from the baseline grid.

This heading and the heading on the page on the right (page 2) are formatted using the Head 1 style. To automatically update the second heading so that it uses the same spacing values as the heading you just edited, you'll redefine the style.

5 Click the Paragraph Styles palette tab (or choose Type > Paragraph Styles) to make the palette visible.

6 Click an insertion point in the heading "The Northeast Tour Group Partnership." Notice that a plus sign appears after the Head 1 style name in the palette. This sign indicates that the formatting for the selected text has been modified from the original formatting for the style.

7 Click the Palette Menu button (⊙), and choose Redefine Style from the Paragraph Styles palette menu. The Head 1 style now takes on the formatting of the current text.

Notice that the plus sign disappears and that space is added above the heading on page 2.

8   To apply all the same alignment characteristics to another heading, click the Type tool in the "Our Newest Packages" heading on page 2, and then select the Head 1 style in the Paragraph Styles palette to apply the redefined style.

9   Save the file.

Changing fonts and type style

Changing the fonts and type styles of text can make a dramatic difference in the appearance of your document. Here you'll change the font family, type style, and size for the text in one of the pull-quotes along the border of the spread. You'll make these changes using the Control palette.

1   Make sure the Control palette is visible. (If it's not, click Window > Control to make it visible).

2   Using the Type tool (T), click inside the pull-quote on the left side of page 1, and then choose Edit > Select All to select the entire paragraph.

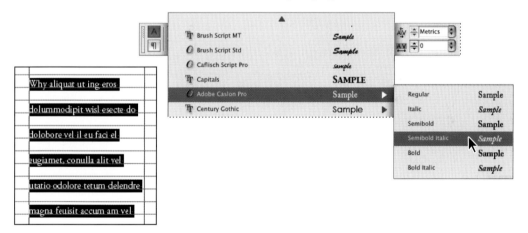

3   In the Control palette, make sure the Character Formatting Controls button is active (A). Select Adobe Caslon Pro from the Font Family menu and Semibold Italic from the Type Style menu.

4   In Font Size, type **15,** and press Enter or Return.

5   Choose Edit > Deselect All to deselect the text. Notice how the text stays aligned to the grid even after changing these attributes.

Because Adobe Caslon Pro is an OpenType font, you can use the Glyphs palette to select alternatives for many characters.

6   Select the first character (the "W") of the pull-quote, and then choose Type > Glyphs.

7   In the Glyphs palette, select Alternates for Selection in the drop-down menu, just to see the alternates for "W." Then double-click the more script-like "W" alternate to replace the original character in the pull-quote.

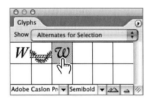

💡 *Some of the more commonly used glyphs, such as the copyright and trademark symbols, are also available from the context menu by right-clicking (Windows) or Ctrl+clicking (Mac OS) at the text insertion point.*

8   You won't be using the baseline grid for the remainder of the lesson, so you can hide it from view. To hide it, choose View > Grids & Guides > Hide Baseline Grid. Then save the file.

Changing paragraph alignment

You can easily manipulate how a paragraph fits in its text frame by changing the horizontal alignment. You can align text with one or both edges of a text frame or text-frame inset. Justifying text aligns both the left and right edges. In this section, you'll justify the pull-quote.

1   Using the Type tool (T), click an insertion point in the pull-quote on page 1.

2   In the Control palette, make sure the Paragraph Formatting Controls button is active (¶), and then click the Justify All Lines button (≡).

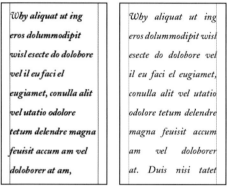

Before and after justifying text.

Adding a decorative font and special character

Now you'll add a decorative font character and a flush space (special character) to the end of the pull-quote. Used together, a decorative font and flush space can make a dramatic difference in the look of a justified paragraph.

1   Using the Type tool (T), click an insertion point in the pull-quote, just after the final period.

2   If the Glyphs palette is not still open, choose Type > Glyphs.

3 In the Glyphs palette, for Show, select Ornaments.

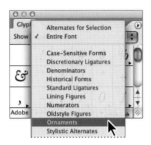

4 From the scrollable list, select the ❀ character and double-click to insert the character. The character appears at the insertion point in the document. You're finished with the Glyphs palette for this lesson, so you can close it now, and then save your work.

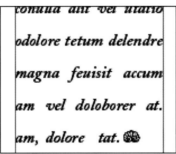

Note: This font may display many more glyphs than you are accustomed to seeing because it is an OpenType font. OpenType fonts are able to carry many more characters and glyph alternates than earlier PostScript typefaces. Adobe's OpenType fonts are built on the same foundation as PostScript. For more information about OpenType fonts, visit Adobe.com/type.

Notice how the last line of the pull-quote has overly large spaces between the words. You can address this by adding a flush space to the end of the paragraph. A flush space adds a variable amount of space to the last line of a fully justified paragraph. You'll insert the flush space between the period and the decorative end-of-story character you just added.

You could add a flush space using the Type menu, but this time you'll use the Context menu to do the job.

5   Using the Type tool, click an insertion point between the final period and the Wood Type decorative character.

6   Right-click (Windows) or Ctrl+click (Mac OS) and choose Insert White Space > Flush Space.

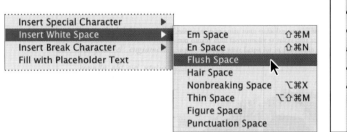

Applying special font features

You can add creative touches to your document using the special InDesign font features. For example, you can make the first character or word in a paragraph a drop cap, or apply a gradient or color fill to text. Other features include superscript and subscript characters, along with ligatures and old-style numerals for font families with these features.

Applying a gradient to text

InDesign makes it easy to apply gradients to the fill and stroke of text characters. You can apply gradients to an entire text frame or to different character ranges within a frame. Here you'll apply a gradient to the pull-quote on page 1. You'll use a gradient swatch that was previously created and added to the Swatches palette.

For more on working with gradients, see Chapter 6 "Working with Color."

1   Click the Swatches palette tab (or choose Window > Swatches) to make the palette visible.

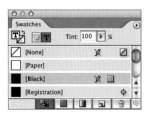

2   Make sure that the Type tool (T) is still selected, click in the text of the pull-quote on page 1, and then select all the text in the paragraph.

3   Select the Fill box (🖹) in the toolbox, and then select the Text Gradient swatch in the Swatches palette (you may need to scroll). To see the gradient, choose Edit > Deselect All.

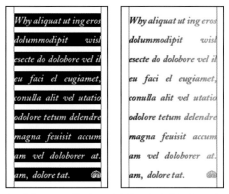

Applying a gradient swatch to selected text creates a left-to-right gradient fill.

Notice how the gradient flows from the left to right. If you want to change the direction of the gradient, you can use the gradient tool. You'll do that now to make the gradient flow from top to bottom, like the pull-quote on page 1.

4   Using the Type tool, reselect all the text in the pull-quote.

5 Select the Gradient tool (⬛) in the toolbox, and drag a line from the top to the bottom of the highlighted text. Holding down the Shift key as you drag, ensures that you'll draw a straight line.

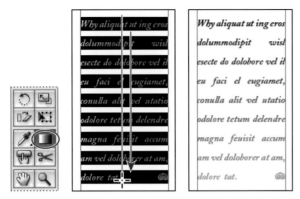

The Gradient tool (left) lets you set the direction of the gradient fill.

To view the gradient fill, you'll use a keyboard shortcut to deselect all the text.

6 Press Shift+Ctrl+A (Windows) or Shift+Command+A (Mac OS) to deselect the text.

7 Select File > Save.

Creating a drop cap

Here you'll create a three-letter drop cap in the first paragraph of the document.

1 Using the Type tool (T), click an insertion point anywhere in the first paragraph on page 1.

2   In the Control palette, type **3** for Drop Cap Number of Lines to make the letters drop down three lines. Then type **3** for Drop Cap One or More Characters (⧉) to enlarge the first three letters. Press Enter or Return.

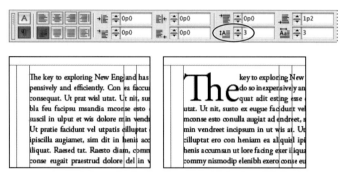

Before and after applying the drop cap.

Applying a fill and stroke to text

Next, you'll add a fill and stroke to the drop cap letters you just created.

1   With the Type tool (**T**) still selected, select the drop cap characters on page 1.

2   If necessary, select the Fill box (⧉) in the Swatches palette.

3   In the Swatches palette, select TravelNE Green. InDesign fills the letters with green, though you can't see it yet because the text is still selected.

Note: If you don't see TravelNE Green in the palette, click the Show All Swatches button (⧉).

4   Select the Stroke box (⧉) in the toolbox.

5   In the Swatches palette, select Black. A stroke appears around each of the letters.

The default size of the stroke is 1 point, which is a little thick for the letters. You'll change the stroke to 0.5 point.

6   Choose Window > Stroke to open the Stroke palette.

7 In the Stroke palette, choose 0.5 pt for Weight. Then, press Shift+Ctrl+A (Windows) or Shift+Command+A (Mac OS) to deselect the text to view the fill and stroke effect.

Original drop cap (left), drop cap with color fill (middle), and drop cap with fill and stroke (right).

8 Close the Stroke palette, and then save the file.

Adjusting letter and word spacing

You can change the spacing between words and letters using InDesign's kerning and tracking features. You can also control the overall spacing of text in a paragraph by using the single-line or paragraph composers.

Adjusting the kerning and tracking

With InDesign, you can control the space between letters by using the kerning and tracking features. Kerning is the process of adding or subtracting space between specific letter pairs. Tracking is the process of creating an equal amount of spacing across a range of letters. You can use both kerning and tracking on the same text.

Here you'll manually kern some letters in the heading "The Northeast Tour Group Partnership" to close up noticeable gaps. Then you'll track the heading.

1 To distinguish the amount of space between letters more easily and to see the results of the kerning more clearly, select the Zoom tool (🔍) in the toolbox and drag a marquee around the heading "The Northeast Tour Group Partnership."

2 If necessary, increase the zoom level in the magnification menu in the lower left corner of the document window.

3 Select the Type tool (T) and click an insertion point between the "N" and the "o" in the word "Northeast."

4   Press Alt+Left Arrow (Windows) or Option+Left Arrow (Mac OS) to move the letter "o" to the left. Press this key combination repeatedly until the two adjacent letters look visually pleasing to you. We pressed it twice.

Note: You can also use the Control palette to make these changes if you prefer.

Before and after kerning.

5   If you've moved the letter too far, press Alt+Right Arrow (Windows) or Option+Right Arrow (Mac OS) to move the letter to the right.

6   Click an insertion point between the "P" and the "a" in the word "Partnership."

7   Press Alt/Option+Left Arrow to move the letter "a" to the left. Press this key combination repeatedly until the two adjacent letters look visually pleasing to you. We pressed it four times.

Before and after kerning.

Now you'll set a tracking value for the entire heading "The Northeast Tour Group Partnership" to condense the overall spacing. To set tracking, you must first select the entire range of characters you want to track.

8   Choose 200% from the magnification menu at the lower left corner of the document window to view more of the page on-screen.

9   With the Type tool, click four times on "The Northeast Tour Group Partnership" to select the entire heading.

10 In the Control palette, click the Character Formatting Controls button (**A**), then enter **-15** for Tracking (**A V**) and press Enter or Return.

The heading after tracking is applied.

Now you'll use a keyboard shortcut to deselect the text.

11 Press Shift+Ctrl+A (Windows) or Shift+Command+A (Mac OS).

12 Press Ctrl+1 (Windows) or Command+1 (Mac OS) to return to a 100% view.

13 Save the file.

Applying the paragraph and single-line composers

The density of a paragraph (sometimes called its color) is determined by the composition method used. When composing text, InDesign considers the word spacing, letter spacing, glyph scaling, and hyphenation options you've selected, and then evaluates and chooses the best line breaks. InDesign provides two options for composing text: the paragraph composer, which looks at all the lines in the paragraph, or the single-line composer, which looks separately at each individual line.

When you use the paragraph composer, InDesign composes a line by considering the impact on the other lines in the paragraph; in the end, the best overall arrangement of the paragraph is established. As you change type in a given line, previous and subsequent lines in the same paragraph may break differently, making the overall paragraph appear more evenly spaced. When you use the single-line composer, which is the standard for other layout and word-processing programs, only the lines following the edited text are recomposed.

The text in this lesson was composed using the default, the Adobe Paragraph Composer. To see the difference between the two, you'll recompose the pull-quote text using the single-line composer.

1 Using the Type tool (T), click an insertion point in the pull-quote text on page 1.

2 Choose Type > Paragraph, then choose Adobe Single-line Composer from the Paragraph palette menu.

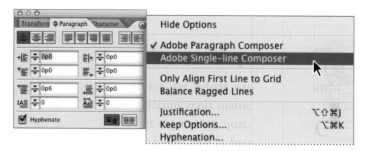

The single-line composer looks at each line individually and, consequently, can make some lines in a paragraph appear more dense or sparse than others.

Because the paragraph composer looks at multiple lines at once, it makes the density of the lines in a paragraph more consistent.

3 From the Paragraph palette menu, choose Adobe Paragraph Composer. Notice that the lines of text now have a consistent density and all the text fits neatly in the text frame.

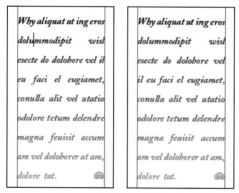

Pull-quote formatted using the Adobe Single-line Composer (left), and the Adobe Paragraph Composer (right).

4 Choose File > Save to save your file.

Working with tabs

You can use tabs to position text in specific horizontal locations in a frame. Using the Tabs palette, you can organize text and create tab leaders, indents, and hanging indents. Here you'll format the information at the top of page 2 using the Tabs palette. The tab markers have already been entered in the text, so all you will be doing is setting the final location of the text.

1   If necessary, scroll to the top of page 2 until the table appears on-screen.

2   To view the tab markers in the table, choose Type > Show Hidden Characters, and make sure that Normal View Mode (🖺) is selected in the toolbox. If you decide not to keep them showing as you work, choose Type > Hide Hidden Characters.

3   Using the Type tool (T), click in the word "Category" at the top of the table.

4   Choose Type > Tabs to open the Tabs palette. When an insertion point is in a text frame and there is enough space at the top of the frame, the Tabs palette snaps to the border of the frame so that the measurements in the palette's ruler exactly match the text.

5   To center the page on your screen, double-click the page 2 icon in the Pages palette. Because the Tabs palette moves independently of the table, the two are no longer aligned.

6   Click the magnet icon in the Tabs palette to realign the palette with the text.

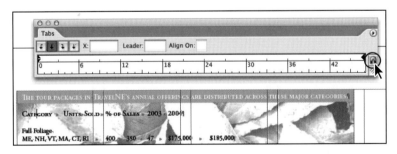

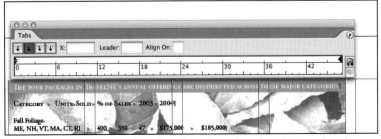

Clicking the magnet icon in the Tabs palette aligns the ruler with the selected text.

Note: If the Tabs palette did not snap to the text frame, part of the text block may be hidden from view, or there may not be enough room for the Tabs palette between the text frame and the top of the document window. Scroll as necessary, and then click the magnet icon (⬛) again.

7 Using the Type tool, select all the text in the table's text frame, from the word "Category" to the number "$110,000."

8 In the Tabs palette, click the Center-Justified Tab button (⬛) so that when you set the new tab positions, they will align from the center.

9 In the Tabs palette, position the pointer in the top portion of the ruler, just above the numbers, and then click to set tab markers at the following locations: 24, 29, 34, 40, and 45. You can view the location of the pointer on the ruler in the X: text box (above the left side of the ruler). To precisely set the value, drag in the ruler while watching the X value before releasing the mouse button, or type the value directly into the X value of the Tabs palette.

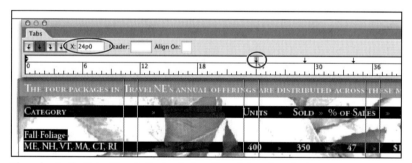

The value in the X: text box indicates the location of the selected tab.

Note: If you don't get the tab locations correct the first time, you can select the tab in the ruler and type the location in the X value. You can also click on a tab in the Tabs palette and drag up to remove a tab.

10 Press Shift+Ctrl+A (Windows) or Shift+Command+A (Mac OS) to deselect the text and view the new tab settings.

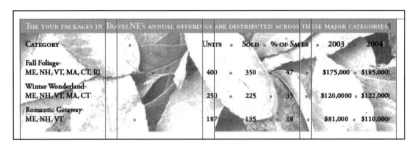

Now you'll set a tab leader for some of the tabs.

11 Select all the text in the table from "Fall" to "$110,000."

12 In the Tabs palette, click the first tab arrow along the ruler to select it so that the leader you create will affect any selected tabs at that tab marker.

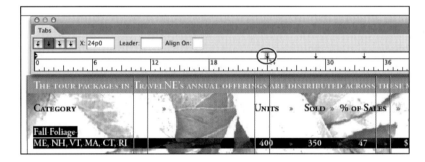

13 In the Leader text box, type ._ (period, space) and press Enter or Return. You can use any character as a tab leader. We used a space between periods to create a more open dot sequence.

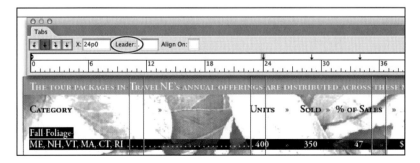

14 Deselect the table text and view the leaders.

Creating a hanging indent

Now you'll use the Tabs palette to create hanging indents. The text frame for this table has an inset value of 6 points at the top and 9 points on the sides and bottom. (To see the inset values, choose Object > Text Frame Options.) An inset sets the text apart from the frame; now you'll set it apart even more by indenting the three categories in the table.

You can set an indent in the Tabs palette or the Control palette. You'll keep the Control palette visible so you can see how the values change there, too.

1 Make sure that the Control palette is visible. If necessary, select Window > Control.

2 In the table, use the Type tool (T) to select all the text from "Fall" to "$110,000."

3 Make sure that the Tabs palette is still aligned directly above the table. If it has moved, click the magnet icon (ⓐ).

4 In the Tabs palette, drag the indent markers on the left side of the ruler to the right until the X value is 2p0. Dragging the bottom marker moves both at once. Notice how all the text shifts to the right and the indent option in the Paragraph palette changes to 2p0. Keep the text selected.

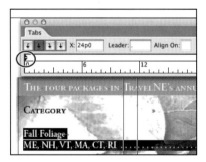 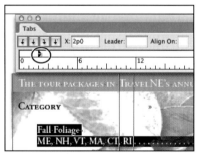

Now you'll bring just the category headings back to their original location in the table to create a hanging indent.

5   In the Tabs palette, drag the top half of the indent marker to the left until the X value is -2p0. Deselect the text and view the hanging indent.

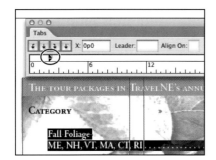 

6   Close the Tabs palette and save the file.

Note: You can also create tables of information using the Table menu and Table palette. For more information, see Lesson 9, "Creating Tables."

Adding a rule below a paragraph

You can also add a rule, or line, above or below a paragraph. Here you'll add a rule under the table headings.

1   Using the Type tool (T), click an insertion point in the word Category in the table.

2   From the palette menu in the Paragraph section of the Control palette, choose Paragraph Rules.

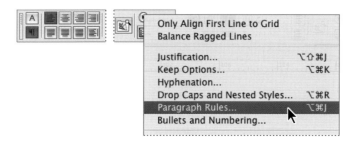

3   In the Paragraph Rules dialog box, choose Rule Below from the menu at the top of the dialog box, and then select Rule On to activate the rule.

4   To view the rule as you select your options, select Preview and move the dialog box so that it is not obstructing your view of the heading.

5   For Weight, choose 1 pt; for Color, choose TravelNE Green; for Width, choose Column; and for Offset, type **0p9**. Then click OK.

6   Save the file.

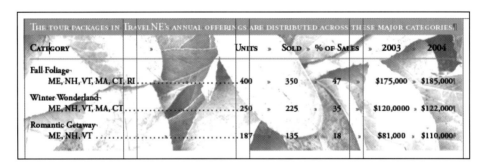

Category		Units	Sold	% of Sales	2003	2004
Fall Foliage ME, NH, VT, MA, CT, RI		400	350	47	$175,000	$185,000
Winter Wonderland ME, NH, VT, MA, CT		250	225	35	$120,0000	$122,000
Romantic Getaway ME, NH, VT		187	135	18	$81,000	$110,000

Congratulations. You have finished the lesson.

Exploring on your own

Now that you have learned the basics of formatting text in an InDesign document, you're ready to apply these skills on your own. Try the following tasks to improve your typography skills.

1   Click your cursor within various paragraphs and experiment with enabling and disabling hyphenation from the Paragraph palette. Select a hyphenated word and choose No Break from the Character palette menu to individually stop a word from hyphenating.

2   Click your cursor within the body copy and choose Edit > Edit in Story Editor. Make some edits to the text and then select Edit > Edit in Layout. Notice how the edits made in the story editor are reflected back in the layout. Explore the formatting and editing commands that are available while working in the Story Editor.

3   Apply Optical Margin Alignment to each paragraph in the main story (everything except the pull-quotes and tables). You can access the Optical Margin Alignment feature by choosing the Story command in the Type menu.

Optical Margin Alignment—the text visually aligns along the edges of the text frame, allowing some of the text, such as punctuation and quotation marks, to be positioned outside of the text frame.

Review

▶ **Review questions**

1 How do you view a baseline grid?

2 When and where do you use a flush space?

3 How do you apply a gradient to only a few words or characters in a paragraph?

4 What is the difference between the paragraph composer and the single-line composer?

▶ **Review answers**

1 To view a baseline grid, choose View > Grids & Guides > Show Baseline Grid. The current document view must be at or above the View Threshold set in the Baseline Grid preferences. By default, that value is 75%.

2 You use a flush space on justified text. For example, if used with a special character or decorative font at the end of a paragraph, it absorbs any extra space in the last line.

3 To apply a gradient to a specific range of characters, you first select the text with the Type tool. Next, you apply the gradient to the text. If the entire range of colors does not appear, select the Gradient tool and drag from one end of the selected text to the other in the direction you want the gradient to flow.

4 The paragraph composer evaluates multiple lines at once when determining the best possible line breaks. The single-line composer looks at only one line at a time when determining line breaks.

You can create, save, and apply process and spot colors, including tints, and blended gradients.

When your document must meet color standards set by clients and designers, color consistently becomes critical. A color management system reconciles color differences among devices so that you can be reasonably certain of the colors in your documents.

6 | Working with Color

In this introduction to working with colors and color management, you'll learn how to do the following:

- Add colors to the Swatches palette.

- Apply colors to objects.

- Create dashed strokes.

- Create and apply a gradient swatch.

- Adjust the direction of the gradient blend.

- Create a tint.

- Create a spot color.

- Specify a color management engine.

- Specify default source ICC profiles.

- Assign ICC profiles in InDesign CS2.

- Embed ICC profiles in graphics created in other Adobe programs.

Getting started

In this lesson, you'll work on and set up color management for an advertisement for a fictitious chocolate company called Tifflins Truffles. Color management is important in environments where you must evaluate image color reliably in the context of your final output. Color correction is a different issue that involves images with tonal or color-balance problems, and is usually handled in the original graphics application, such as Photoshop CS2.

The ad will run in a variety of publications, so getting consistent and predictable color is your goal. You will set up the color management system using a CMYK press-oriented workflow, build the document using graphics from other Adobe products, and specify ICC profiles for individual graphics to ensure color integrity.

The ad consists of graphics created in InDesign CS2 and other Adobe applications. You will color-manage those graphics to achieve consistent color output from InDesign CS2.

Before you begin, you'll need to restore the default preferences for Adobe InDesign CS2. Then you'll open the finished document for this lesson to see what you'll be creating.

1   To ensure that the tools and palettes function exactly as described in this lesson, delete or deactivate (by renaming) the InDesign CS2 Defaults file and the InDesign CS2 SavedData file. See "Restoring default preferences" on page 2.

2   Start Adobe InDesign CS2.

3   Choose File > Open, and open the 06_a.indd file in the Lesson_06 folder, located inside the Lessons folder within the InDesignCIB folder on your hard disk.

Note: If you have not already copied the resource files for this lesson onto your hard disk from the Lesson_06 folder from the Adobe InDesign CS2 Classroom in a Book CD, do so now. See "Copying the Classroom in a Book files" on page 4.

4   Choose File > Save As, rename the file **06_Color.indd**, and save it in the Lesson_06 folder.

Note: This lesson is designed for users who work with InDesign CS2 in environments that also involve Adobe Illustrator (version 9 or later) and Adobe Photoshop (version 5.0 or later). If you do not have those programs installed on your computer, you will skip some of these step-by-step instructions for color-managing graphics from Illustrator and Photoshop.

5   If you want to see what the finished document will look like, open the 06_b.indd file in the same folder. You can leave this document open to act as a guide as you work. When you're ready to resume working on the lesson document, choose its name from the Window menu.

*A. InDesign CS2 object. **B.** Photoshop PSD file.*
*C. Legacy (archived) CMYK file. **D.** Illustrator file exported as a bitmap.*

Note: As you work through the lesson, feel free to move palettes around or change the magnification to a level that works best for you. For more information, see "Changing the magnification of your document" and "Using the Navigator palette" in Lesson 1.

Defining printing requirements

It's a good idea to know printing requirements before you start working on a document. For example, meet with your prepress service provider and discuss your document's design and use of color. Because your prepress service provider understands the capabilities of their equipment, they may suggest ways for you to save time and money, increase quality, and avoid potentially costly printing or color problems. The magazine article used in this lesson was designed to be printed by a commercial printer using the CMYK color model.

Adding colors to the Swatches palette

You can add color to objects using a combination of palettes and tools. The InDesign CS2 color workflow revolves around the Swatches palette. Using the Swatches palette to name colors makes it easy to apply, edit, and update colors for objects in a document. Although you can also use the Color palette to apply colors to objects, there is no quick way to update these colors, called unnamed colors. Instead, you'd have to update the color of each object individually.

You'll now create most of the colors you'll use in this document. Since this document is intended for a commercial press, you'll be creating CMYK process colors.

1 Make sure that no objects are selected, and then click the Swatches palette tab. (If the Swatches palette is not visible, choose Window > Swatches.)

The Swatches palette stores the colors that have been preloaded into InDesign CS2, as well as the colors, tints, and gradients you create and store for reuse.

2 Choose New Color Swatch from the Swatches palette menu.

3 Deselect Name With Color Value, and for Swatch Name, type **Brown**. Make sure that Color Type and Color Mode are set to Process and CMYK, respectively.

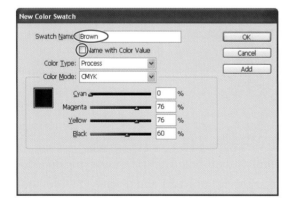

The Name With Color Value option names a color using the CMYK color values that you enter, and automatically updates the name if you change the value. This option is available only for process colors and is useful when you want to use the Swatches palette to monitor the exact composition of process-color swatches. For this swatch, you deselected the Name With Color Value option, so that you can use a name (Brown) that's easier to read for this lesson.

4   For the color percentages, type the following values: C = **0**, M = **76**, Y = **76**, K = **60**, and then click OK.

5   Repeat the previous three steps to name and create the following colors:

	C	M	Y	K
Blue	60	20	0	0
Tan	2	13	29	0

💡 *If you forget to type the name for a color or if you type an incorrect value, double-click the swatch, change the name or value, and then click OK.*

New colors added to the Swatches palette are stored only with the document in which they are created. You'll apply these colors to text, graphics, and frames in your document.

Applying colors to objects

There are three general steps to applying a swatch color: (1) selecting the text or object, (2) selecting the stroke or fill in the toolbox, depending on what you want to change, and (3) selecting the color in the Swatches palette. You can also drag swatches from the Swatches palette to objects.

1   Choose the Selection tool (➤), and click the path or one of the lines in any one of the diamond shapes at the top right of the page to select it.

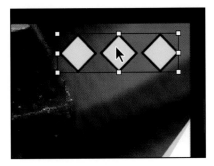

Notice that these three objects are grouped, so all are now selected. You will ungroup these objects and lock them in place. Locking objects prevents you from accidentally moving them.

2   With the group of objects still selected, choose Object > Ungroup and then choose Object > Lock Position.

3   Deselect the objects. To deselect an object, you can choose Edit > Deselect All, you can click a blank area in your document window, or you can press Shift+Ctrl+A (Windows) or Shift+Command+A (Mac OS).

4   Choose the Zoom tool (🔍) in the toolbox and drag across the three diamonds to draw a marquee around the shapes. The view magnification changes so that the area defined by the marquee now fills the document window. Make sure that you can see all three diamond shapes.

💡 *To fine-tune the zoom magnification, you can press Ctrl+= (Windows) or Command+= (Mac OS). To zoom out, you can press Ctrl+- (Windows) or Command+- (Mac OS).*

5   Choose the Selection tool, and click the border of the middle diamond to select it. Select the Stroke box (🔲) in the toolbox, and then click Green in the Swatches palette.

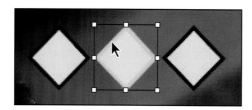

The stroke of the diamond shape is now green.

6   Deselect the object.

7   Click the border of the left diamond to select it. Select Brown in the Swatches palette to apply a brown stroke.

8   With the left diamond still selected, select the Fill box (◼) in the toolbox, and then select Green in the Swatches palette (you may need to scroll down the list of swatches).

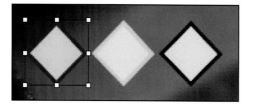

The right diamond requires the same Brown stroke and Green fill. You'll use the eyedropper to copy the stroke and fill attributes from the left diamond in one quick step.

9 Select the Eyedropper tool (✐), and click the left diamond. Notice that the eyedropper is now filled (✎), indicating that it picked up the attributes from the clicked object.

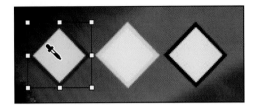

10 With the filled Eyedropper tool, click the gray background of the rightmost diamond. The right diamond takes on the left diamond's fill and stroke attributes.

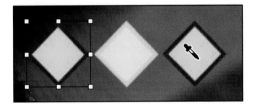

Now you'll change the color of the middle diamond.

11 Choose the Selection tool, and then deselect the objects.

12 Using the Selection tool, click the border of the middle diamond to select it. Select the Fill box in the toolbox, and then click [Paper] in the Swatches palette.

[Paper] is a special color that simulates the paper color on which you're printing. Objects behind a paper-colored object won't print where the paper-colored object overlaps them. Instead, the color of the paper on which you print shows through.

Creating dashed strokes

You'll now change the black line that borders the ad to a custom dashed line. Because you will be using the custom dashed line on only one object, you will create it using the Stroke palette. If you need to save a stroke for repetitive use throughout a document, you can easily create a stroke style. For more information about saving Stroke styles, including dashes, dots, and stripes, see InDesign Help, "To define custom stroke styles."

1   Deselect any selected objects and Zoom out to fit window. Choose the Selection tool (⬆) and select the black outline that borders the ad.

2   If the Stroke palette is not already visible, choose Window > Stroke to open it and drag the tab onto the page for better visibility.

3   For Type, select Dashed.

Six dash and gap boxes appear at the bottom of the Stroke palette. To create a dashed line, you specify the length of the dash, and then the gap, or spacing, between the dashes.

4   Type the following values in the Dash and Gap boxes: **16**, **4**, **2**, **4** (press Tab after you type each value to move to the next box). Leave the last two dash and gap boxes empty.

5   Select Brown from the Gap Color to fill the gap with brown.

6   Deselect the line and close the Stroke palette. Then choose File > Save.

Working with gradients

A gradient is a graduated blend between two or more colors, or between tints of the same color. You can create either a linear or a radial gradient.

A
B

A. Linear gradient.   *B. Radial gradient.*

Creating and applying a gradient swatch

Every InDesign CS2 gradient has at least two color stops. By editing the color mix of each stop and by adding additional color stops in the Gradient palette, you can create your own custom gradients.

1   Make sure no objects are selected, and choose New Gradient Swatch from the Swatches palette menu.

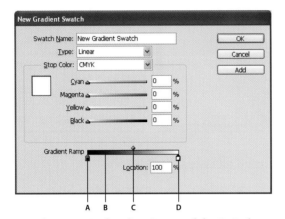

A. Left stop. B. Gradient bar. C. Ramp slider. D. Right stop.

Gradients are defined by a series of color stops in the gradient bar. A stop is the point at which a gradient changes from one color to the next and is identified by a square below the gradient bar.

2   For Swatch Name, type **Brown/Tan Gradient**.

3   Click the left stop marker (⬧). For Stop Color, select Swatches, and then scroll down the list of color swatches and select Brown.

Notice that the left side of the gradient ramp is brown.

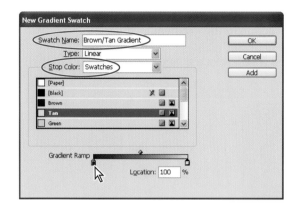

4   Click the right stop marker. For Stop Color, select Swatches, and then scroll down the list and select Tan.

The gradient ramp shows a color blend between brown and tan.

5   Click OK.

Now you'll apply the gradient to the fill of the middle diamond in the upper right hand corner.

6   Zoom in on the upper right hand corner, bringing the three diamond shapes into view.

7   Use the Selection tool (▸), to select the middle diamond.

8   Select the Fill box (◼) in the toolbox, and then click Brown/Tan Gradient in the Swatches palette.

Adjusting the direction of the gradient blend

Once you have filled an object with a gradient, you can modify the gradient by using the Gradient tool to "repaint" the fill along an imaginary line you drag. This tool lets you change the direction of a gradient and change the beginning point and endpoint of a gradient. You'll now change the direction of the gradient.

1   Make sure the middle diamond is still selected, and then select the Gradient tool (◼) in the toolbox.

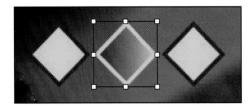

Now you'll experiment with the Gradient tool to see how you can change the direction and intensity of the gradient.

2   To create a more gradual gradient effect, place the pointer outside the selected diamond and drag across and past it.

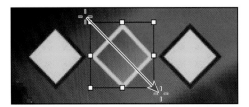

When you release the mouse button, you'll notice that the blend between brown and tan is more gradual than it was before you dragged the Gradient tool.

3   To create a sharper gradient, drag a small line in the center of the diamond. Continue to experiment with the Gradient tool so that you understand how it works.

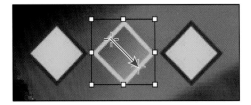

4   When you have finished experimenting, drag from the top corner of the diamond to the bottom corner. That's how you'll leave the gradient of the middle diamond.

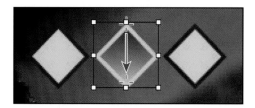

5   Choose File > Save.

Creating a tint

In addition to adding colors, you can also add tints to the Swatches palette. A tint is a screened (lighter) version of a color. You'll now create a 30% tint of the brown swatch you saved earlier in this lesson.

Tints are helpful because InDesign CS2 maintains the relationship between a tint and its parent color. For example, if you changed the brown color swatch to a different color, the tint swatch you create in this procedure would become a lighter version of the new color.

1   Deselect all objects.

2   Choose View > Fit Page in Window to center the page in the document window.

3   Click Brown in the Swatches palette. Choose New Tint Swatch from the Swatches palette menu. For Tint percentage, type **30** and then click OK.

The new tint swatch appears at the bottom of the list of swatches. The top of the Swatches palette displays information about the selected swatch, with a Fill/Stroke box showing that the brown tint is currently the selected fill color and a Tint option showing that the color is 30% of the original Brown color.

4 Use the Selection tool (▶), to click the outlined text "Si" in the center of the page to select it.

5 Make sure the Fill box (■) is selected, and then click the Brown tint that you just created in the Swatches palette; notice the color change.

About spot and process colors

A spot color is a special premixed ink that is used instead of, or in addition to, CMYK inks, and requires its own printing plate on a printing press. Use spot color when few colors are specified and color accuracy is critical. Spot color inks can accurately reproduce colors that are outside the gamut of process colors. However, the exact appearance of the printed spot color is determined by the combination of the ink as mixed by the commercial printer and the paper it's printed on, so it isn't affected by color values you specify or by color management. When you specify spot color values, you're describing the simulated appearance of the color for your monitor and composite printer only (subject to the gamut limitations of those devices).

A process color is printed using a combination of four standard process inks: cyan, magenta, yellow, and black (CMYK). Use process colors when a job requires so many colors that using individual spot inks would be expensive or impractical, such as when printing color photographs. Keep the following guidelines in mind when specifying a process color:

- For best results in a printed document, specify process colors using CMYK values printed in process color reference charts, such as those available from a commercial printer.

- The final color values of a process color are its values in CMYK, so if you specify a process color using RGB or LAB, those color values will be converted to CMYK when you print color separations. These conversions will work differently if you turn on color management; they'll be affected by the profiles you've specified.

- Don't specify a process color based on how it looks on your monitor, unless you are sure you have set up a color management system properly, and you understand its limitations for previewing color.

- Avoid using process colors in documents intended for online viewing only, because CMYK has a smaller color gamut than a typical monitor.

Sometimes it's practical to print process and spot inks on the same job. For example, you might use one spot ink to print the exact color of a company logo on the same pages of an annual report where photographs are reproduced using process color. You can also use a spot color printing plate to apply a varnish over areas of a process color job. In both cases, your print job would use a total of five inks—four process inks and one spot ink or varnish. You can mix process and spot colors together to create mixed ink colors.

—From InDesign Help

Creating a spot color

This publication will be printed by a commercial printer using the standard CMYK color model, which requires four separate plates for printing—one each for cyan, magenta, yellow, and black. However, the CMYK color model has a limited range of colors, which is where spot colors come in handy. Because of this, spot colors are used to create additional colors beyond the range of CMYK or to create consistent, individual colors such as those used for company logos.

In this publication, the design calls for a spot ink not found in the CMYK color model. You'll now add a spot color from a color library.

1   Deselect all objects.

2   In the Swatches palette menu, select New Color Swatch.

3   In the New Color Swatch dialog box, select Spot on the Color Type drop-down menu.

4   In Color Mode, select PANTONE solid coated.

5   In the PANTONE C text box, type **567** to automatically scroll the list of Pantone swatches to the color you want for this project, which is PANTONE 567 C.

6   Click OK. The spot color is added to your Swatches palette. Notice the icon (◉) next to the color name in the Swatches palette. This icon indicates that it is a spot color.

Note: The color you see on your monitor does not reflect the actual printed color. To determine the color you want to use, look at a chart provided by the color system, such as a PANTONE Color Formula Guide, or an ink chart obtained from your printer. Each spot color you create generates an additional spot-color plate for the press. In general, commercial printers typically produce either 2-color, using black and one spot color, or 4-color CMYK work with the possibility of adding one or more spot colors. Using spot colors generally increases your printing costs. It is a good idea to consult with your printer before using spot colors in your document.

Applying color to text

As with frames, you can apply a stroke or fill to text itself. You'll apply colors to the text on the top and bottom of the document.

1 Choose the Selection tool (↖), click the word "Indulgent?" then hold down the shift key and click the text "Paris • Madrid • New York" to select.

2 In the toolbox, make sure the Fill box (◼) is selected and then click the small "T" icon (the formatting affects text button) in the row below the Fill box.

3 In the Swatches palette, click PANTONE 567 C, and then click a blank area to deselect. The text now appears in the spot color.

4 Choose File > Save.

Applying colors to additional objects

Now you'll apply the same color used by the outlined text "Yes!" to color the outlined text "Oui!" First you'll magnify the view of the outlined text "Yes!" to see which color is used.

1 In the toolbox, choose the Zoom tool (🔍), and then drag across the outlined text in the middle of the page.

2   Select the Direct Selection tool (↖), and then click on the outlined text "Yes!" to select. Notice that the corresponding swatch in the Swatches palette becomes highlighted when you select the object to which the swatch is applied.

Now you'll apply this color to the outlined text "Oui!"

3   Drag the Green fill swatch from the Swatches palette to the outlined text "Oui!" Be sure to drop it inside the object and not on the object's stroke.

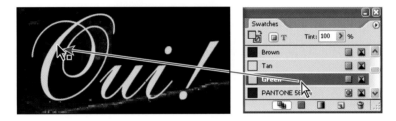

Dragging and dropping can be a more convenient way to apply color, because you don't have to select the object first.

💡 *If you applied the color to the wrong object, choose Edit > Undo Apply Attribute and try again.*

Creating another tint

You'll now create a tint based on the Blue color. When you edit the Blue color, the tint that is based on the color will also change.

1　Deselect all objects.

2　Click Blue in the Swatches palette. Choose New Tint Swatch from the Swatches palette menu. Type **40** in the Tint box, and then click OK.

3　Choose the Selection tool (⬆) and select the outlined text "Si!" shown below and apply the Blue 40% fill.

Next you'll change the Blue color. Blue 40% is based on the Blue swatch, so the tint will also change.

4　Deselect all objects.

5　Double-click Blue (not the Blue tint) to change the color. For Swatch Name, type **Violet Blue**. For the color percentages, type the following values: C = **59**, M = **80**, Y = **40**, K = **0**. Click OK.

Notice that the color change affects all objects to which Blue and Blue 40% were applied. As you can see, adding colors to the Swatches palette makes it easy to update colors in multiple objects.

6　Choose File > Save.

Using advanced gradient techniques

Earlier you created and applied a gradient and adjusted its direction using the Gradient tool. InDesign CS2 also lets you create gradients of multiple colors, and control the point at which the colors blend. In addition, you can apply a gradient to individual objects or to a collection of objects.

Creating a gradient swatch with multiple colors

Earlier in this lesson, you created a gradient with two colors—brown and tan. Now you'll create a gradient with three stops so that a brown color on the outside will fade to white in the middle. Make sure that no objects are selected before you begin.

1 On the Swatches palette menu, choose New Gradient Swatch, and then type **Brown 30/White Gradient** for Swatch Name.

The colors from the previous blend appear in the dialog box.

2 Click the left stop marker (⌂), select Swatches for Stop Color, and make sure that Brown 30% is selected in the list box. Click the right stop marker (⌂), select Swatches for Stop Color, and make sure that Brown 30% is selected in the list box.

The gradient ramp is now entirely Brown 30%. Now you'll add a stop marker to the middle so that the color fades toward the center.

3 Click just below the center of the gradient bar to add a new stop. For Location, type **50** to make sure the stop is centered.

4 For Stop Color, select CMYK and then drag each of the four color sliders to 0 (zero) to create white.

5 Click OK, and then choose File > Save.

Applying the gradient to an object

To apply the new gradient fill we just created, you'll create a box containing the gradient fill. First, change the view size so that you can see the entire page.

1   Choose 100% from the magnification pop-up list at the bottom of the document window or double-click the Zoom tool (🔍).

Before you create the graphics frame, make sure that the Artwork layer is selected. It's a good idea to get into the habit of making sure that your objects are placed on the appropriate layer, so you can hide or lock a set of objects easily.

2   Choose Edit > Deselect All to be sure nothing is selected. Choose Window > Layers to bring the Layers palette to the front, and then select Artwork. (Do not select either box to the left of Artwork, or you'll hide or lock the objects on the Artwork layer.)

3   Select the Fill box (■) in the toolbox, and then select Brown 30/White Gradient in the Swatches palette, if it's not already selected. Select the Stroke box (🔳) in the toolbox, and then click the None button (☑) at the bottom of the toolbox.

A. *Apply last-used color.*
B. *Apply last-used gradient.*
C. *Remove color or gradient.*

Now that the Fill box is set to the gradient and the Stroke box is set to none, the next object you draw will contain the gradient fill with no stroke.

4　Select the Rectangle tool (▢), and then draw a frame that covers the text "Indulgent?" located in the upper left corner of the page; you may need to zoom in.

5　To zoom in, press Z to switch to the Zoom tool, and drag across the text "Indulgent?", then press M to switch back to the rectangle tool.

6　Choose Edit > Deselect All, then choose File > Save.

Applying a gradient to multiple objects

Previously in this lesson, you used the Gradient tool to change the direction of a gradient, and to change the gradient's beginning point and end point. You'll now use the Gradient tool to apply a gradient across multiple objects in the three diamond shapes on the bottom of the page.

1　Double-click the Hand tool (✋) to fit page to window.

2　Select the Selection tool (▶), and then click the left diamond shape to select it, then while holding the Shift key, select the other two diamond shapes.

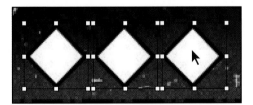

Now you'll apply the Brown/Tan Gradient to the three different diamond objects.

3 Confirm that the Fill box () is selected in the Swatches palette, then select the Brown/Tan Gradient swatch as the fill.

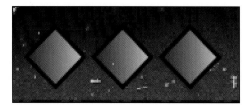

Notice that the gradient affects each object on an individual basis. Now you'll use the Gradient tool to apply the gradient across the three selected objects as one.

4 With the three objects still selected, select the Gradient tool (⬛) in the toolbox. Drag an imaginary line as shown.

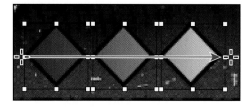

Now the gradient runs across all three selected objects.

5 Save the file by choosing File > Save.

Ensuring Consistent Color

Color management is important in environments where you must evaluate image color reliably in the context of your final output. Color correction is a different issue that involves images with tonal or color-balance problems, and is usually handled in the original graphics application, such as Photoshop.

Do you need color management?

Use the following guidelines to determine whether or not you need color management:

- Color accuracy in your working environment isn't required if you rely completely on prepress service providers and commercial printers for all your color work.

- Color management is recommended for maintaining color accuracy in monitor display, the ability to soft-proof colors, and color consistency in large workgroups.

- Color management is recommended if you reuse color graphics for print and online media, use various kinds of devices within a single medium (such as different printing presses), or print to different domestic and international presses.

If you decide to use color management, consult with your production partners—such as graphic artists and prepress service providers—to ensure that all aspects of your color management workflow integrate with theirs.

—From InDesign Help

See also "About color management in Adobe applications" in InDesign Help.

Color management: An overview

Devices and graphics have different color gamuts. Although all color gamuts overlap, they don't match exactly, which is why some colors on your monitor can't be reproduced in print or online. The colors that can't be reproduced in print are called out-of-gamut colors because they are outside the spectrum of printable colors. For example, you can create a large percentage of colors in the visible spectrum using programs such as InDesign CS2, Photoshop CS2, and Illustrator CS2, but you can reproduce only a subset of those colors on a desktop printer.

The printer has a smaller color space or gamut (the range of colors that can be displayed or printed) than the application that created the color.

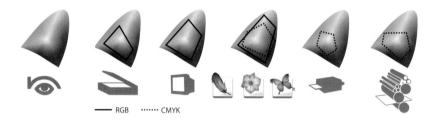

Visible spectrum containing millions of colors (far left) compared with color gamuts of various devices and graphics.

To compensate for these differences and to ensure the closest match between on-screen colors and printed colors, applications use a color management system (CMS). Using a color management engine, the CMS translates colors from the color space of one device into a device-independent color space, such as CIE (Commission Internationale d'Éclairage) LAB. From the device-independent color space, the CMS fits that color information to another device's color space by a process called color mapping, or gamut mapping. The CMS makes any adjustments necessary to represent the color consistently among devices.

A CMS uses three components to map colors across devices:

• A device-independent (or reference) color space.

• ICC profiles that define the color characteristics of different devices and graphics.

• A color management engine that translates colors from one device's color space to another's.

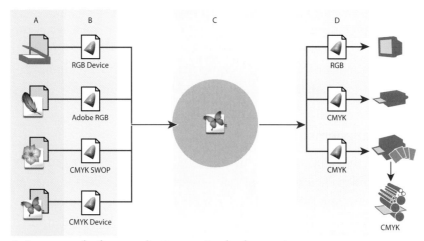

A. Scanners and software applications create color documents.
B. ICC source profiles describe document color spaces.
C. A color management engine uses ICC source profiles to map document colors to a device-independent color space through supporting applications.
D. The color management engine maps document colors from the device-independent color space to output-device color spaces using destination profiles.

About the device-independent color space

To successfully compare gamuts and make adjustments, a color management system must use a reference color space—an objective way of defining color. Most CMS use the CIE LAB color model, which exists independently of any device and is big enough to reproduce any color visible to the human eye. For this reason, CIE LAB is considered device-independent.

About ICC profiles

An ICC profile describes how a particular device or standard reproduces color using a cross-platform standard defined by the International Color Consortium (ICC).

ICC profiles ensure that images appear correctly in any ICC-compliant applications, and on color devices. This is accomplished by embedding the profile information in the original file or assigning the profile in your application.

At a minimum, you must have one source profile for the device (such as a scanner or digital camera) or standard (such as SWOP or Adobe RGB) used to create the color, and one destination profile for the device (such as monitor or contract proofing) or standard (SWOP or TOYO, for example) that you will use to reproduce the color.

About color management engines

Sometimes called the color matching module (CMM), the color management engine interprets ICC profiles. Acting as a translator, the color management engine converts the out-of-gamut colors from the source device to the range of colors that can be produced by the destination device. The color management engine may be included with the CMS or may be a separate part of the operating system.

Translating to a gamut—particularly a smaller gamut—usually involves a compromise, so multiple translation methods are available. For example, a color-translation method that preserves correct relationships among colors in a photograph will usually alter the colors in a logo. Color Management engines provide a choice of translation methods, known as rendering intents, so that you can apply a method appropriate to the intended use of a color graphic. Examples of common rendering intents include Perceptual (Images) for preserving color relationships the way the eye does, Saturation (Graphics) for preserving vivid colors at the expense of color accuracy, and Relative and Absolute Colorimetric for preserving color accuracy at the expense of color relationships.

Components of a CMYK press-oriented workflow

In a CMYK workflow, you work with CMYK images prepared for a specific printing press or proofing device, or legacy (archived) CMYK images. You generate a source profile based on your press or contract-proofing standard and embed it into the CMYK images or assign the profile in InDesign CS2. The profile enables consistent CMYK printing at other color-managed sites, such as when printing a widely distributed magazine on presses in many different cities. Because you use color management, the reliability and consistency of color display improves across all your workstations.

For final printed output, you select a printer profile in the Print dialog box that describes your contract-proofing standard or your printing press.

Setting up color management in InDesign CS2

No mechanical device can produce the full range of color visible to the human eye: no monitor, film, printer, copier, or printing press. Each device has a specific capability, so that different devices make different kinds of compromises in reproducing color images. The unique color-rendering abilities of a specific output device are known collectively as its gamut or color space.

InDesign CS2 and other graphics applications, such as Adobe Photoshop CS2, Adobe Illustrator CS2, and others, use color numbers to describe the color of each pixel in an image. The color numbers correspond to the color model, such as the familiar RGB values for red, green, and blue or the CMYK values for cyan, magenta, yellow, and black.

Color management is simply the designation of a consistent way of translating the color numbers for each pixel from the source (the document or image stored on your computer) to the output device (such as your monitor, color printer, or high-resolution printing press, each with its own specific gamut).

In an ICC workflow—that is, one that follows the conventions of the ICC—you specify a color management engine and a color profile. The color management engine is the software feature or module that does the work of reading and translating colors between different color spaces. A color profile is the description of how the color numbers map to the color space (capabilities) of output devices.

Adobe Creative Suite 2 applications give you new, easy-to-use color management features and tools that help achieve good, sellable color without the need to become a color management expert. With color management now enabled out-of-the-box, you'll be able to view colors consistently across applications and platforms while ensuring more accurate color from edit to proof to final print.

A look at the Bridge

The Adobe Bridge application in Adobe Creative Suite 2 is a central location where users can select a color settings file with preset color management policies and default profiles. Selecting a Color Settings File (CSF) in Adobe Bridge ensures that color is handled consistently and that color displays and prints the same way from all Adobe Creative Suite 2 applications.

When users select a CSF, the file's preset values determine the color management behavior in all applications, such as how embedded profiles are handled, what the default RGB and CMYK working spaces are, and whether to display warning dialogs when embedded profiles don't match the default working space. Selecting the correct CSF depends on your workflow. For more information on the Adobe Bridge application, see Lesson 14, "Working with Adobe Bridge and Version Cue."

Specifying the Adobe ACE engine

Different companies have developed various ways to manage color. To provide you with a choice, you use a color management system to designate a color management engine that represents the approach you want to use. Remember that the color management engine translates colors from the source. InDesign CS2 now offers the Adobe ACE engine as one of your choices. This engine uses the same architecture as in Photoshop and Illustrator, so that your color management choices are integrated across these Adobe graphics applications.

1   Choose Edit > Color Settings.

The color management engine and other settings you choose in the Color Settings dialog box are saved with InDesign CS2 and apply to all InDesign CS2 documents you work on in the future.

By default, color management in InDesign CS2 is enabled.

2 Select the North America Prepress 2 from the Settings drop-down menu.

3 Select the Advanced Mode check box.

4 Under Conversion Options in the lower part of the dialog box, select Adobe (ACE) in the Engine drop-down menu.

5 For Intent, select Perceptual from the drop-down menu. Later in this lesson, you'll explore the Intent options in more detail.

6 Leave the dialog box open so you can use it in the next section.

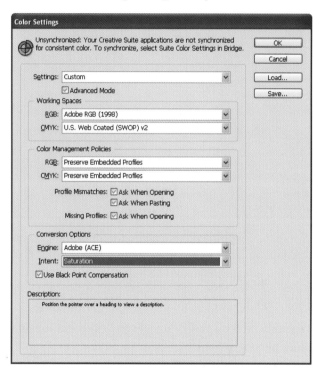

Choose Adobe ACE unless your prepress service provider recommends another engine. Use the same engine throughout your workflow in Photoshop CS2, Illustrator CS2, Acrobat CS2 and InDesign CS2.

Setting up default working spaces

To complete the application-wide color management setup, you'll choose profiles for the devices you will use to reproduce the color, including your monitor, composite proofing device, and final separations standard. InDesign CS2 refers to these preset profiles as working spaces. These working spaces are also available in other Adobe graphics applications, including Illustrator CS2 and Photoshop CS2. Once you designate the same working space in all three applications, then you've automatically set up consistent color for illustration, digital images, and document layouts.

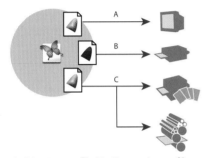

A. *Monitor profile.* **B.** *Composite profile.*
C. *Separations profile (which can be an output device or press standard, such as SWOP or TOYO).*

First, you'll select a monitor profile. If the Color Settings dialog box is not still open from the previous procedure, reopen it now.

1   Under Working Spaces, for CMYK select U.S. Web Coated (SWOP) v2.

In a later section, you'll set the on-screen display of images to full resolution so that InDesign CS2 can color-manage all available image data.

2   Move the dialog box out of your way and study the colors in the ad.

Notice the heavy use of brown. You'll see a noticeable difference in the browns when you apply color management by closing the dialog box in the next step.

3   Click OK.

4   Choose View > Proof Colors. This will show soft-proof colors on your monitor. Depending upon your viewing conditions, this can give you a more accurate preview of how your image will print.

Several colors change in the ad, but most noticeably the browns; they appear to have more detail. It's important to note that although the images look better than they did when you opened the document, the images themselves have not been altered—only the display of the images has changed. Specifically, what you see now represents the color characteristics of the following devices:

- The program or scanner that saved the image, using the source profile embedded in the image.

- The final output device for the document, using the destination profile you set up earlier in the lesson.

It's easy to see that the success of color management ultimately depends on the accuracy of your profiles.

Assigning source profiles

Source profiles describe the color space InDesign CS2 uses when you create colors in InDesign CS2 and apply them to objects, or when you import an RGB, CMYK, or LAB color graphic that wasn't saved with an embedded profile. When you import an image with embedded profiles, InDesign CS2 will color-manage the image using the embedded profiles rather than the profiles you choose here, unless you override the embedded profiles for an individual image.

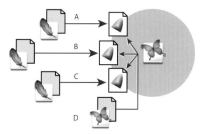

A. LAB profile.
B. RGB profile.
C. CMYK profile.
D. InDesign CS2 document applying a profile that matches the color model of each image that lacks a profile.

1   Choose Edit > Assign Profiles. In both the RGB Profile and CMYK Profile areas of the dialog box, select the Assign Current Working Space options which should be set to Adobe RGB (1998) and U.S. Web Coated (SWAP) v2, as shown.

Notice that the text following the words "working space" contains the same working-space information that you entered in the Color Settings dialog box. With these settings, the Adobe ACE engine won't unnecessarily convert colors for which you've already specified a profile.

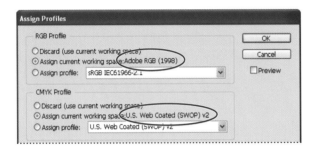

2   Leave the dialog box open so you can use it in the next section.

Specifying the rendering intent

The rendering intent determines how the color management engine converts colors, based on the source and destination profiles you specify in InDesign CS2. You'll specify the color-translation method for the InDesign CS2 color management engine to apply to the graphics in the advertisement.

1   In the lower area of the Assign Profiles dialog box, leave Relative Colorimetric selected for the Solid Color Intent option. This option preserves individual colors at the expense of color relationships, so it's appropriate for business logos and other such graphics.

2   Make sure that Use Color Settings Intent is selected in both the Default Image Intent and After-Blending Intent options. These options are appropriate for this photo-intensive page spread.

3   Click OK to close the Assign Profiles dialog box, and then save your work.

Using full-resolution display with color management

When you use image-display resolutions lower than High Quality so that screen redraw is faster, image-color display is also made faster by displaying their colors less precisely. Image colors display most precisely when you view images at the fullest resolution (in addition to turning on color management).

Choose View > Display Performance > High Quality Display.

It's especially important to view color-managed images at full resolution when you work with duotones.

When color management is on, image display is set to full resolution, and you use accurate profiles that are applied properly, you see the best possible color representation that your monitor is capable of showing.

Note: To save disk space, the sample files for this lesson are 150 pixels per inch (ppi), so the colors are not as precise as they would be using a higher resolution.

Color-managing imported graphics in InDesign CS2

When you import a graphic, you can control its color management in your document. If you know that an imported graphic contains an accurate embedded profile with an appropriate rendering intent, you just import it and continue working. InDesign CS2 will read and apply the embedded profile to the graphic, integrating it into the CMS for the document. If an imported bitmap image does not include an embedded profile, InDesign CS2 applies the default source profile (CMYK, RGB, or LAB) to the image.

InDesign CS2 also applies a default source profile to InDesign CS2-drawn objects. You can assign a different profile within InDesign CS2—using Edit > Assign Profiles to open the Assign Profiles dialog box—or open the graphic in the original application and embed the profile there.

The ad already includes two images that were saved without embedded profiles. You'll integrate those images into the document CMS using two different methods: assigning a profile within InDesign CS2 and opening the original image so that you can embed the profile. Later in the lesson, you'll import two additional graphics and practice two methods of assigning a profile before you place them in the ad.

Assigning a profile after importing an image

When you import images that were saved without embedded profiles into InDesign CS2, InDesign CS2 applies its default source profile to the image. If an imported image was not created in the default color space, you should assign the profile that describes the image's original color space.

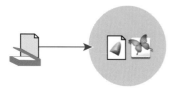

InDesign CS2 applies its default source profile to any bitmap image without embedded profiles.

You'll work with an image that was imported into InDesign CS2 before you turned on color management. First, you'll confirm the default profile InDesign CS2 is using to color-manage the image. Then, within InDesign CS2, you'll assign a new profile because the image's original color space is different from the default color space.

1   Using the Selection tool (↖), select the plate of truffles on the left side of the ad.

2   Choose Object > Image Color Settings.

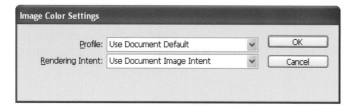

Notice that Use Document Default is selected for Profile. InDesign CS2 enables color management for each imported image and assigns the default source profile you set up earlier in this lesson. You can also assign a new profile here. Because you are assigning the profile within InDesign CS2, the change will apply only to the selected image in this document.

3   For Profile, choose U.S. Sheetfed Coated v2 to match the image's original color space. This profile represents the color-lookup tables used by the scanner operator who originally scanned this as a CMYK image.

4   Leave the Rendering Intent set as Use Document Image Intent, and click OK. The colors deepen noticeably.

InDesign CS2 will color-manage the image using the newly assigned profile.

Embedding a profile in a Photoshop image

As a general rule, you should embed ICC profiles in files before importing the files into another document that uses color management. That way, images with embedded profiles will more likely appear as intended in InDesign CS2 or other color-managed programs without requiring any additional work.

In this section, you'll work with a previously imported, color bitmap image that does not contain an embedded profile.

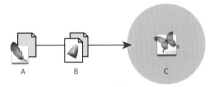

A. Image's working CMYK color space.
B. Image with embedded ICC profile.
C. InDesign CS2 uses embedded profile.

Note: If you don't have Photoshop installed on your system, you can use the Photoshop files provided in the lesson folder. The steps indicate when to do so.

Setting up color management in Photoshop CS2

First, you'll define the working color spaces (used for viewing and editing) for the image's RGB and CMYK color modes.

1　Start Photoshop, and choose Edit > Color Settings (Mac OS: Photoshop > Color Settings).

2　For Settings, select U.S. Prepress Defaults on the drop-down menu. Click More Options to view all the selections available.

3　For the CMYK option under Working Spaces, select U.S. Web Coated (SWOP) v2, if it is not already selected, so that the embedded profile matches the default separations profile you specified in InDesign CS2.

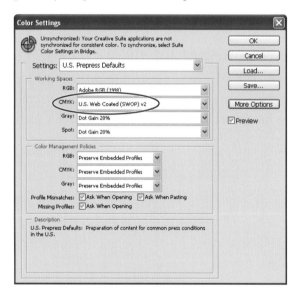

4　Leave the other settings as they are, and click OK.

Embedding the profile

Now that you have specified the working color spaces for the Photoshop image, you'll embed the specified profile.

1   From Photoshop, choose File > Open and select 06_d.psd inside the Lesson_06 Folder.

2   In Photoshop, if the Missing Profile dialog box appears, select Assign Working CMYK. Notice that it is already set to U.S. Web Coated (SWOP) v2, which is the profile you selected in the previous procedure, "Setting up color management in Photoshop." Click OK. If you do not receive a Missing Profile warning, choose Image > Mode > Convert to Profile and choose U.S. Web Coated (SWOP) v2 as the Destination Profile and click OK.

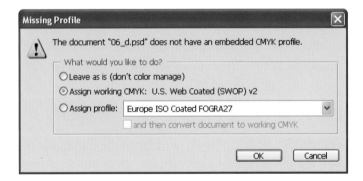

3   To embed the profile, choose File > Save As. Select your Lesson_06 folder in your InDesignCIB folder, and then choose TIFF from the Format drop down menu. Type **06_dprof.tif** for File Name. Make sure that the ICC Profile: U.S. Web Coated (SWOP) v2 check box (Windows) or the Embed Color Profile check box (Mac OS) is selected, and click Save.

4   In the TIFF Options dialog box, click OK to accept the default.

5   Close the image, exit Photoshop and return to InDesign CS2.

Updating the image within InDesign CS2

Now that you've embedded the ICC profile in the Photoshop file, you can update the image in InDesign CS2. InDesign CS2 will color-manage the image using the embedded profile.

1   In InDesign CS2, select the large chocolate image.

2   Do one of the following:

• If you followed Photoshop instructions in the previous sections, click the Relink button (⟐⟶▣) at the bottom of the Links palette. Click Browse and locate the 06_dprof.tif file you just saved in the Lesson_06 folder. Double-click the file.

Note: When relinking to a file using a different file format, you need to select All Files under the Files of Type drop-down menu when browsing for the file on the Windows operating system.

• If you don't have Photoshop, or skipped the previous two sections, click the Relink button (▣⟶) at the bottom of the Links palette. Click Browse and locate 06_dprof.psd in the Final folder. Double-click the file.

Note: You may need to select All Files for Files of Type.

3   To confirm that the embedded profile is being used, open the Links palette menu (choose Window > Links if the Links palette is not visible), select a file, and choose Link Information. In the Link Information dialog box, make sure that the Profile says U.S. Web Coated (SWOP) v2, and then click Done.

A quick way to check profiles for all graphics in a document is by using the Preflight feature to view document components.

Now that you have fixed existing graphics in the document, you will finish the ad by importing two additional graphics and setting options as you import.

Assigning a profile while importing a graphic

If you know that a color-managed image uses a color space that is different from the color space described by the default source profile, you can assign a profile to it while you're importing the image into InDesign CS2. In this section, you'll import a legacy (archived) CMYK image scanned without a profile, and assign a profile before you place it in the ad.

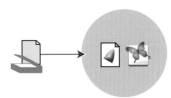

You can assign a profile while you import an image.

1   In InDesign CS2, choose View > Show Frame Edges to show the outline of the frame for the graphic you're about to place—and the outlines for all the graphics frames in the ad.

2   If necessary, adjust your view so that you can easily see the frames in the lower right area of the spread. Using the Selection tool (**↖**), select the topmost of these three frames.

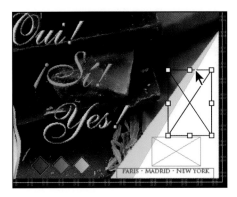

3   Choose File > Place to open the Place dialog box, and do the following:

•   Open Lesson_06 folder in the InDesignCIB folder and select the 06_e.psd file.

•   Select the Show Import Options check box, so that you'll have an opportunity to specify a profile.

•   Click Open.

4   In the Image Import Options dialog box, select the color tab in the middle of the dialog box.

5   Select the following options:

•   For Profile, select U.S. Sheetfed Coated v2 to match the image's original color space.

Note: If you selected a different profile in "Assigning a profile after importing an image," select the same profile here.

•   For Rendering Intent, select Perceptual (Images).

•   Click OK.

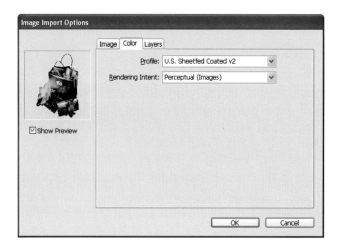

The image appears in the selected frame. InDesign CS2 will color-manage the image using the profile you assigned.

Embedding a profile in an Illustrator graphic

In this lesson, you'll set up Illustrator (version 9 or later) so that its color-management settings match InDesign CS2. You'll then save a color-managed Illustrator graphic and place it in an InDesign CS2 document.

InDesign CS2 can color-manage vector graphics created in Illustrator 9 or later when you save them in formats that embed profiles, such as PDF or TIFF. In this lesson, you'll save a file as PDF and then place the graphic in InDesign CS2.

Note: *If you don't have Illustrator 9 or later installed on your system, you can read the information in the next two sections, and then skip to step 2 in "Placing a color-managed Illustrator file into InDesign CS2" later in this lesson to use the Illustrator file provided in the Lesson_06 folder.*

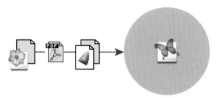

InDesign CS2 color-manages a PDF file using the
profiles saved with the PDF version of the file.

Setting up color management in Illustrator CS2

Now you'll set up color management in Illustrator CS2 so that it matches color management settings in InDesign CS2. This ensures that the colors are consistent from Illustrator to InDesign CS2 on-screen and in print. Setting up color management in Illustrator also enables you to embed an ICC profile in an exported version of the Illustrator file. When you place the exported Illustrator file in the InDesign CS2 layout, InDesign CS2 color-manages the logo using the embedded profile.

1 Start Adobe Illustrator CS2, and choose Edit > Color Settings.

2 Select the Advanced Mode check box to expand the dialog box so that you see more options, and then in the Color Settings dialog box, select U.S. Prepress Defaults.

3 Under Working Spaces, for RGB select sRGB IEC61966-2.1. Leave CMYK set for U.S. Web Coated (SWOP) v2.

4 Review the conversion options and make sure that the Adobe (ACE) engine, and Relative Colorimetric intent are selected.

5 Click OK.

You have finished setting up color management in Illustrator.

Embedding a profile in a graphic from Illustrator

You can embed an ICC profile in files that you create in Illustrator and export in PDF or bitmap (.bmp) formats. Then, InDesign CS2 can use the profile to color-manage the graphic. In this task, you'll export a file to PDF format, and then place the graphic in an InDesign CS2 document.

1   In Illustrator, choose File > Open. Locate and double-click the 06_f.ai file in the Lesson_06 folder inside the InDesignCIB folder on your hard disk.

2   When the Missing Profile dialog box opens, select Assign current working space: U.S. Web Coated (SWOP) v2, and click OK.

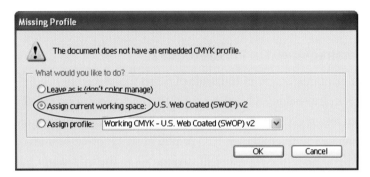

3   Choose File > Save As.

4   Name the file **06_Logo.pdf**, and choose Adobe PDF from the Save as Type (Windows) or Format (Mac OS) menu. Make sure that the Lesson_06 folder is targeted, and then click Save to close the Save As dialog box, and the Adobe PDF Format Options dialog box will appear next.

5   Make sure that the PDF compression options are appropriate for your final print production by clicking General on the left side of the dialog box.

6 For Compatibility, choose Acrobat 5.0, if it is not already selected, and match the settings shown below. This setting ensures that the profile is saved with the PDF file. Then click Save PDF.

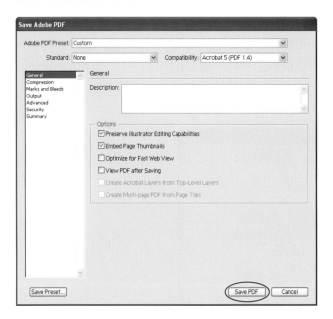

7 Close the file and quit Illustrator.

Placing a color-managed Illustrator file into InDesign CS2

Now that you have created a PDF file of the Illustrator document, you'll place it in InDesign CS2.

1 In InDesign CS2, select the remaining empty frame in the bottom right area of the ad.

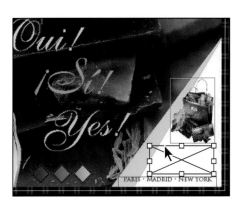

2 Do one of the following:

• If you followed Illustrator instructions in the previous sections, choose File > Place and select the 06_Logo.pdf file that you created. Make sure that Show Import Options is checked when you place the graphic.

• If you don't have Illustrator, or skipped the previous two sections, choose File > Place and select the 06_Logo.pdf file in the Final folder in the Lesson_06 folder, located inside the Lessons folder within the InDesignCIB folder on your hard disk. Make sure that Show Import Options is selected before you click Open.

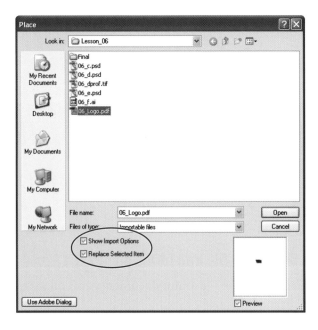

3 In the Place PDF dialog box, for Crop To, choose Bounding Box. This option places only the logo's bounding box—the minimum area that encloses the logo.

4   Make sure that Transparent Background is selected so that you can see any text or graphics behind the bounding box, and then click OK.

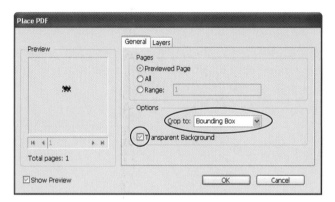

The logo appears in the selected frame. InDesign CS2 will color-manage the PDF file using the embedded profile.

5   Choose File > Save to save the file.

In this lesson, you have learned how to set up color management across three Adobe applications—an admirable achievement. You have learned several methods for incorporating graphics so that they can be color-managed when placed in InDesign CS2 documents. Because you described your color environment to the other Adobe applications whose graphics you imported, you can expect predictable, consistent color for those graphics across the applications.

At this time, you could either hand off the native InDesign CS2 file with all the linked files, or export the InDesign CS2 file as PDF, embedding the ICC profiles you assigned. If you create a PDF file of the document, the colors in the ad will look the same across all publications that use the ad, regardless of the color-management settings used by the publication's layout application. Other users can preview and proof your color-managed files more accurately, and repurpose them for different print conditions when that is useful, or when it is a requirement of your project.

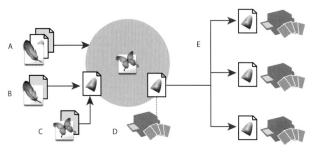

A. *Image with embedded CMYK profile.*
B. *Image with CMYK profile assigned in InDesign CS2.*
C. *InDesign CS2 document using a CMYK profile based on a separation profile.*
D. *Separation profile.*
E. *Different separation profiles when targeting different presses.*

Other information resources for color management

You can find additional information on color management on the web and in print. Here are a few resources that are available as of the date of publication of this book:

• At the Adobe web site (Adobe.com), search for color management.

• At the Apple web site (Apple.com), search for ColorSync.

• At your local library or bookstore, look for *Real World Color Management* (ISBN 0201773406).

Exploring on your own

Follow these steps to learn more about importing colors and working with gradients.

1   To create a new document, choose File > New > Document, and then click OK in the New Document dialog box.

2   To import the colors from a different InDesign CS2 document, use the following procedure:

• Use the Swatches palette menu and choose New Color Swatch.

• In the Color Mode drop-down menu, select Other Library and browse to find the Lesson_06 folder.

• Double-click 06_Color.indd (or 06_b.indd). Notice that the colors you created earlier in this lesson appear in this dialog box list for the new document.

• Select the Brown/Tan Gradient and click OK to close the dialog box and add the color to the Swatches palette.

• Repeat this entire process a few more times to add other colors to the Swatches palette.

3   Using the lesson files or your own InDesign CS2 document, double-click the color swatch Paper and change its composition. Notice how the color of the document changes to reflect the color of the paper on which the document will be reproduced.

Review

▶ **Review questions**

1   What is the advantage of applying colors using the Swatches palette instead of the Color palette?

2   What are the pros and cons of using spot colors versus process colors?

3   After you create a gradient and apply it to an object, how do you adjust the direction of the gradient blend?

4   What does the color management engine do?

5   What do source profiles describe?

6   What are three ways to attach an ICC profile to a graphic so that InDesign CS2 can color-manage the graphic?

7   Why would you embed an ICC profile in a graphic?

8   Which file formats embed ICC profiles for use in both Windows and Mac OS?

▶ **Review answers**

1   If you use the Swatches palette to apply a color to several objects, and then decide you want to use a different color, you don't need to update each object individually. Instead, change the color in the Swatches palette and the color of all the objects will be updated automatically.

2   By using a spot color, you can ensure color accuracy. However, each spot color requires its own plate at the press, so using spot colors is more expensive. Use process colors when a job requires so many colors that using individual spot inks would be expensive or impractical, such as when printing color photographs.

3   To adjust the direction of the gradient blend, use the Gradient tool to repaint the fill along an imaginary line in the direction you want.

4   The color management engine translates colors from the color space of one device to another device's color space by a process called color mapping.

5   Source profiles selected in the Assign Profiles dialog box describe the color space InDesign CS2 assigns to objects you create using the drawing tools, or when you import an RGB, CMYK, or LAB color graphic that wasn't saved with an embedded profile.

6   You can embed the profile in the original file, assign a profile within InDesign CS2, or use the default profile you specified when you set up color management in InDesign CS2.

7   Embedding an ICC profile ensures that the graphic displays correctly in any application that uses ICC-compliant color management. The application that uses the graphic honors the embedded profile rather than applying a default one.

8   A growing number of formats can contain an embedded ICC profile, but the most widely supported formats to use with embedded ICC profiles at this time are bitmap image formats such as Photoshop (PSD), TIFF, and JPEG.

With Adobe InDesign CS2 you can create styles, or sets of bundled formatting attributes, that can be applied in multiple instances. Applying styles to a document allows you to change the look and feel of its graphics and text with a single action.

7 Working with Styles

In this introduction to working with InDesign styles, you'll learn how to do the following:

- Create and apply Object styles.

- Create and apply Character styles.

- Create and apply Paragraph styles.

- Nest Character styles inside Paragraph styles.

- Globally update Object, Character, and Paragraph styles.

- Import and apply styles from other InDesign documents.

Getting started

In this lesson, you'll work on a 6-panel menu for Pisano Bistro, a fictitious Italian restaurant. Several items in the menu, including text and graphics, have already been placed for you. Your objective is to apply styles, or grouped attributes, to these items. Before you begin, you'll need to make several preparations:

• If you have not already copied the resource files for this lesson from the Lesson_07 folder of the Adobe InDesign CS2 Classroom in a Book CD, do so now. See "Copying the Classroom in a Book files" on page 4.

• Restore the default preferences for Adobe InDesign.

When your preparations are complete, you're ready to start work on the lesson.

1   To ensure that the tools and palettes function exactly as described in this lesson, delete or deactivate (by renaming) the InDesign Defaults file and the InDesign SavedData file. See "Restoring default preferences" on page 2.

2   Start Adobe InDesign.

To begin working, you'll open an existing InDesign document.

3   Choose File > Open, and open the 07_a.indd file in the Lesson_07 folder, located inside the Lessons folder within the InDesignCIB folder on your hard disk.

4   Choose File > Save As, rename the file **07_menu.indd**, and save it in the Lesson_07 folder.

5   If you want to see what the finished document will look like, open the 07_b.indd file in the same folder. You can leave this document open to act as a guide as you work. When you're ready to resume working on the lesson document, choose its name from the Window menu.

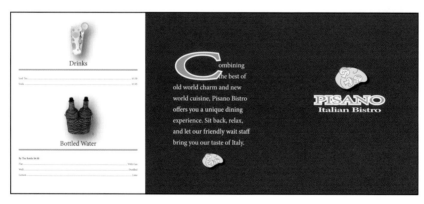

Creating and applying object styles

Object styles allow you to apply and globally update formatting, on the object level, to graphics, text, and frames. These formatting attributes, including fill, stroke, transparency, and text wrap options, create a more consistent overall design, and speed up tedious production tasks.

Creating an object style

The menu document consists of two 3-panel spreads. Panels 1-3 represent the outside of the menu, while panels 4-6 represent the inside. In this section, you'll be creating and applying an object style to both spreads.

1   Double-click on the numbers "4-6" beneath the second spread to center those panels in the document window.

2   Double-click the Zoom tool (⌕) to increase the magnification to 100%.

3   You want to apply a soft-edged drop shadow to the photographs of the dishes served at Pisano Bistro, and apply text wrap to break the text around the images. To begin, open the Object Styles palette by choosing Window > Object Styles.

4 In the Object Styles palette, create a new object style by choosing "New Object Style" from the palette menu. The New Object Style window opens, offering you formatting options to be built into the style.

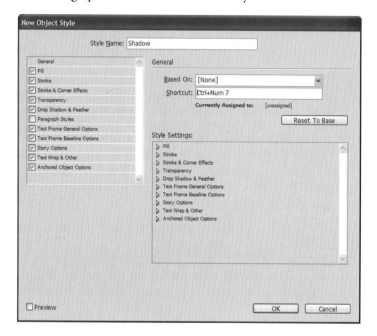

5 First assign a name to the style by typing it into the Style Name field at the top of the window. Name this style **Shadow** to describe the attributes to be applied.

6 In the General section of this window, note that you can base a new object style on a previously created style. Since you're creating a style from scratch, leave this setting at the default "None."

7 Also in the General section, you can create a keyboard shortcut for easy application of this style. Click inside the Shortcut field, hold down Ctrl (Windows) or Command (Mac OS), and type the number **7** from the numeric keypad on your keyboard.

Note: Use of a modifier key, such as Ctrl (Windows) or Command (Mac OS) along with another key when creating style shortcuts. If you use a laptop and do not have a numeric keypad you can skip the steps of creating keyboard shortcuts.

8 If you were creating this style based on existing formatting in the document, you'd see those settings displayed in the Style Settings section of this window. Since this style is created from scratch, clicking on the triangles next to each setting shows the defaults for that attribute.

9   The check boxes to the left of this window show the attributes that will be applied when this style is used. To add a drop shadow to the style, click once on the Drop Shadow & Feather option in this column.

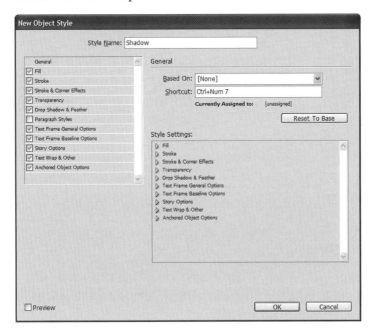

10   In the Drop Shadow & Feather settings that appear to the right, click in the Drop Shadow check box to activate the feature, and specify the following:

• Set the Opacity to 50%.

• Change the X and Y Offset values to .125 inches.

• Set the Blur value to .25 inches.

• Leave all other settings at their defaults, making sure Black is chosen as the shadow color.

11   Next you'll add a text wrap attribute to the style. From the formatting options on the left, click once on the Text Wrap & Other option.

12   In the Text Wrap settings that appear to the right, click on the fourth button from the left, the Jump object option. This will make text appear only above and below the image when the style is applied. Leave all other settings in this section at their default values.

13 You have now created your first object style. Click OK to close the New Object Style window, and you should see the new Shadow style appear in the Object Styles palette.

Applying an object style

Now you'll apply your object style to the previously placed photographs of dishes served at Pisano Bistro. The use of an object style prevents you from having to manually apply the shadow and text wrap attributes to each image individually.

1 In the Pages palette, double-click on Panel 1 of the menu to center it in your document window.

2 Using the Selection tool (↖), click once on the drinking glass image at the top of the panel to select it.

3 In the Object Styles palette, click once on the Shadow style to apply it to this image. You should see a soft-edged drop shadow added to the image, and when you later reflow the menu text, you'll see the text jumping over the image.

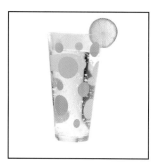

4 Now click once to select the jug near the bottom of Panel 1.

5 This time you'll use the keyboard shortcut you defined earlier to apply the Shadow style. Hold down Ctrl (Windows) or Command (Mac OS), and type the number **7** from the numeric keypad on your keyboard. Because this was the keyboard shortcut you specified for the Shadow style, the style is applied to the jug image.

6 Using either method described above, apply the Shadow object style to the images placed on Panels 4, 5, and 6. Notice that the text is pushed above and below each image on Panels 4 and 5 as a result of the Text Wrap option you included in the style.

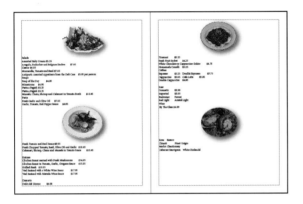

7 Choose File > Save.

Creating and applying character styles

In the previous exercise, object styles allowed you to apply object-level formatting to graphics with a single click or a key press. Similarly, character and paragraph styles are a way to apply multiple attributes to text using a single action. Unlike paragraph styles (which are covered later in this lesson), character styles apply formatting to ranges of text smaller than a paragraph (i.e., a character, a word, or a group of words). Because of this, character styles are best used for character formatting you use over and over again when creating a document.

Creating a character style

The text for items listed on the Pisano Bistro menu was previously created in a word processing application and imported into the lesson file for you. The object of this exercise is for you to create and apply a character style to selected text in the menu, and to recognize the advantages in efficiency and consistency that character styles have to offer.

1 With your menu document (07_menu.indd) open, double-click on Panel 3 in the Pages palette to center the menu's cover in your document window.

2 If it's not already visible, open the Character Styles palette by choosing Window > Type & Tables > Character Styles. Note that the only style listed in this palette is the default, [None].

Unlike the object style you built from scratch in the previous exercise, you'll build your character style based on existing text formatting. This approach allows you to effectively "see" the style before you build it. In this case, you'll pick up the formatting already applied to the "Pisano" logotype and build it into a character style, so that it can be reused efficiently throughout the menu document.

3 Choose the Type tool (T) from the toolbox, and drag-select over the word "Pisano" on Panel 3 to select it.

4 In the Character Styles palette, create a new character style by choosing "New Character Style" from the palette menu. The New Character Style window opens, offering you formatting options to be built into the style.

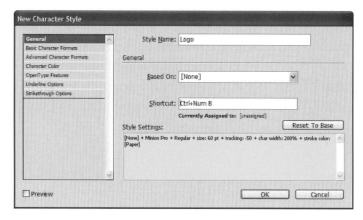

5 First assign a name to the style by typing it into the Style Name field at the top of the window. Name this style **Logo** to define the text to which it is to be applied.

6 In the General section of this window, note that you can base a new character style on a previously created style. Since you're creating a new style, leave this setting at the default "None."

7 Also in the General section, you can create a keyboard shortcut for easy application of this style. Click inside the Shortcut field, hold down Ctrl (Windows) or Command (Mac OS), and type the number **8** from the numeric keypad on your keyboard. (InDesign requires the use of a modifier key for style shortcuts.)

8 Since you are creating this style based on formatting already applied to formatted text in the document, you'll see those settings displayed in the Style Settings section below. Among the attributes listed are font, style, spacing, and color.

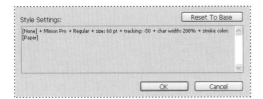

You want to create a style that applies these attributes to selected text while maintaining the original size of that selected text. However, when you told InDesign to build the character style based on the 60-point type on the cover, it built that sizing into the style. Your next step will be to edit the Logo style to remove the type sizing attribute.

9 The categories to the left of this window provide a means for editing the formatting that have been included in the Logo style. Click on the Basic Character Formats category to access the type sizing attribute.

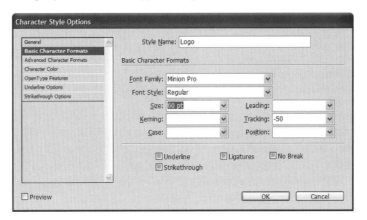

10 Click-drag over the "60 pt" value that appears in the Size field of this section to select it. Press the Delete or Backspace key on your keyboard to delete this value and leave the field blank. Since you've removed the size formatting from the style, the size of the selected type will not change when the style is applied.

11 Next you'll change the color formatting applied by the Logo style. From the list on the left, click on the Character Color category to access this option.

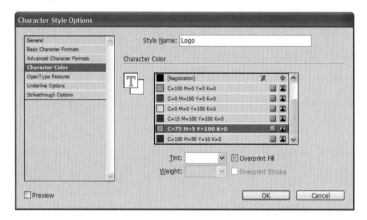

12 In the Character Color settings that appear to the right, select the default Green (C=75, M=5, Y=100, K=0). When this style is applied, the color of the specified characters will turn to green.

13 You have now created (and edited) your first character style. Click OK to close the New Character Style window. You should see the new Logo style appear in the Character Styles palette.

Applying a character style

Now you'll apply your character style to selected text already placed in the menu. As with object styles, using character styles prevents you from having to manually apply multiple type attributes to each run of text individually.

1 In the Pages palette, double-click on Panel 1 of the menu to center it in your document window.

At the bottom of the panel, you'll see the word "Pisano" placed as a footer. To give this footer the same appearance as the logo on the menu's cover, you'll apply the Logo character style.

2 Choose the Type tool (T) from the toolbox, and drag-select over the word "Pisano" on Panel 1 to select it.

3 In the Character Styles palette, click once on the Logo style to apply it to this image. You should see the font, style, spacing, and color of the footer change to reflect the character style you've just created.

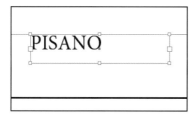 

Note: You also could have used the keyboard shortcut you defined earlier (Ctrl/Command+8) to apply the Logo style.

4 Using either method described above, apply the Logo character style to the footers placed on Panels 4, 5 and 6 and complete this exercise.

 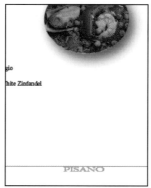

5 Choose File > Save.

Creating and applying paragraph styles

Although they're used for the same general purpose (to speed up your workflow and provide consistency throughout your InDesign document), paragraph styles are more comprehensive than object styles or character styles. This is because paragraph styles incorporate all elements of text formatting. Paragraph styles often include character attributes like font, size, style, and color, combined with paragraph attributes like indents, alignment, tabs, and hyphenation. They also differ from character styles in that they are applied to entire paragraphs at once, not just to selected characters.

Creating a paragraph style

In this exercise you'll apply additional text formatting to your document by creating and applying a paragraph style to selected paragraphs that have already been placed in the menu.

1 With your menu document (07_menu.indd) open, double-click on Panel 4 in the Pages palette to center the panel in your document window.

As with the character style you built in the previous exercise, the easiest way to create a paragraph style is to format an example paragraph using local (i.e., not style-based) formatting, then create a new style based on that example paragraph. Again, this allows you to effectively "see" the style before you build it. In this case, you'll style the text in the first part of the menu locally, and then have InDesign pick up this existing formatting and build it into a new paragraph style. The new style can then be reused efficiently throughout the rest of the menu document.

2 Choose the Type tool (T) from the toolbox and drag to select from "Assorted Baby Greens" to (and including) "$5.95 per person" in the first (Salads) section of the menu.

Note: *InDesign considers a paragraph to be all text that exists between paragraph returns. Each line in the menu's imported text is followed by a paragraph return, so each line is treated as a separate paragraph. If the original text had been built with soft returns (Shift+Return) between lines, you would have been able to simply click once inside the paragraph to select it for styling. In this case, we had to drag-select over all the lines to select them.*

3 In the Control palette, click on the Character formatting button, and specify the following:

- Font: Minion Pro

- Style: Regular

- Size: 12 pt

- Leading: 24 pt

Leave all other settings at their defaults.

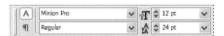

4 Choose Type > Tabs to bring up the Tab ruler palette. Position the palette at the top of the text frame in Panel 4. If necessary, click the magnet icon (🔒) to align it with the text frame margins. In the Tab ruler palette, specify the following:

- Click the 3rd button from the left to establish a Right-aligned tab.

- In the X field, enter **7.5 in** and press Enter or Return to accept this entry.

- In the Leader field, type "**..**" and press Enter or Return to accept this entry.

- Close the Tab ruler palette.

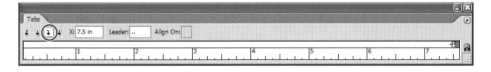

Note: *The magnet icon moves the palette only if there is enough space above the text frame to accommodate the Tabs palette.*

The prices for all the dishes in the menu should now be aligned on the right at the 7.45 inch mark, and each price should be separated from the name of its corresponding dish by a line of dots, or a leader.

Salads

Assorted Baby Greens... $5.25

Arugula, Radicchio and Belgium Endive.. $7.95

Caesar.. $6.95

Mozzarella, Tomato and Basil.. $7.95

Antipasti: Assorted Appetizers from the Deli Case ....$5.95 per person

Now you'll build this formatting into a paragraph style so you can use it to format the other sections of the menu.

5   If it's not already visible, open the Paragraph Styles palette by choosing Window > Type & Tables > Paragraph Styles. Note that the only style listed in this palette is the default, [Basic Paragraph].

6   In the Paragraph Styles palette, create a new paragraph style by choosing "New Paragraph Style" from the palette menu. The New Paragraph Style window opens, offering you formatting options to be built into the style.

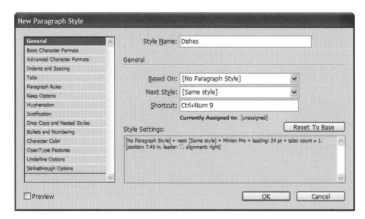

7   First assign a name to the style by typing it into the Style Name field at the top of the window. Name this style **Dishes** to define the text to which it is to be applied.

8 In the General section of this window, note that you can base a new style on a previously created style. Since you're creating a new style, leave this setting at the default. You can also have InDesign switch to another style automatically when you press Return or Enter. Since this is your first paragraph style, you should leave the Next Style setting at its default, [Same style].

9 Also in the General section, you can create a keyboard shortcut for easy application of this style. Click inside the Shortcut field, hold down Ctrl (Windows) or Command (Mac OS), and type the number **9** from the numeric keypad on your keyboard. (InDesign requires the use of a modifier key for style shortcuts.)

10 Since you are creating this style based on formatting already applied to highlighted text in the document, you'll see those settings displayed in the Style Settings section below. Note that the attributes for font, leading, and tabs have been added to the default [Basic Paragraph] style.

11 As with the other types of styles you've created in this lesson, the "Dishes" style can be edited in the New Paragraph Style window. Simply click on a category from the list to the left to make changes to the settings within that category.

12 You have now created your first paragraph style. Click OK to close the New Paragraph Style window. You should see the new Dishes style appear in the Character Styles palette.

Applying a paragraph style

Now you'll apply your paragraph style to selected text in the other sections of the menu.

1 In the Pages palette, double-click on Panel 4 of the menu to center it in your document window.

2 Using the Type tool (T), drag-select over the lists of dishes and prices in each remaining section of the menu, being careful not to select their headings (Soups, Pasta, Entrées, Desserts, Coffees, Drinks, and Bottled Water). You'll format these headings with another style later in this lesson.

3   For each selected section, click once on the Dishes style in the Paragraph Styles palette to apply the style to the text. You should see the text attributes change to reflect the paragraph style you've just created.

Note: You also could have used the keyboard shortcut you defined earlier (Ctrl/Command+9) to apply the Dishes style.

4   Choose File > Save.

Nesting character styles inside paragraph styles

To make the use of styles more convenient and powerful for you, InDesign provides for the nesting of character formatting within paragraph styles. These nested styles allow you to apply character formatting to portions of a paragraph, whether it's the first character, the second word, or the third sentence. This makes nested styles ideal for applying to run-in headings (where the first portion of a line or paragraph is styled differently from the rest of the line or paragraph), structured paragraphs, or as you're about to see, drop caps.

Creating a paragraph style for nesting

The two prerequisites for using nested styles are that you have first created a character style, and that you then have built a paragraph style in which to nest it. Since you created the Logo character style earlier in this lesson, your next step is to build a new paragraph style in which to nest that style.

1   With your menu document (07_menu.indd) open, double-click on Panel 2 in the Pages palette to center the back cover of the menu in your document window.

The welcoming copy on the back cover is obviously too small and simple to catch the reader's eye. In this exercise, you'll create a new nested style that makes this copy more appealing.

2   Choose the Type tool (T) and click anywhere within the paragraph that begins with "Combining the best of…" on Panel 2. Choose Edit > Select All to select the entire contents of this text frame. You'll see in the Paragraph Styles palette that the copy is styled (by default) with the [Basic Paragraph] style. You'll now format the copy locally so that you can base the new nested style on it.

3   In the Control palette, click on the Character formatting button (A), and specify the following:

- Font: Minion Pro

- Style: Regular

- Size: 30 pt

- Leading: 48 pt

Leave all other settings at their defaults.

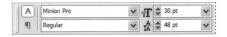

4   Also in the Control palette, click on the Paragraph formatting button (¶), and specify the following:

- Drop Cap Number of Lines: 2

- Drop Cap One or More Characters: 1

Leave all other settings at their defaults.

5   Your locally formatted text should now be ready to serve as the basis for a new paragraph style. If it's not already visible, open the Paragraph Styles palette by choosing Window > Type & Tables > Paragraph Styles.

6   In the Paragraph Styles palette, create a new paragraph style by choosing "New Paragraph Style" from the palette menu. The New Paragraph Style window opens, offering you formatting options to be built into the style.

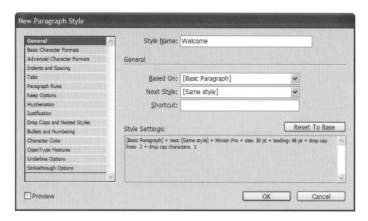

7   First assign a name to the style by typing it into the Style Name field at the top of the window. Name this style **Welcome** to define the text to which it is to be applied.

8   Since you are creating this style based on formatting already applied to highlighted text in the document, you'll see those settings displayed in the Style Settings section below. Note that the attributes for font, size, leading, and drop caps have been added to the default [Basic Paragraph] style.

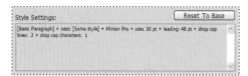

9   As with the other types of styles you've created in this lesson, the Welcome style can be edited in the Paragraph Style Options window. To compensate for the dark red background, you'll now change the color formatting applied by the Welcome style from black to white. From the list on the left, click on the Character Color category to access this option.

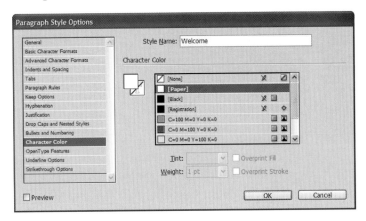

10   In the Character Color settings that appear to the right, select the default Paper (White) color.

11   Click OK to close the Paragraph Style Options window. You should see the new Welcome style appear in the Paragraph Styles palette.

12   You won't, however, see the type on the menu's back cover change until you actually apply the new paragraph style to it. Click anywhere within the welcoming paragraph on Panel 2, and then click on the "Welcome" style in the Paragraph Styles palette. You should now see the copy turn white and become more legible.

You have successfully created and applied another new paragraph style. But to add more visual impact to the welcoming copy, you'd like to style the drop cap to match the Pisano logo. This is best achieved by nesting the Logo character style inside the Welcome paragraph style.

Creating a nested style

When you create a nested style within an existing paragraph style, you're essentially building a secondary set of rules for InDesign to follow while formatting a paragraph. In this exercise, you'll build a nested style into the Welcome style you created in the last exercise.

1   If it's not already centered on your screen, double-click on Panel 2 in the Pages palette to center the back cover of the menu in your document window.

2   Choose the Type tool (T) and click anywhere within the paragraph that begins with "Combining the best of..." on Panel 2. (The Paragraph Styles palette should still be open from the previous exercise.) Note that this paragraph is formatted with the Welcome style you created in the last exercise.

3 In the Paragraph Styles palette, double-click on the Welcome style to open the Paragraph Style Options dialog box.

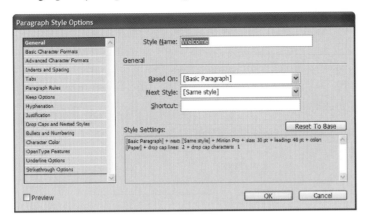

4 From the categories on the left, choose Drop Caps and Nested Styles by clicking once on it. You'll see options for applying drop caps and nested styles appear on the right.

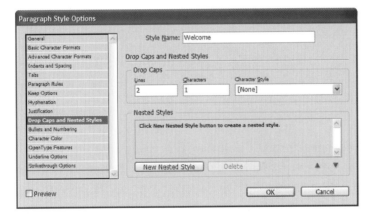

5 Earlier in this exercise, you applied a drop cap to this text using local formatting from the Control palette. These settings are reflected in the Drop Caps section at the top of this window. You won't make any changes in this section. Note, however, that the drop cap is set to apply to one character and be two lines high. No provision is made for the font used in the drop cap, so it defaults to the font applied by the Welcome style (Minion Pro).

You'll now create a nested style that changes the font and other attributes of the drop cap to match the Pisano logo on the front of the menu.

6   In the Nested Styles section below, click on the New Nested Style button to create a new nested style.

7   When it appears below, click on the [None] entry to reveal a drop-down menu. Click and hold on the arrow to the right to expand the drop-down menu, exposing your choices of the character styles available for nesting.

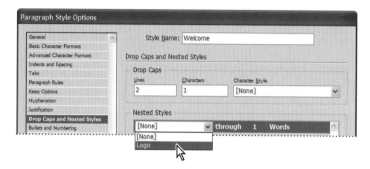

8   In this case, since you've created only one character style; "Logo" is the only choice available. Click on "Logo" to select it as your nested style.

9   Click on the "through" entry to expose another drop-down menu. This menu contains only two choices: "through" and "up to." Leave this setting at the default "through."

10   Click on the number "1" entry to expose a text field into which you can type a number. The number defines "through" or "up to" how many units the style will apply. Units are defined in the next step, so leave this setting at the default "1."

11   Click on the "Words" entry to expose another drop-down menu. This menu contains many choices of units to which the style will be applied, including sentences, characters, and spaces. Since we simply want to change the style of the singular drop cap character that begins any paragraph to which the nested style is applied, choose "Characters" from this menu.

12 Click on the OK button to accept these changes. You have now finished creating a nested style that will apply the "Logo" character style "through" the first ("1") "Character" of any paragraph styled with the "Welcome" paragraph style.

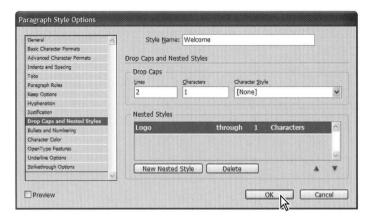

13 To view the results of your efforts, look at the welcoming paragraph on Panel 2. The paragraph that was originally styled with the "Welcome" paragraph style now includes a stylized drop cap that matches the logotype on the cover, thanks to the nested style you just created.

14 Select File > Save.

Globally updating styles

There are two ways to update object, character, or paragraph styles in InDesign. The first is simply to open the style itself and make changes to the formatting options, as you did when you created a nested style in the previous exercise. Because there's a parent-child relationship between the style and the instance(s) in which it's applied, all instances are updated to reflect a modified style.

The other way to update object, character, or paragraph styles is to use local formatting to change an instance, and then redefine the style based on that instance. In this exercise, you'll make a change to the Shadow object style by using local formatting to redefine the style.

1   With your menu document (07_menu.indd) open, double-click on the numbers "4-6" in the Pages palette to center the inside spread of the menu in your document window. Then choose View > Fit Spread in Window so that you can see all three panels.

2   Using the Selection tool (⬆), click once on the top image on Panel 4 (the antipasto) to select it.

3   If it's not already visible, choose Window > Object Styles to access the Object Styles palette. Note that the Object Styles palette shows the "Shadow" style you applied to this image earlier in the lesson.

4   Choose Object > Drop Shadow to access the Drop Shadow dialog box. Changes made in this dialog box affect only the selected image, and InDesign will not redefine the actual "Shadow" style until we instruct it to.

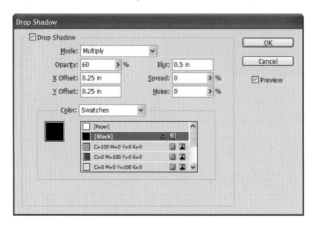

5   In the Drop Shadow dialog box, change the following settings to:

- Opacity: 60%

- X Offset: 0.25 in

- Y Offset: 0.25 in

- Blur: 0.5 in

Leave all other settings at their defaults and click OK. You should see the drop shadow on the antipasto image move slightly, darken somewhat, and spread out more.

Note: You'll also see a "+" appear next to the style name in the Object Styles palette. This indicates that local formatting has been applied (and added to the previously applied "Shadow" style).

6   Now you'll redefine the object style so that the local change applies to all the food images previously styled with the "Shadow" style. In the palette menu of the Object Styles palette, choose "Redefine Object Style." The "+" should no longer appear next to the "Shadow" style in the Object Styles palette. All images in the menu that have been styled with "Shadow" should globally update to reflect the changes you made to the drop shadow.

Note: The same process can be used to redefine character and paragraph styles based on local text formatting.

7   Select File > Save.

Loading styles from another document

Styles appear only in the document in which you create them. However, it's easy to share styles between InDesign documents by loading, or importing, styles from other InDesign documents. In this exercise, you will import and apply a menu header style from the finished menu document (07_b.indd). Instead of having to manually add formatting to style the header type, you'll save time by loading the styles from the other document and applying them to each header using a single action.

1   With your menu document (07_menu.indd) open, double-click on Panel 4 in the Pages palette to center the first page of the menu in your document window.

2   If it's not already visible, select Window > Type & Tables > Paragraph Styles to access the Paragraph Styles palette.

3   Click the palette menu button in the Paragraph Styles palette and choose Load All Styles from the Paragraph Styles palette menu.

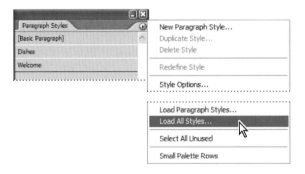

4   In the Open a File dialog box, double-click 07_b.indd from the Lesson_07 folder. The Load Styles dialog box appears. To avoid overwriting existing styles on import, make sure only Headers is checked in this dialog box, and click OK. In the Paragraph Styles palette, notice the new style called Headers. This style contains both character and paragraph formatting, including font, alignment, spacing, and rule below attributes.

5   Using the Type tool (T), click an insertion point in the header for Salads, and then choose the new Headers style from the Paragraph Styles palette. The text and the spacing around it should change to correspond with the imported style you've applied.

6   Repeat Steps 1-5 to apply the Headers style to the following text:

• Soups

• Pasta

• Entrées

• Desserts

• Coffees

• Drinks

• Bottled Water

7   Select File > Save.

Finishing up

To complete the menu, you will add a drop shadow to the mushrooms artwork on the front and back covers and create an object style that reflects this formatting.

1   With the Selection tool (⬆), click on the mushrooms artwork on the front cover (Panel 3).

2   Shift+click on the mushrooms logo on the back cover (Panel 2) to select it as well.

3   In the Object menu, choose Drop Shadow to access the Drop Shadow dialog box. Click the Drop Shadow check box and accept the default drop shadow settings, then click OK.

4   In the Object Styles palette, choose New Object Style from the palette menu.

5   Name the style **Mushrooms**, add a keyboard shortcut if you desire, and click OK to save the new object style. With the mushrooms logo still selected, click the Mushrooms object style to attach the style to this object.

Even though the formatting of the mushrooms logo was used as the foundation for the style, you should confirm that the style is also applied to this object in the event that the style is modified.

6   Select File > Save.

Congratulations. You have finished the lesson.

Exploring on your own

Follow these steps to gain more experience in working with styles.

In the Finishing Up section, you created a new object style based on a locally applied drop shadow. If you want to edit just one of the two applications of this style, you can break the link to the style for that one instance. This enables you to locally re-format that instance without interfering with the object style itself. Try this:

1 Go to Panel 2 and using the Selection tool (➤) click on the Mushrooms artwork to select it.

Notice in the Object Styles palette that the artwork is styled with the "Mushrooms" style you created in the last exercise.

2 From the palette menu in the Object Styles palette, choose Break Link to Style.

Now notice that the artwork is styled with the "None" style and shows local formatting (with the "+").

3 With the Mushrooms artwork on Panel 2 still selected, go to the Object menu and choose Drop Shadow. The Drop Shadow dialog box appears.

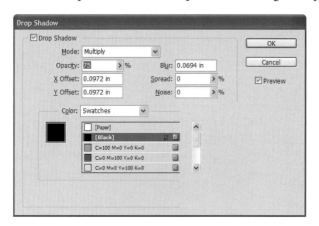

4 Since the artwork on the back cover is smaller than that on the front, you'll want to tone down the effect of the drop shadow. Try experimenting with different Opacity, Offset, and Blur settings to achieve the desired result. Click OK to close the Drop Shadow dialog box.

Note: The changes you make locally to this artwork do not affect the "Mushrooms" object style, because you broke the link beforehand.

Modifying an object style

The images of the dishes that head each section in the menu were silhouetted in Photoshop before being imported into InDesign. Sometimes this can have the effect of leaving jagged edges on the images. You can compensate for this by adding a slight Feather value to the "Shadow" object style you created earlier in this lesson. Remember, when you make changes to a style, InDesign will globally update all applications of that style to reflect those changes.

1   With nothing selected, locate the "Shadow" style in the Object Styles palette and click once on it to select the style.

2   From the palette menu in the Object Styles palette, choose Object Style Options. This is an alternate way of accessing the options for this style.

3   Click on the Drop Shadow & Feather category to the left to access these settings.

4   Click in the check box next to Feather to activate this feature, and experiment with different Width, Corners, and Noise settings to slightly blur the images' edges.

Note: Make sure the Preview option is checked so you can see how much feathering is applied before you accept the change to your style.

5   Click OK to apply the style change, and globally update all images to which "shadow" has been applied.

Review

▶ **Review questions**

1 How can using object styles speed your workflow?

2 What must you have created previously in order to create a nested style?

3 What are the two ways to globally update a style you've applied to an InDesign document?

4 How would you import styles from another InDesign document?

▶ **Review answers**

1 Object styles save time by letting you keep a group of formatting attributes together that you can quickly apply to images. If you need to update the formatting, you don't have to change each image formatted with the style individually. Instead, you can simply modify the style.

2 The two prerequisites for using nested styles are that you have first created a character style, and that you then have built a paragraph style in which to nest it.

3 There are two ways to update object, character, or paragraph styles in InDesign. The first is simply to open the style itself and make changes to the formatting options. The other is to use local formatting to change an instance, and then redefine the style based on that instance.

4 Importing styles is easy. Simply choose Load All Styles from the Object, Character, or Paragraph palette menus and locate the InDesign document from which you want to load them. The styles are then loaded into the respective palette(s) and are immediately available for use inside your document.

You can easily enhance your document with photographs and artwork imported from Adobe Photoshop, Adobe Illustrator, or other graphics programs. If these imported graphics change, InDesign can tell you that a newer version of a graphic is available. You can update or replace imported graphics at any time.

8 Importing and Linking Graphics

In this lesson, you'll learn how to do the following:

- Distinguish between vector and bitmap graphics.

- Place layered Adobe Photoshop and Adobe Illustrator graphics.

- Import clipping paths with graphics, and create clipping paths.

- Manage placed files using the Links palette.

- Use and create libraries for objects.

- Import graphics using Adobe Bridge.

Getting started

In this lesson, you'll assemble a booklet for a compact disc by importing and managing graphics from Adobe Photoshop, Adobe Illustrator, and Adobe Acrobat. After printing and trimming, the insert will be folded so that it fits into a CD case.

This lesson includes a procedure that you can perform using Adobe Photoshop, if you have a copy of that program installed on your computer.

Before you begin, restore the default preferences for Adobe InDesign, using the procedure in "Restoring default preferences" on page 2.

1 Start Adobe InDesign CS2.

2   Choose File > Open, and open the 08_a.indd file in the Lesson_08 folder, located inside the Lessons folder within the InDesignCIB folder on your hard disk.

Note: If you have not already copied the resource files for this lesson onto your hard disk from the Lesson_08 folder from the Adobe InDesign CS2 Classroom in a Book CD, do so now. See "Copying the Classroom in a Book files" on page 4.

3   A message appears, saying that the publication contains missing or modified links. Click Don't Fix; you will fix this later in the lesson.

4   If necessary, move the Links palette out of the way so it doesn't obscure your view of the document. The Links palette opens automatically whenever you open an InDesign document that contains missing or modified links.

5   To see what the finished document will look like, open the 08_b.indd file in the same folder. If you prefer, you can leave the document open as you work to act as a guide. When you're ready to resume working on the lesson document, select 08_a.indd from the Window menu.

6   Choose File > Save As, rename the file **08_cdbook.indd**, and save it in the Lesson_08 folder.

Note: As you work through the lesson, feel free to move palettes around or change the magnification to a level that works best for you. For more information, see "Changing the magnification of your document" and "Using the Navigator palette" in Lesson 1, "Getting to Know the Work Area."

Adding graphics from other programs

InDesign supports many common graphics file formats. While this means that you can use graphics that were created using a wide range of graphics programs, InDesign works most smoothly with other Adobe professional graphics programs, such as Photoshop, Illustrator, and Acrobat.

By default, imported graphics are linked, which means that InDesign displays a graphics file on your layout without actually copying the entire graphics file into the InDesign document.

There are two major advantages to linking resource files. First, it saves disk space, especially if you reuse the same graphic in many InDesign documents. Second, you can edit a linked document in the program you used to create it and then simply update the link in the InDesign Links palette. Updating a linked file maintains the current location and settings for the resource so you don't have to redo that work.

All linked graphics and text files are listed in the Links palette, which provides buttons and commands for managing links. When you create final output using PostScript® or PDF, InDesign uses the links to produce the highest level of quality available from the original, externally stored versions of placed graphics.

Comparing vector and bitmap graphics

The drawing tools of Adobe InDesign and Adobe Illustrator create vector graphics, which are made up of shapes based on mathematical expressions. Vector graphics consist of smooth lines that retain their clarity when scaled. They are appropriate for illustrations, type, and graphics, such as logos that are typically scaled to different sizes.

Bitmap images are based on a grid of pixels and are created by image-editing applications, such as Adobe Photoshop. In working with bitmap images, you edit individual pixels rather than objects or shapes. Because bitmap graphics can represent subtle gradations of shade and color, they are appropriate for continuous-tone images, such as photographs or artwork created in painting programs. A disadvantage of bitmap graphics is that they lose definition and appear "jagged" when enlarged. Additionally, bitmap images are typically larger in file size than a similar vector file.

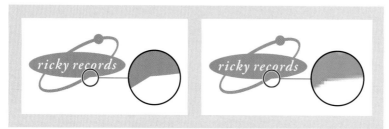

Logo drawn as vector art (left), and rasterized as bitmap art (right).

In general, use vector drawing tools to create art or type with clean lines that look good at any size, such as a logo used on a business card and also on a poster. You can create vector artwork using the InDesign drawing tools, or you might prefer to take advantage of the wider range of vector drawing tools available in Illustrator. You can use Photoshop to create bitmap images that have the soft lines of painted or photographic art and for applying special effects to line art.

Managing links to imported files

When you opened the document, you saw an alert message about problems with linked files. You'll resolve those issues using the Links palette, which provides complete information about the status of any linked text or graphics file in your document.

Identifying imported images

To identify some of the images that have already been imported into the document, you'll use three different techniques involving the Links palette. Later in this lesson, you'll also use the Links palette to edit and update imported graphics.

1 If necessary, zoom or scroll the document window so that you can see both spreads in the document. Alternatively, choose View > Entire Pasteboard.

2 If the Links palette is not visible, choose Window > Links.

3 Using the Selection tool (↖), select the Orchard of Kings logotype on page 4, the far right page of the first spread. Notice that the graphic's filename, 08_i.ai, becomes selected in the Links palette when you select it on the layout.

 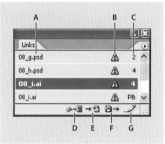

*A. Linked file name. **B.** Alert icon. **C.** Page on which linked item appears.*
*D. Relink button. **E.** Go To Link button. **F.** Update Link button. **G.** Edit Original button.*

Now you'll use the Links palette to locate a graphic on the layout.

4 In the Links palette, select 08_g.psd, and then click the Go To Link button (⋯→🗐). The graphic becomes selected and centered on the screen. This is a quick way to find a graphic when you know its file name.

If the Links palette is still in the center of the document window, you can move it now so that it doesn't block your view of the page as you work through the rest of the lesson.

These techniques for identifying and locating linked graphics are useful throughout this lesson and whenever you work with a large number of imported files.

Viewing information about linked files

You can use the Links palette to manage placed graphics or text files in many other ways, such as updating or replacing text or graphics. All the techniques you learn in this lesson about managing linked files apply equally to graphics files and text files that you place into your document.

1 If the Links palette is not visible, choose Window > Links to display it. If you cannot see the names of all the linked files without scrolling, drag the lower right corner of the palette to enlarge it so that all the links are visible.

2 Double-click the link 08_g.psd. The Link Information dialog box appears, describing the linked file.

3 Click Next to view information about the following file on the Links palette list, 08_h.psd. You can quickly examine all the links this way. Some of the other links may display an alert icon (⚠) under Content Status; this icon indicates a linking problem, which you'll address in the next topic. After you've examined the link information, click Done.

By default, files are sorted in the Links palette so that files listed first are those that may need to be updated or relinked. You can use commands in the Links palette menu to sort the file list in different ways.

4 In the Links palette, choose Sort by Page from the Links palette menu. The palette now lists the links in numerical order by the page on which the linked item appears.

Showing Files in the Explorer (PC) or Finder (Mac OS)

Although the Links palette gives you information on the attributes and location of a specific file, it does not give you access to the file itself. You can access a file directly from your hard drive with the Reveal in Finder option.

1   Select the graphic 08_g.psd if it is not currently chosen. Right-click or Ctrl+click on the graphic and choose Graphics > Reveal in Explorer (PC) or Graphics > Reveal in Finder (Mac OS). This opens the window where the linked file is currently stored. This feature is useful for locating documents on your hard drive and renaming them if necessary.

2   Close the window and, if necessary, click on the document to return to InDesign.

Updating revised graphics

Even after you place text or graphic files in your InDesign document, you can still use other programs to modify those files. The Links palette indicates which files have been modified outside of InDesign and gives you the choice of updating your document with the latest versions of those files.

In the Links palette, the file 08_i.ai has an alert icon (⚠), indicating that the original has recently been modified. This is the file, as well as some others, that caused the alert message when you opened this document. You'll update its link so that the InDesign document uses the current version.

Viewing link status in the Links palette

A linked graphic can appear in the Links palette in any of the following ways:

• An up-to-date graphic displays only the file name and its page in the document.

• A modified file displays a yellow triangle with an exclamation point (⚠). This alert icon means that the version of the file on disk is more recent than the version in your document. For example, this icon will appear if you import a Photoshop graphic into InDesign, and then another artist edits and saves the original graphic using Photoshop.

• A missing file displays a red hexagon with a question mark (❓). The file isn't at the location from which it was originally imported, though the file may still exist somewhere. This can happen if someone moves an original file to a different folder or server after it's been imported into an InDesign document. You can't know whether a missing graphic is up to date until its original is located. If you print or export a document when this icon is displayed, the graphic may not print or export at full resolution.

1 In the Links palette, select the second instance of the file 08_i.ai (on page 4), and click the Go To Link button (⋯➜🖺). You don't have to do this step to update a link, but it's a quick way to double-check which imported file you are about to update.

2   Click the Update Link button (🖻⋯→). The appearance of the image in the document changes to represent its newer version. However, the new image is larger than the previous version, so the existing frame now crops the updated graphic, you will change this in the next step. Select the other files displaying the alert icon (⚠) and click the update button. You can hold down the Shift key to select multiple consecutive files to be updated in a single step, or Ctrl+click (Windows) or Command+click (Mac OS), to select non-consecutive items in the Links palette.

💡 *All the buttons at the bottom of the Links palette are also available as commands in the Links palette menu.*

3   Select the 08_i.ai graphic on the page and choose Object > Fitting > Fit Content Proportionally. The larger graphic is now visible.

You'll replace the image of the hands that spans the first spread (pages 2-4) with a modified image. You'll use the Relink button to reassign the link to another graphic.

4   Go to pages 2-4 (the first spread) and choose View > Fit Spread in Window.

5   Select the 08_h.psd image, which is the photograph of the interlocked hands that sits on page 4. You can tell when you've selected the right image because the filename becomes selected in the Links palette.

6   Click the Relink button (📷⋯→🗔) in the Links palette.

7   Browse to find the 08_j.psd file in the Lesson_08 folder, and then click Open. The new version of the image (which has a different background) replaces the original image, and the Links palette is updated accordingly.

8   Click a blank area of the pasteboard to deselect all objects in the file.

9   Choose File > Save to save your work.

Adjusting view quality

Now that you've resolved all the file's links, you're ready to start adding more graphics. But first, you will adjust the view quality of the Illustrator file 08_i.ai you updated in the last step.

As you place an image into a document, InDesign automatically creates a low-resolution (proxy) version of it, corresponding to the current settings in the Preferences dialog box. This and any other images in this document are currently low-resolution proxies, which is why the image appears to have jagged edges. You can control the degree of detail InDesign uses to display placed graphics. Reducing the on-screen quality of placed graphics displays pages faster, and doesn't affect the quality of final output.

1 In the Links window, select the image 08_i.ai file you updated in the last exercise (on page 4). Click the Go To Link button to view the document in magnified view.

2 Right-click (Windows) or Ctrl+click (Mac OS) the Orchard of Kings image, and then choose Display Performance > High Quality Display from the context menu that appears. The image appears at full resolution. Use this process to confirm the clarity, appearance, or position of an individual placed graphic in your InDesign layout.

On-screen display using Typical Display (left) and High Quality Display (right).

3 Choose View > Display Performance > High Quality Display. This setting changes the default display performance for this document. All graphics will be displayed at the highest quality. On older computers, or for designs with many imported graphics, this setting can sometimes tax the system, resulting in slower screen redraw. In most cases, it is advisable to set your Display Performance to Typical Display and then change the display quality of individual graphics as needed.

4 Choose File > Save.

Working with clipping paths

You can remove unwanted backgrounds from images using InDesign. You'll get some experience doing this in the following procedure. In addition to removing the background using Adobe InDesign, you can also create paths or alpha channels in Photoshop, which can then be used to silhouette an image in an InDesign layout.

The image you will be placing has a solid rectangular background that blocks your view of the area behind it. You can hide unwanted parts of an image using a clipping path—a drawn vector outline that acts as a mask. InDesign can create clipping paths from many kinds of images:

- If you drew a path in Photoshop and saved it with the image, InDesign can create a clipping path from it.

- If you painted an alpha channel in Photoshop and saved it with the image, InDesign can create a clipping path from it. An alpha channel carries transparent and opaque areas and is commonly created with images used for photo or video compositing.

- If the image has a light or white background, InDesign can automatically detect its edges and create a clipping path.

The pear image you will be placing doesn't have a clipping path or an alpha channel, but it does have a solid white background that InDesign can remove.

Removing a white background using InDesign

You can use the Detect Edges option of the Clipping Path command to remove a solid white background from an image. The Detect Edges option hides areas of an image by changing the shape of the frame containing the image, adding anchor points as necessary. For more information about frames and anchor points, see the "About frames, paths, and selections" sidebar in Lesson 3, "Working with Frames."

1   Navigate to page 7 of your document by double-clicking on the Page 7 icon in the Pages palette. Choose File > Place and double-click the file 08_c.psd in the Lesson_08 folder.

2   Position the loaded graphics icon outside the purple square—to the left and slightly below the top edge (make sure you are not placing the cursor in the square itself), and click to place an image of a pear on a white background. If you need to reposition the image, do so now.

3   Choose Object > Clipping Path. If necessary, drag the Clipping Path dialog box so that you can see the pear image.

4   In the Type drop-down menu, choose Detect Edges. If the Preview checkbox is not selected, do so now. The white background is almost entirely eliminated from the image.

5   For Threshold, drag the slider and watch the image on page 7 until the Threshold setting hides as much of the white background as possible without hiding parts of the subject (darker areas). We used a Threshold value of 20.

Note: If you can't find a setting that removes all the background without affecting the subject, specify a value that leaves the entire subject visible along with small bits of the white background. You'll eliminate the remaining white background by fine-tuning the clipping path in the following steps.

The Threshold option works by hiding light areas of the image, starting with white. As you drag to the right to choose a higher value, increasingly darker tones are included within the range of tones that become hidden. Don't try to find a setting that matches the pear perfectly. You'll learn how to improve the clipping path a little bit later.

6   For Tolerance, drag the slider slightly to the left until the Tolerance value is between about 1 and 1.8.

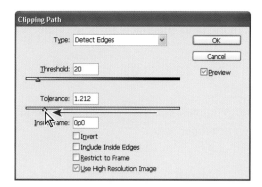

The Tolerance option determines how many points define the frame that's automatically generated. As you drag to the right, InDesign uses fewer points so that the clipping path fits the image more loosely (higher tolerance). Using fewer points on the path may speed up document printing, but may also be less accurate.

7   For Inset Frame, specify a value that closes up any remaining background areas. We specified a value of 0p1 (zero picas, one point). This option shrinks the current shape of the clipping path uniformly, and is not affected by the lightness values in the image. Then click OK to close the Clipping Path dialog box.

Before and after applying an inset of 1 point.

8 (Optional) You can refine the clipping path manually. Switch to the Direct Selection tool (↳) to activate it. You can then drag individual anchor points and use the Drawing tools to edit the clipping path around the pears. With images which have complex edges, you will want to magnify the document in order to effectively work with the anchor points.

9 Choose File > Save to save the file.

💡 *You can also use the Detect Edges feature to remove a solid black background. Just select the Invert option and specify a high threshold value.*

Working with alpha channels

When an image has a background that isn't solid white or black, the Detect Edges feature may not be able to remove the background effectively. With such images, hiding the background's lightness values may also hide parts of the subject that use the same lightness values. Instead, you can use the advanced background-removal tools in Photoshop to mark transparent areas using paths or alpha channels, and let InDesign make a clipping path from those areas.

Note: If you place a Photoshop file (.psd) that consists of an image placed on a transparent background, InDesign honors the transparency with no dependence on clipping paths or alpha channels. This can be especially helpful when you place an image with a soft or feathered edge.

Importing a Photoshop file and alpha channels

You imported the previous image using the Place command. This time, use an alternate method: You'll simply drag a Photoshop image directly onto an InDesign spread. InDesign can use Photoshop paths and alpha channels directly—you don't need to save the Photoshop file in a different file format. For more information see "To drag and drop graphics" in InDesign Help.

1 In the Layers palette, make sure that the Photos layer is selected so that the image will appear on that layer.

2 Go to page 2 of your document. Then resize and arrange your Explorer window (Windows), Finder window (Mac OS), and your InDesign windows, as needed, so that you can simultaneously see the list of files on the desktop and the InDesign document window. Make sure that the lower left quarter of page 2 in your document is visible.

3 In Explorer (Windows) or the Finder (Mac OS), open the Lesson_08 folder, which contains the file 08_d.psd file.

4 Drag the file 08_d.psd to page 2 in the InDesign document. Then use the Selection tool (➤) to reposition the graphic so that it is in the lower left corner of the page.

Note: When you place the file, be careful to drop it onto the white pasteboard. If you drop it in an object drawn using InDesign, it will be placed inside the object. If this happens, choose Edit > Undo, and try again.

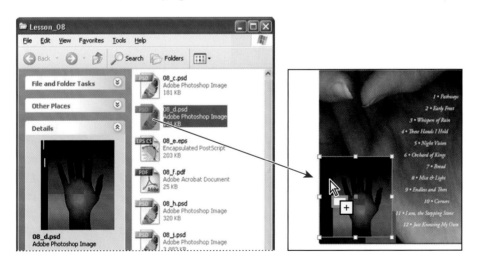

5 If necessary, you can now maximize the InDesign window to its previous size, because you've finished importing the file.

Examining Photoshop paths and alpha channels

In the Photoshop image that you just dragged into InDesign, the hand and the background share many of the same lightness values. Therefore, the background can't easily be isolated using the Detect Edges option in the Clipping Path command.

Instead, you'll set up InDesign to use a path or alpha channel from Photoshop. First you'll use the Links palette to open the image directly in Photoshop to see what paths or alpha channels it already includes.

The procedure in this topic requires a full version of Photoshop 4.0 or later, and is easier if you have enough RAM available to leave both InDesign and Photoshop open as you work. If your configuration doesn't include these two standards, you can still read these steps to help you understand what Photoshop alpha channels look like and do, and resume your work in the next section of this lesson.

1   If necessary, use the Selection tool (✸) to select the 08_d.psd image in InDesign.

2   If the Links palette is not already open, choose File > Links. The image filename appears selected in the Links palette.

3   In the Links palette, click the Edit Original button (✐). This opens the image in a program that can view or edit it. This image was saved from Photoshop, so if Photoshop is installed on your computer, InDesign starts Photoshop with the selected file.

Note: Sometimes the Edit Original button opens an image in a program other than Photoshop or the program that created it. When you install software, some installer utilities change your operating system's settings for associating files with programs. The Edit Original command uses these settings for associating files with programs. To change these settings, see the documentation for your operating system.

4   If an Embedded Profile Mismatch dialog box appears as the image opens in Photoshop, do one of the following:

•   If you are not using color management, select Use the Embedded Profile (Instead of the Working Space).

•   If you've properly configured all Photoshop and InDesign color-management settings for your workflow using accurate ICC profiles, select Convert Document's Colors to the Working Space to reproduce the image properly in Photoshop.

5   In Photoshop, choose Window > Channels to display the Channels palette, or click the Channels palette tab.

Scroll down the Channels palette if necessary to view the three alpha channels in addition to the standard RGB channels. These channels were drawn using the masking and painting tools in Photoshop.

Photoshop file saved with three alpha channels.

6   In the Channels palette in Photoshop, click Alpha 1 to see how it looks, then click Alpha 2 and Alpha 3 to compare them.

7   In Photoshop, choose Window > Paths to open the Paths palette, or click the Paths palette tab.

The Paths palette contains two named paths, "Shapes" and "Circle." These were drawn using the Pen tool (✿) and other Path tools in Photoshop, although they could also be drawn in Illustrator and pasted into Photoshop.

8   In the Photoshop Paths palette, click Shapes to view that path. Then click Circle. You're finished using Photoshop, so you can now quit that program.

Using Photoshop alpha channels in InDesign

Now you'll return to InDesign and see how you can create different clipping paths from the Photoshop paths and alpha channels.

1   Switch to InDesign. Make sure that the 08_d.psd Photoshop file is still selected on the page; if necessary, select it using the Selection tool (➤).

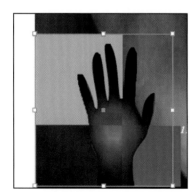

2   (Optional) Right-click (Windows) or Ctrl+click (Mac OS) the hand image, and choose Display Performance > High Quality from the context menu that appears. This step isn't necessary, but it lets you precisely preview the following steps.

3   With the hand image still selected, choose Object > Clipping Path to open the Clipping Path dialog box. If necessary, move the Clipping Path dialog box so that you can see the image as you work.

4   Make sure that Preview is selected in the Clipping Path dialog box, and then choose Alpha Channel from the Type menu. The Alpha menu becomes available, listing the three alpha channels you saw in Photoshop by the names used in that program.

5   In the Alpha menu, choose Alpha 1. InDesign creates a clipping path from the alpha channel. Then choose Alpha 2 from the same menu, and compare the results.

The first clipping path you see represents the default settings for defining the edges of an alpha channel. You can fine-tune the clipping path that InDesign creates from an Alpha Channel by adjusting the Threshold and Tolerance options, as you did for the Detect Edges feature earlier in this lesson. For Alpha Channels, start with a low Threshold value, such as 1.

6   Choose Alpha 3 from the Alpha menu, and then select the Include Inside Edges option. Notice the changes in the image.

Selecting the Include Inside Edges option makes InDesign recognize a butterfly-shaped hole painted into alpha channel 3, and adds it to the clipping path.

You can see how the butterfly-shaped hole looks in Photoshop by viewing Alpha Channel 3 in the original Photoshop file.

7   Choose Photoshop Path from the Type menu, and then choose Shapes from the Path menu. InDesign reshapes the image's frame to match the Photoshop path.

8   Choose Circle from the Path menu. Since this is the effect wanted for this design, click OK.

Placing native files

InDesign works with native Adobe files such as Photoshop, Illustrator, and Acrobat in unique ways. A document may have different requirements for graphics, and InDesign allows you to import different file types, and provides options for controlling how the file is imported. For example, a Photoshop file with layers can be imported as a complete document, or you have the option of importing one (or more) of the layers separately.

Importing a Photoshop file with layers and layer comps

In the last exercise, you worked with a Photoshop file with saved paths and alpha channels; however, the file had only a single background layer. When you work with a layered Photoshop file, you can adjust the visibility of the individual layers. Additionally, you can view different layer comps.

Layer comps were introduced with Photoshop CS and are often used when a designer wants to create multiple compositions of an image in order to compare different styles or artwork. Layer comps are created in Photoshop and saved as part of the file; when the file is placed into InDesign you have the ability to preview the different comps in relation to your entire layout.

1   In the Links palette, click on the link for 08_j.psd and click the Go To Link button (⸱⸱⸱⸱⸢) to select the file and center it on your screen. This file, which you relinked in a previous exercise, has four layers and three layer comps.

2   Choose Object > Object Layer Options to open the Object Layer Options window. This window allows you turn layers off and on, as well as switch between layer comps.

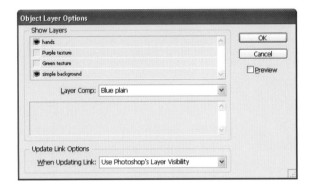

3   Click and drag the Object Layer Options window to the bottom of your screen in order to see the selected image more clearly. Check the Preview checkbox. This will allow you to view changes while keeping the Object Layer Options window open.

4   Click on the eye icon (◉) to the left of the hands layer. This turns off the hands layer, leaving only the simple background layer visible. Direct your attention to the Links palette and note that in the link for the current graphic (08_j.psd) there is an eye icon. This icon appears when the visibility of a layered document is modified by the user and is a visual cue that the default state of the graphic has been changed.

5   Click on the square next to the hands layer to turn visibility back on. The eye icon disappears from the Links palette because the image's original state has been restored.

6   In the Layer Comp section of the Object Layer window, click on the drop-down menu and choose the Green Glow option. This layer comp has a different background and the hands layer has a green glow added to it. The glow was added as a layer style in Photoshop to the Green Textured layer comp.

7   From the Layer Comp section, choose the Purple Opacity option. This layer comp has a different background and the hands layer is partially transparent. Layer comps are not merely an arrangement of different layers, but are able to save Photoshop layer styles, visibility, and position values.

8   From the Layer Comp section, choose the Blue Plain option. This layer comp was the original version of the document. Click OK.

Placing inline graphics

Inline graphics are graphics that flow with the text when placed. In this exercise you will place the album logo into the paragraph text.

1   In the Pages palette double-click on the second spread and choose View > Fit Spread in Window. Scroll down if necessary. At the bottom of the pasteboard is a text frame with the logo Orchard of Kings. You will be inserting this graphic into the paragraph above.

2   Click on the logo named Orchard of Kings and choose Edit > Cut to place the graphic into your clipboard.

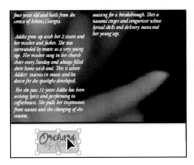 

3   Click on the Zoom tool (🔍) and click on the text frame to magnify the view; we used 150%. Choose Type > Show Hidden Characters to view the spaces and paragraph returns in the text. This will help you locate where you want to paste the inline graphic.

Note: Show Hidden Characters is not a necessary step when placing inline graphics; it is used here to help identify structure of the text.

4   Choose the Type tool (T) and click on the second paragraph return following the words "Athens, Georgia." You will see a blinking text cursor. Choose Edit > Paste to place the graphic between the two paragraphs. Notice that the text after the graphic reflows when the image is placed.

5   You will now create space between the graphic and the surrounding text by using Space Before. At the top of your screen, in the Control palette, click on the Paragraph button (¶) to switch to the paragraph formatting controls. In the Space Before property, click the up arrow to change the value to 0p4. As you increase the value, the inline graphic and following text shift downwards slightly.

Adding text wrap to an inline graphic

Text Wrap can be added to an inline graphic quite easily. This feature allows a designer to experiment with different layouts and see the results immediately.

1 Choose the Selection Tool (↖) and click on the Orchard of Kings graphic you placed in the last exercise. Hold down the Ctrl and the Shift keys (PC) or the Command and the Shift keys (Mac) on your keyboard and click and drag the top right anchor point of the frame up and to the right. This key combination allows you to proportionally scale the graphic and the frame simultaneously. You should scale the graphic until it is roughly 25% into the second column.

2 Choose Window > Text Wrap to access the text wrap options. Even though the graphic is inline, it is placed beneath the existing text.

3 In the Text Wrap window, click on the third option Wrap around object shape (⬚) to add text wrap to the graphic.

4 To increase space around the bounding box of the graphic, press the up arrow in the Top Offset option and change the value to 1p0.

5 Text can also wrap around the shape of the graphic rather than just the bounding box. To see this more clearly, click on the white pasteboard to deselect and then click back on the Orchard Kings logo, then press the forward slash key (/) to apply no fill color.

6   In the Contour Options of the Text Wrap window, choose Detect Edges from the drop-down menu. Because this image is a vector graphic, the text wrap honors the edges of the text. To view the document clearly, click on the background to deselect the graphic and choose Type > Hide Hidden Characters to hide the paragraph returns and space.

7   (Optional) Click on the Direct Selection tool ( ) and then click on the graphic to view the anchor points used for the text wrap. When using the Detect Edges option, you can always manually adjust the anchor points used to define the text wrap by clicking on the anchor points and adjusting them.

8   Close the Text Wrap palette.

Importing an Illustrator file

InDesign takes full advantage of the smooth lines provided by EPS (Encapsulated PostScript) vector graphics such as those from Adobe Illustrator. When you use InDesign's high-quality screen display, EPS vector graphics and type appear with smooth edges at any size or magnification. Most EPS vector graphics don't require a clipping path because most programs save them with transparent backgrounds. In this section, you'll place an Illustrator graphic into your InDesign document.

1   Select the Layers palette and click on the Graphics layer to target it. Choose Edit > Deselect All to make sure nothing is selected in your document. Then choose File> Place and select the Illustrator file 08_e.ai from the Lesson_8 folder and click Open.

2   Place your loaded cursor on the top left corner of page 5 and click to add the Illustrator file. Position it as shown below. Graphics created in Illustrator are transparent in the areas where there is no artwork.

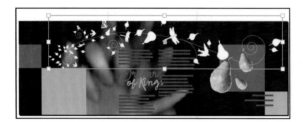

3   If you want, resize the InDesign window once you've finished importing the file.

Importing an Illustrator file with layers

If you want to import an Illustrator file with layers, you must save the original Illustrator file in layered PDF format. This will allow you to control the visibility of the layers and reposition the graphic; however, you will not be able to edit the paths, objects, or text.

1   Be sure nothing is selected by clicking in the white area of your document. Choose File > Place. In the bottom left corner of the Place window, select the checkbox Show Import Options. Select the file 08_n.pdf and click the Open button. The Place PDF window appears when Show Import Options box is checked.

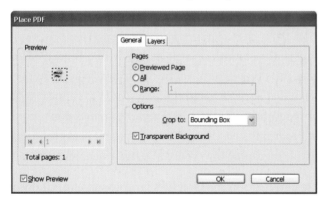

To create a layered PDF in Adobe Illustrator

You can save an Illustrator CS2 graphic as a layered PDF file, and control the visibility of the top-level layers in InDesign. Adjusting layer visibility in InDesign lets you vary an illustration depending on context. Rather than create multiple versions of the same illustration, say for a multilingual publication, you can place the same illustration where needed, and adjust the visibility of the layers as appropriate.

You can transform a PDF file as a single object (you can rotate or resize it, for example), but you cannot edit the paths, objects, or text within the illustration.

Note: Keep the layers that you want to adjust in InDesign in the top level or within a layer set at the top level. Do not place them in nested layer sets.

1 *In Illustrator CS2, choose File > Save As.*

2 *In the Save As dialog box, type a file name and choose a location for the file.*

3 *For Format, choose Adobe PDF (.pdf), and click Save.*

4 *In the Adobe PDF Options dialog box, choose Acrobat 7 (1.6) or Acrobat 6 (1.5) for Compatibility.*

5 *Select Create Acrobat Layers from Top-Level Layers, and click Save PDF.*

—From InDesign Help

2   In the Place PDF window, make sure in the Pages Section, Show Preview is selected; in the General section, be sure Crop to: Bounding Box and Transparent Background are selected.

3   Click the Layers tab to view the layers in this file. This file has three layers: A background image of trees (Layer 3), a layer of text in English (English Title) and a layer of text in Spanish (Spanish Title). Although you can designate which layers you would like to import at this point, the small Preview area makes it difficult to see the results, so you will do so in the document itself. Click OK.

4   With the loaded graphic icon (⌐), place your cursor to the left of the large blue box on page 5, do not place your cursor inside the blue box or you will insert the graphic into the frame. Click once to place the graphic and then position the graphic so that it is centered over the blue box.

5   With the graphic still selected, choose Object > Object Layer Options. Move the window if necessary so you can see the graphic in the document. Select the Preview checkbox and then click the eye icon (👁) next to the English Title layer to turn it off. Now click the empty box next to the Spanish Title to turn on that layer. Click OK and deselect the graphic by clicking on the white pasteboard. Using layered Illustrator files allows you to re-purpose illustrations without having to create two separate documents.

Using a library to manage objects

Object libraries let you store and organize graphics, text, and pages that you frequently use. You can also add ruler guides, grids, drawn shapes, and grouped images to a library. Each library appears as a separate palette that you can group with other palettes any way you like. You can create as many libraries as you need—for example, different libraries for each of your projects or clients. In this section, you'll import a graphic currently stored in a library, and then you'll create your own library.

1   If not currently on page 5, type **5** into the page navigation box at the bottom of the InDesign document window to go to that page, and then press Enter or Return.

2   Choose File > Open, select the file 08_k.indl in the Lesson_08 folder, and then click Open. Drag the lower right corner of the palette to reveal more of the items it contains.

3   In the 08_k.indl library palette, click the Show Library Subset button (🔍). In the last box for the Parameters option, type **tree**, and click OK.

4   Make sure that the Links palette is visible. In the Layers palette, make sure that the Graphics layer is targeted.

5   Out of the two objects visible in the 08_k.indl library palette, drag Tree.psd to page 5. The file is added to the page, and notice how the file name appears in the Links palette.

Note: Because you copied the Tree.psd from its original location to your hard drive, InDesign may alert you to the fact that the file is in a new location by displaying an alert icon (⚠) in the links palette. You can remove the warning by choosing the Update Link command from the Links palette menu.

6   Using the Selection tool (▸), position the Tree.psd image as shown below.

Creating a library

Now you'll create your own library.

1   Choose File > New > Library. Type **CD Projects** as the library filename, navigate to the Lesson_08 folder, and click Save. The library appears in its own floating palette, labeled with the filename you specified.

2   Go to page 3 and, using the Selection tool (⬉), drag the "ricky records" logo to the library you just created. The logo is now saved in the library for use in other InDesign documents.

3   In the CD Projects library, double-click the "ricky records" logo. For Item Name, type **Logo**, and then click OK.

4   Using the Selection tool, drag the address text block to the library you created. It appears in the CD Projects library palette.

5   In the CD Projects library, double-click the address text block. For Item Name, type **Address**, and then click OK. Now your library contains both text and graphics. As soon as you make changes to the library, InDesign saves the changes.

Note: Graphics stored using an InDesign library still require the original, high-resolution file for printing. The entire graphic file is not copied into the library, and it maintains a link to the original source file.

6   Close the Library.

Using Adobe Bridge to import graphics

Adobe Bridge is a separate application which is installed with Adobe InDesign CS2. Bridge allows you to browse your local and networked computers for images and then place them into InDesign.

1   Choose File > Browse to launch Adobe Bridge.

2   In the upper left corner in the Favorites section is a list of the various locations you can browse for documents in Bridge. If you placed the Lesson_08 folder used for this chapter on your desktop, locate the folder and double-click on it to view the contents. If you placed the Lesson_08 folder in a different location, double-click on My Computer (PC) or Computer (Mac OS) and navigate to the Lesson_08 folder, double-click on the folder to view its contents.

3   Bridge allows you to view the thumbnails of all your images. Click once on the graphic named Leaf.psd to select it. Then click once on the file name to select the file name field. Rename the file 08_o.psd and press the Return key to commit the change. Renaming files directly in Bridge can be very useful.

4   If necessary, resize the Bridge window so the InDesign document is visible in the background, then click and drag the o8_o.psd file into the white pasteboard area of your document. Click once in the document to return to InDesign.

5   Position the leaf graphic in the upper right corner of page 3.

6   Click on the 08_j.psd file in the Links palette to select it. Then select the Go To Link button at the bottom of the Links palette. Right-click or Ctrl+click (Mac OS) on the graphic in the document and choose Graphics > Reveal in Bridge. You will switch from InDesign to Bridge and the 08_j.psd file will be selected.

7   Save the file.

Congratulations! You've created a CD booklet by importing, updating, and managing graphics from many different graphics file formats.

Exploring on your own

Now that you've had some practice working with imported graphics, here are some exercises to try on your own.

1   Place different file formats with Show Import Options turned on in the Place dialog box, and see what options appear for each format. For a full description of all the options available for each format, see InDesign Help.

2   Place a multiple-page PDF file with Show Import Options turned on, and import different pages from it.

3   Create libraries of text and graphics for your work.

Review

▶ **Review questions**

1   How can you determine the filename of an imported graphic in your document?

2   What are the three options in the Clipping Path window, and what must an imported graphic contain for each option to work?

3   What is the difference between updating a file's link and replacing the file?

4   When an updated version of a graphic becomes available, how do you make sure that it's up to date in your InDesign document?

▶ **Review answers**

1   Select the graphic and then choose File > Links to see if the graphic's filename is highlighted in the Links palette. The graphic will appear in the Links palette if it takes up more than 48KB on disk and was placed or dragged in from the desktop.

2   The Clipping Path window in InDesign allows you to create a clipping path from an imported graphic by using:

• The Detect Edges option when a graphic contains a solid white or solid black background.

• The Photoshop Path option when a Photoshop file contains one or more paths.

• The Alpha Channel option when a graphic contains one or more alpha channels.

3   Updating a file's link simply uses the Links palette to update the on-screen representation of a graphic so that it represents the most recent version of the original. Replacing a selected graphic uses the Place command to insert another graphic in place of the selected graphic. If you want to change any of a placed graphic's import options, you must replace the graphic.

4   Check the Links palette and make sure that no alert icon is displayed for the file. If an alert icon appears, you can simply select the link and click the Update Link button as long as the file has not been moved. If the file has been moved, you can locate it again using the Relink button.

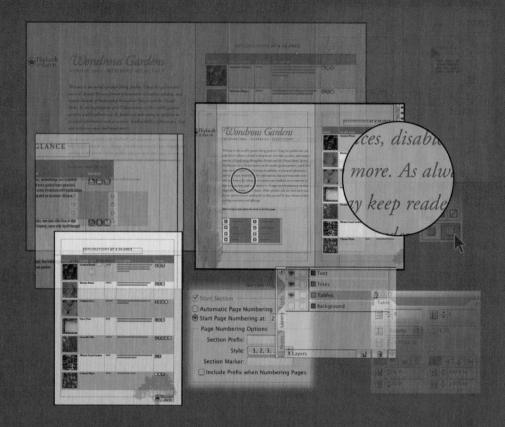

Tables are an efficient and effective
way to communicate large amounts of
information. With InDesign, you can
easily create visually rich tables. You
can either create your own tables or
import tables from other applications.

9 | Creating Tables

In this lesson you'll learn how to do the following:

- Import formatted tables from other applications, such as Microsoft Word and Microsoft Excel.

- Format tables with alternating row colors.

- Format cell and border strokes.

- Apply colors to individual rows.

- Delete and resize columns.

- Set precise column dimensions.

- Place single or multiple graphics within a cell.

- Format text in tables by columns and by rows.

Getting started

In this lesson you'll work on a fictional magazine spread that takes tables of information and brings them into the world of effective visual design. You'll develop tables using the Table palette which gives you complete control over table features.

To ensure that the tools and palettes function exactly as described in this lesson, delete or deactivate (by renaming) the InDesign Defaults file and the InDesign SavedData file. See "Restoring default preferences" on page 2.

1 Start Adobe InDesign.

2   Choose File > Open, and open the 09_a.indd file in the Lesson_09 folder inside the Lessons folder located in the InDesignCIB folder on your hard disk. This layout contains specific information about a garden tour.

Note: If you have not already copied the resource files for this lesson onto your hard disk from the Lesson_09 folder from the Adobe InDesign CS2 Classroom in a Book CD, do so now. See "Copying the Classroom in a Book files" on page 4.

3   Choose File > Save As, name the file **09_Gardens**, and save it in the Lesson_09 folder in the InDesignCIB folder on your hard disk.

4   To see what the finished document will look like, open the 09_b.indd file in the same folder. You can leave this document open to act as a guide as you work. When you're ready to resume working on the lesson document, choose Window > 09_ Gardens.indd.

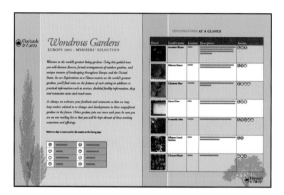

In the Pages palette of your 09_Gardens.indd document, notice that page 1 and page 2 are on different spreads. You want those pages to face each other in a single spread, numbering them pages 2 and 3.

5 In the Pages palette, click to select page one. From the palette menu, choose Numbering & Section Options, and then select the Start Page Numbering At option and type **2**. Click OK to close the dialog box.

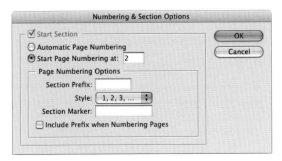

6 From the Pages palette menu, choose Keep Spread Together. If you were to add or remove pages, doing this would keep this pair of pages together.

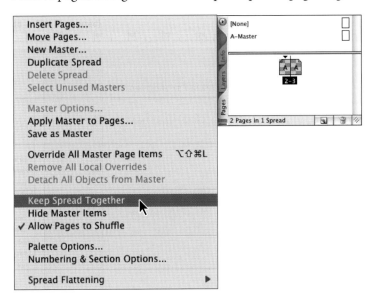

7 Open the Layers palette, and make the following adjustments:

- (Optional) Click the eye icon (👁) for the Background layer to hide that layer. This will make it easier to see guides and frame edges.

- Select the Tables layer to target it.

- Click to lock the Text and Trees layers so that you don't accidentally change them while you work on the first table.

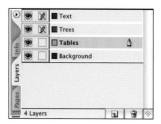

Importing and formatting a table

If you've worked with tables before, you already know that tables are grids of individual cells set in rows (horizontal) and columns (vertical). The border of the table is a stroke that lies on the outside perimeter of the entire table. Cell strokes are lines within the table that set the individual cells apart from each other. Many tables include special rows or columns that describe the category of information they contain. Typically, these are in the top row or the first column.

InDesign CS2 can import tables from other applications, including Microsoft Word and Microsoft Excel. In this section, you'll import a table that was created in Word. This table contains all the information about the garden tour that you want in your InDesign layout, organized into rows and columns.

1 Click on the Pages palette tab, then double-click page 3 to center it in the document window.

2 Select View > Grids & Guides, and make sure that the Snap to Guides command is selected, as indicated by a check mark. If the Show Guides command is available in the View menu, select it now.

3   Choose File > Place, and then navigate to the Lesson_09 folder and double-click the 09_c.doc file. If the Microsoft Word Import Options dialog box appears, click OK.

4   Move the pointer, which now appears as a loaded text icon (▦), to the intersection of the left margin of page 3 and the guide at the 1.5-inch mark of the vertical ruler. Click once to place the Microsoft Word table into your InDesign document.

Because it is a table, text wraps within the cells. You can edit text and make selections according to rows, columns, or the entire table.

The frame for the table fills the page from margin to margin, although the table itself does not cover that much space. Leave the frame in its current size because your table will grow larger as you set cell dimensions, add graphics, and format text.

Formatting borders and alternating row colors

InDesign CS2 includes many easy-to-use formatting options for tables. You can use these to make your tables attractive and easy for readers to understand so that they find the information they need quickly and comfortably.

1   Using the Zoom tool (🔍), click the upper left area of page 3 to increase the magnification to 100% or more. Then select the Type tool (T).

2   Move the pointer to the upper left corner of the imported table, so that the pointer appears as a heavy diagonal arrow, and click once to select the entire table.

Increase the magnification if you experience difficulty getting the diagonal arrow to appear. An alternate way to select an entire table is to click the Type tool anywhere in the table and then choose Table > Select > Table. If the Type tool is not selected, this command is not available.

3   Choose Table > Table Options > Table Setup. (Or, choose the same command on the Table palette menu.) The Table Options dialog box opens at the Table Setup tab.

4   Under Table Border, set the following options: the Weight as 1, the Type as Solid, and the Color as [Black].

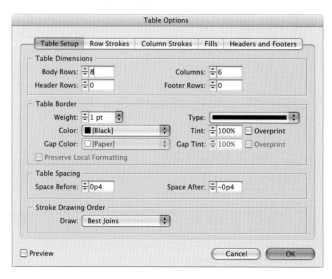

5   Then click the Fills tab and set the following options:

- For Alternating Pattern, select Every Other Row.

- On the left side, select Color as C = 75, M = 5, Y = 100, K = 0, and then type **25%** for Tint.

- On the right side, select Color as [Paper].

- In Skip First, type **1** so that the alternating colors start on row 2 (the row below the headings).

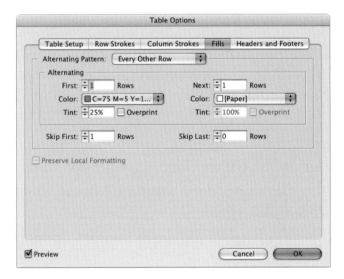

6   Click OK to close the dialog box, and then choose Edit > Deselect All so that you can see the results.

The even-numbered rows now have a pale green fill color behind the black text.

Adding cell strokes

Another way you can help your readers to interpret table information is to add strokes around each cell.

1 Select the Type tool (T) and move the pointer to the upper left corner of the table until it turns into a diagonal arrow, then click to select the entire table.

2 Choose Table > Cell Options > Strokes and Fills (or choose the same command from the Table palette menu).

3 In the Cell Stroke area of the dialog box, select the following options:

• For Weight, select 0.5 pt.

• For Type, select Solid.

• For Color, select [Black], and then click OK.

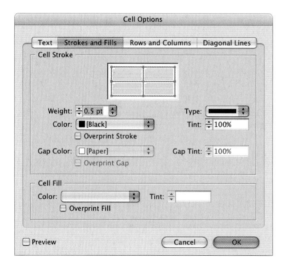

4 Choose Edit > Deselect All to see the results of your formatting.

Formatting the heading cells

Another element that makes reading a table easier is to set the categories apart from the table data. By making the categories visually distinctive, your readers are more likely to comprehend the table information more easily. In this procedure, you'll create insets so that the text doesn't run into the strokes on each cell, and then you'll give the heading row a unique color fill.

1   Using the Type tool (T), move the pointer over the left edge of the first row until it appears as a heavy horizontal arrow (→). Then click to select the entire first row.

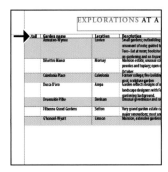

2   Choose Table > Cell Options > Text.

3   On the Text tab, set the following options:

• Under Cell Insets, type **0.075"** (or 0.075 in) for Bottom. If the Top, Left, and Right values are not already 0.05", type that number in each of those options.

• Under Vertical Justification, for Align, select Bottom.

• For First Baseline, make sure that the Offset is set as Ascent. Leave the dialog box open.

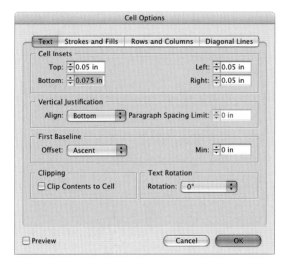

4 On the Strokes and Fills tab, leave the Cell Stroke value as it is (0.5 pt, Solid, [Black], 100%). For the Color option under Cell Fill, select C = 15, M = 100, Y = 100, K = 0. Leave the Tint at 100%, and leave the dialog box open.

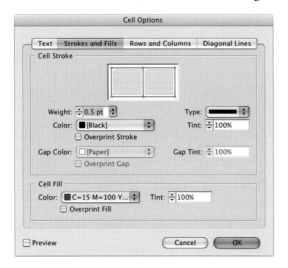

5 On the Rows and Columns tab, for Row Height, select Exactly on the drop-down menu, and then type **0.5"**.

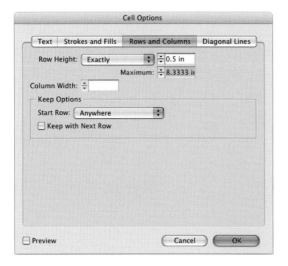

6 Click OK to close the dialog box, and then deselect to see the results of your work.

The heading row of the table now appears formatted with white type against a deep red background.

Deleting a column

After you create or import a table, you can add or delete entire rows or columns to or from your table structure. Sometimes, you'll want to delete just the contents of a cell, row, or column. Other times, you'll want to delete the cell, row, or column itself, including its contents. The techniques for these two procedures differ slightly so that you make the exact edits that you intend.

The information in the column on the far right of this table is out of date and no longer relevant, so you'll delete the entire column now.

1 Using the Type tool (T), move the pointer to the top edge of column 6 (the last column, on the right) until the pointer turns into a heavy downward-pointing arrow (↓). Then click to select the entire column.

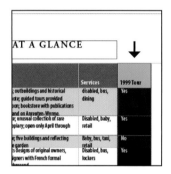

2 Choose Table > Delete > Column. Now the entire column disappears.

Note: To delete only the contents of a column, you can select the column and use the Delete key on your keyboard.

You'll find additional commands on the Table menu and Table palette menu for inserting additional columns and rows, for deleting rows and entire tables, and for selecting rows, columns, cells, and entire tables.

Using graphics within tables

You can use InDesign tables to create effective tables that combine text, photographs, and illustrations. The techniques involved are as easy as working with text.

In this section, you'll adjust your table formatting so that the cells are the correct sizes for the graphics you'll place in them. Then you'll put graphics into those cells.

Setting fixed column and row dimensions

You can define the sizes of cells, columns, or rows to fit precise measurements. In this exercise, you will adjust the size of the first column so that the one-inch photographic images fit nicely within the cells.

1   Using the Type tool (T), select the first column, either by dragging from top to bottom or by clicking the top edge of the column when the heavy downward-pointing arrow (↓) appears. Or, you can click in any cell of the column and select Table > Select > Column.

2   Choose Window > Type & Tables > Table to show the Table palette, if it is not already visible. In the Column Width option (⊟), type **1.15 in** (or **1.15"**), and press Enter. Then click anywhere in the table to deselect the column.

3   Using the Type tool, drag down from the second cell in the first column. Select all the cells except the heading cell at the top of the column.

4   In the Table palette, select Exactly in the Row Height option and type **1.15 in**. Press Enter.

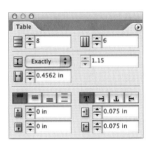

Placing graphics in table cells

To save you some time, most of the images you'll place within the table are already placed on the pasteboard of this document. In this procedure, you'll just cut and paste these images one by one into the cells of the first table column. To begin, you'll import one image that is not yet part of the InDesign file.

1   Using the Type tool (T), click to place the insertion point in the first cell in the second row (just below the "Detail" cell).

2   Choose File > Place, and locate the 09_d.tif file in your Lesson_09 folder. Double-click to open the file. If the Import Image Options dialog box appears, click OK. The photographic image appears in the first cell.

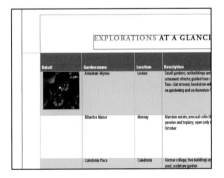

3   Double click on the page 3 thumbnail.

4   Using the Selection tool (↖), select the top photograph on the pasteboard to the right of the spread. Then choose Edit > Cut.

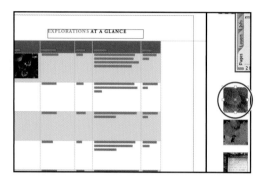

5   Switch to the Type tool and click to place a cursor in the third row of the first column, just below the photograph you placed in the previous step.

6   Choose Edit > Paste.

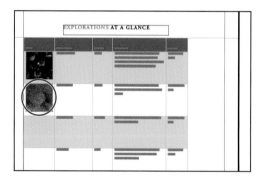

7   Continue cutting and pasting to place each of the remaining five photographs into the empty cells in column 1, proceeding from top to bottom.

💡 *You can temporarily switch between the Selection tool and the Type tool by holding the Ctrl key (Windows) or Command key (Mac OS).*

Note: You cannot simply drag items into table cells. Dragging would merely position the item above or below the table in the layout stacking order, not place the item within a cell. Tables require you to use the Type tool as you place or paste content into cells.

Placing multiple graphics in a cell

Essentially, the images you place or paste into table cells are inline graphics in text. Because of this, you can add as many images to a single cell as you need. You are limited only by the actual size of a cell.

1   Select the Zoom tool (Q), then click and drag to isolate the upper right hand corner of page 3, along with the icons located on the pasteboard.

2   Hide the Pages palette, or any other palettes if necessary, by clicking on the Pages tab, to reveal the graphics on the pasteboard of the document. Using the Selection tool ( ), select the wheelchair graphic on the pasteboard.

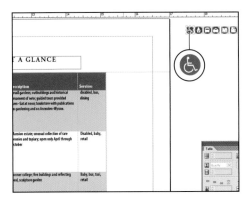

3   Choose Edit > Copy.

4   Switch to the Type tool (T), and look in column 5 for the first instance of the word Disabled. Click and drag to select the entire word and the comma. It is probably easiest to also select the space between that word and the next one.

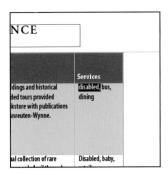

5   Choose Edit > Paste. If you selected the space after the comma, press the spacebar to add a space after the graphic.

6   Find the remaining instances of the word Disabled in the remaining cells of that column, select them, and paste to replace the text with the wheelchair graphic.

7   Repeat this entire process for each of the remaining words and icons: Baby, Bus, Taxi, Lockers, Retail, Coffee, and Dining.

Note: *If you are unsure which icon is which, select the icon with the Selection tool and then look at the Links palette to see which file is selected. The icon files have descriptive names.*

Because you haven't yet adjusted the column widths, your icons may overlap each other vertically at this phase of your work. You'll fix that in the next section.

8   Click on the Pages tab to reveal the Pages palette and double-click on the page 3 thumbnail to center the page.

Formatting text within a table

All that remains in your table project is to make some final adjustments so that the spacing of the text, graphics, and table are in harmony with the rest of the spread.

Applying character styles to text in a table

If you are already comfortable formatting text in text frames, then formatting text in tables will be an easy and natural extension of your InDesign skills.

1   Using the Type tool (T), click anywhere in the words "Garden name" in the first row of your table. Then choose Table > Select > Row.

2   Choose Type > Character Styles to make the Character Styles palette visible, and then select the Table Head character style in that palette to apply that style to the first-row text.

If some of the text no longer fits into the cells, it will be fixed in the next step. Overset text inside of cells is represented by a red dot inside the cell.

3   In the second column, click to insert the cursor before the name Anreuten-Wynne. Click and drag down to select all the garden names in that column, being careful not to include the text in the header at the very top of the column.

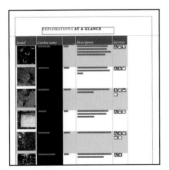

4   In the Character Styles palette, select Table Names to apply that style to the selected text.

5 Select all the cells in columns 3 and 4 except those in the first row, using the same technique as in step 3. Then use the Character Styles palette to apply the style Table Details to this text.

6 Select all the cells except for the headings of each column, using the same technique from steps 3 and 5.

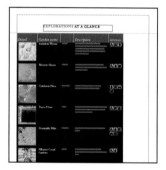

7 In the Table palette, under Top Cell Inset (▤), type **0.05"** and press Enter.

Dragging to adjust column size

When an ordinary text frame contains text that doesn't completely fit into the assigned space, the out port for the frame displays a red plus sign, indicating that there is overset text. You can solve that either by enlarging the text frame or continuing the story in another text frame.

In tables, text or graphics that don't fit into their cells are also called overset but are indicated by a small, colored circle in the lower right corner of the cell. Table cells do not support linking. Overset text must be made smaller, or cells must be made larger, if contents do not fit in a cell.

For this table, you'll resize the columns so that everything fits nicely into the table.

1   Zoom into the page by holding Ctrl+2 (Windows) or Command+2 (Mac OS) to view the page at 200%.

2   Move the Type tool (T) over the vertical line separating columns 2 and 3 until the pointer icon becomes a double arrow (↔), and then drag the column margin to resize it until the words "Garden" and "name" fit on the same line.

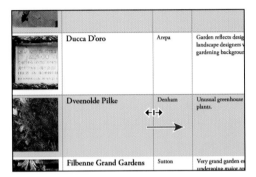

3   Moving from left to right, resize each of the columns so that the contents fit inside. Also set the right edge of the table to snap against the vertical margin guide on the right side of the page. Make sure that the last column on the right is wide enough so that all the Service icons fit on a single line, as shown in the illustration.

4   Choose View > Fit Spread in Window, and then save your work.

Working with tables within existing text frames

The imported table you've been working on is the only text in its frame. Next, you'll make a minor adjustment that affects the other table in the two-page spread. That table, on page 2, is part of a frame that includes other text.

1   In the Layers palette, click the empty box between the eye icon (👁) and the Background layer name to lock that layer. Then reveal the Background layer by clicking in the column immediately to the left of the layer lock icon (🔒). The background colors should now be visible.

2   Select View > Fit Spread in Window.

3   If necessary click the layer lock icon to unlock the Text Layer.

4   Using the Type tool (T), click to place an insertion point immediately in front of the words "As always" (about two-thirds of the way down the long paragraph). Notice the position of the table near the bottom of the page.

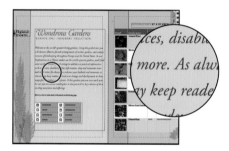

5   Press Enter to separate the text into two paragraphs. Choose Edit > Deselect All. Notice how the table moves down the page, adjusting to the new spacing.

Note: Because tables are placed inside of text boxes, their position can be changed by the formatting of the text surrounding them.

Finishing up

You're almost finished with your work on this lesson.

1 In the toolbox, click the Preview Mode button.

2 Press Tab to hide all the palettes and review the results of your work.

Congratulations! You have now completed this lesson.

For more information about working with tables, see "Tables" in InDesign Help, and Adobe.com.

Exploring on your own

Now that you're skilled in the basics of working with tables using InDesign, you can experiment with other techniques to expand your table-building abilities.

1   To create a new table, scroll beyond the spread to the pasteboard, and drag the Type tool (T) to create a new text frame. Then choose Table > Insert Table and enter the number of rows and columns you want in your table.

2   To enter information in your table, make sure that the blinking insertion point is in the first frame and then type. To move forward to the next cell in the row, press Tab. To move to the next cell down in the column, press the Down Arrow key.

3   To add a column by dragging, move the Type tool over the right edge of one of the columns in your table, so that the pointer becomes a double-headed arrow. Hold down Alt (Windows) or Option (Mac OS) and drag a short distance to the right, perhaps half an inch or so. When you release the mouse button, a new column appears, having the same width as the distance you dragged.

4   To combine several cells into one cell, select all the cells in the new column you created in the previous "Exploring on your own" exercise (number 3). Then choose Table > Merge Cells. To convert the table to text, choose Table > Convert Table to Text. You can have tabs separate what were previously columns and have paragraph breaks separate the columns. You can also modify these options. Similarly, you can convert tabbed text into a table by selecting the text and choosing Table > Convert Text to Table.

5   To create rotated text, click the Type tool inside the merged cell you created "Exploring on your own" exercise number 4. Choose Window > Table to bring the Table palette forward, and select the Rotate Text 270° option (⊢). Then type the text you want in this cell.

Review

▶ **Review questions**

1   What are the advantages of using tables rather than just typing text and using tabs to separate the columns?

2   When might you get an overset cell?

3   What tool is used most frequently when you work with tables?

▶ **Review answers**

1   Tables give you much more flexibility and are far easier to format. In a table, text can wrap within a cell, so you don't have to add extra lines to accommodate cells with many words. Also, you can assign styles to individual rows, columns, and cells, including character styles and even paragraph styles, because each cell is considered a separate paragraph.

2   Overset cells occur when the dimensions of the cell are limited and the contents don't fit inside it. For this to occur, you must actively define the width and height of the cell (or its row and column). Otherwise, when you place text in the cell, the text will wrap within the cell, which then expands vertically to accommodate the text. When you place a graphic in a cell that does not have defined size limits, the cell also expands vertically but not horizontally, so that the row column keeps its original width.

3   The Type tool must be selected to do any work with the table. You can use other tools to work with the graphics within table cells, but to work with the table itself, such as selecting rows or columns, inserting text or graphic content, adjusting table dimensions, and so forth, you use the Type tool.

InDesign CS2 delivers an array of transparency features to feed your imagination and creativity. InDesign CS2 provides control over opacity and color blendings and you can also import files that use transparency.

10 | Working with Transparency

In this lesson you'll learn how to do the following:

- Colorize an imported black-and-white graphic.

- Change the opacity of objects drawn in InDesign.

- Apply blending modes to overlapping objects.

- Apply feathering to soften the edges of objects.

- Adjust transparency settings for imported graphics.

- Apply transparency settings to text.

- Apply drop shadows to text and graphics.

Getting started

The project for this lesson is a menu for a fictional restaurant, Bistro nonXista. By applying transparency using a series of layers, you'll create a visually rich design.

To ensure that the tools and palettes function exactly as described in this lesson, delete or deactivate (by renaming) the InDesign Defaults file and the InDesign SavedData file. See "Restoring default preferences" on page 2.

1   Start Adobe InDesign CS2.

2   Choose File > Open, and open the 10_a.indd file in the Lesson_10 folder, which is located within the Lessons folder in the InDesignCIB folder on your hard disk.

Note: If you have not already copied the resource files for this lesson onto your hard disk from the Lesson_10 folder from the Adobe InDesign CS2 Classroom in a Book CD, do so now. See "Copying the Classroom in a Book files" on page 4.

3   Choose File > Save As, name the file **10_Menu.indd**, and save it in the Lesson_10 folder.

The menu appears as a long, blank page because all layers are currently hidden. You'll reveal these layers one by one as you need them, so that it will be easy to focus on the specific objects and tasks that you'll do in this lesson.

4   To see what the finished project will look like, choose File > Open, and open the 10_b.indd file in the Lesson_10 folder, which is located within the InDesignCIB folder on your hard disk.

5   When you are ready to start working, you can either close the 10_b.indd file or choose Window > 10_Menu.indd to switch back to your own lesson document, leaving the sample of the finished file open for reference.

Importing and colorizing a black-and-white image

You'll begin by working with the background layer for the menu. This layer serves as a random textured background that will be visible through the objects layered above it that have transparency settings. Since there's nothing below this layer in the layer stack, you won't change this object's opacity.

1   In the Layers palette, select the Background layer, scrolling as necessary to find it at the bottom of the layer stack. Make sure that the two boxes to the left of the layer name show that the layer is visible (eye icon (👁) appears) and unlocked (layer lock icon (🔒) does not appear). The pen icon (🖉) to the right of the layer name indicates that this is the layer onto which any imported objects will be placed, or where any new frames will be created.

2   Choose File > Place, and then locate, select, and open the 10_c.tif file in your Lesson_10 folder.

3   Move the loaded graphics icon pointer (🖉) to the upper left corner of the page and click, so that the image fills the entire page, including any margins. After you place the graphic, it remains selected. Keep the image selected.

4   With the graphic still selected, choose Window > Swatches to open the Swatches palette and select the Fill box (■). Scroll down the list of swatches to find the Lime 80% tint, and click to select it. The white areas of the image are now the 80% tint of the green color, but the black areas remain black. Choose Edit > Deselect All to deselect the image.

5   In the toolbox, use the Direct Selection tool (⬚) to select the image again, and then select the Aqua color in the Swatches palette. The Aqua color replaces black in the original image, leaving the Lime 80% areas as they were.

Note: *Remember that the Direct Selection tool appears as a hand (☝) when it is over a frame, but it still selects the contents of an image frame when you click.*

6   In the Layers palette, select the empty box to the left of the Background layer name to lock the layer. Leave the Background layer visible so that you can see the results of the transparency work you will be doing above this layer.

You've learned a quick method for colorizing a grayscale image. While this method is effective for creating composites, you may find the color controls available in Adobe Photoshop CS2 more effective for creating your final work.

Applying transparency settings

InDesign CS2 provides extensive transparency controls. You can adjust the opacity of strokes and fills applied to objects, text, and even imported objects. Additional controls for blending modes, drop shadows, and feathering provide creative opportunities to experiment with transparency effects.

In this project, practice using various transparency options on each of the layers of the menu.

Changing the opacity of solid-color objects

With the background graphic complete, you can start adding transparency features to the layers stacked above it. You'll start with a series of simple shapes that were drawn using InDesign CS2.

1 In the Layers palette, select the Art1 layer so that it becomes the active layer, and click the small boxes on the left of the layer name, unlocking the layer. Click in the box to the far left of the Art1 layer name, so the eye icon (👁) is displayed, indicating that the layer is visible.

2 Using the Selection tool (▶), click the gold background on the right side of the page. This background is a rectangular frame with a solid fill, drawn in InDesign.

3 Choose Window > Transparency to open the Transparency palette.

4 In the Transparency palette, click the arrow to the right side of the Opacity percentage, and an Opacity slider adjustment is displayed. Drag the slider to 60%. You can also type **60%** in the Opacity option and press Enter if you do not wish to use the slider to adjust the transparency level.

After you adjust the transparency, the Background layer is now visible beneath the gold frame.

5   Select the black semicircle at the top of the left side of the page. Make sure that the Fill box is selected (■) and select Lime (not Lime 80%) to apply a fill color to the semicircle.

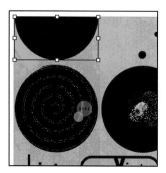

6   With the semicircle still selected, go to the Transparency palette and set the Opacity value at 50%. The semicircle now appears as just a subtle variation in color against the textured background.

7   Repeating the process used in steps 5 and 6, change the remaining solid circles on the Art1 layer, using the following settings to change the colors of each of the circles:

- Left side, middle: color = Navy, Opacity = **80%**
- Left side, bottom: color = Gold, Opacity = **70%**
- Right side, top: color = Aqua, Opacity = **70%**
- Right side, middle: color = Dark Red, Opacity = **60%**
- Right side, bottom (semicircle): color = Black, Opacity = **10%**

Applying the Multiply blending mode

An Opacity setting creates a color that combines the color values of the object with the objects below it. Blending modes give you another way to create color interactions between layered objects.

In this procedure, you'll first change the opacity and then apply the Multiply blending mode to the same objects.

1   Using the Selection tool (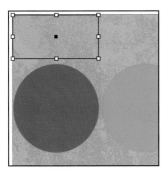), select the subtle green semicircle at the top of the left side of the page.

2   In the Transparency palette, open the blending mode drop-down menu, which currently displays Normal as the selected blending mode, and select Multiply. Notice the change in the appearance of the colors.

3   Select the black half-circle at the bottom of the right side of the page, and apply the Multiply blending mode, using the same method as in step 2.

4   Choose File > Save.

For more information about the different blending modes, see "Blending mode/options" in InDesign Help. This topic describes the results generated by each of the blending modes.

Applying feathering to the margins of an image

Feathering is another way to apply transparency to an object. Feathering applies a gradient transparency to the edges of an object, softening the margins of the object. This creates a more subtle transition between the object and any underlying images.

1   If necessary, select the faint black half-circle at the bottom right side of the menu.

2   Choose Object > Feather. The Feather dialog box opens.

3   Select the Feather check box, and then select the Preview check box so you can see the results as you adjust the settings.

4   In Feather Width, type **0.3 in**. Leave the Corners option set as Diffused. Click in, but do not change the Noise value. Notice how the margins of the faint black circle are now blurred. Click OK to close the Feather dialog box.

5   With the Selection tool (✦), click to select the gold circle at the bottom of the left side of the page.

6   Using the same techniques that you used in steps 1-4 to give the black half-circle a feathered edge, apply a **0.25 in** feather to the gold circle.

7   In the Layers palette, click to the left of the Art1 layer name, locking the layer and then choose File > Save.

Adjusting the transparency settings for EPS images

You have applied various transparency settings to objects drawn using InDesign. You can also set the opacity value, blending mode, and feathering options for imported graphics in programs such as Adobe Illustrator.

1   In the Layers palette, unlock and make visible the Art2 layer.

2   In the toolbox, make sure that the Selection tool (↖) is selected.

3   On the left side of the page, click the black spiral image, which is on top of the navy-colored circle. With the black spiral still selected, press and hold the Shift key and click to select the spiral that is above the red circle on the right side of the page. Both spiral objects should now be selected.

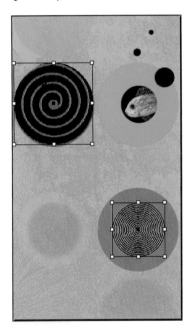

4   In the Transparency palette, select Color Dodge blending mode and set the Opacity to 30%.

5   Zoom in, if necessary, and Ctrl+click (Windows) or Command+click (Mac OS) to select the small black circle above the Navy spiral.

Note: Ctrl+click (Windows) or Command+click (Mac OS) is the keyboard shortcut you use to select an object that is positioned behind another object in the layout. It is especially useful when both objects are on the same layer, as they are in this case.

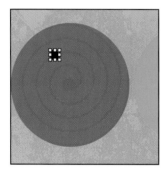

6   Set the following options for the small circle:

• In the Transparency palette, set the Opacity at 80%.

• In the Swatches palette, select Dark Red.

7   Scroll if necessary so that you can see three more small circles in the top right area of the page, and assign the following color swatches and opacity values to them:

• Top small circle: Navy, 50% opacity

• Middle small circle: Dark Red, 35% opacity

• Lowest small circle: Turquoise, 50% opacity. For this circle only, also choose Object > Feather, select the Feather check box, specify **0.21 in** as the Feather Width, and click OK.

8   In the Layers palette, click the box to the left of the Art2 layer name to lock the Art2 layer, and then choose File > Save to save your work.

Adjusting transparency for Photoshop images

In this procedure, you'll apply transparency to an imported Photoshop file. Although this example uses a monochromatic image, you can also apply InDesign transparency settings to complex multicolor photographs.

1   In the Layers palette, select the Art3 layer. Click to unlock this layer and to make it visible. You can hide either the Art1 and Art2 layers to make it easier to work. Be sure to keep at least one underlying layer visible so that you can see the results of the transparency interactions.

2   Using the Selection tool (↖), click the black starburst image on the upper right side of the page.

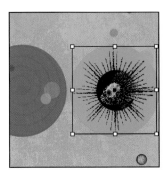

3   On the Transparency palette, enter **50%** as the Opacity value.

4   Switch to the Direct Selection tool (↘), move the pointer over the starburst image so that it changes to a hand (✋), and then click once on the image.

5   In the Swatches palette, select the Dark Red color swatch so that the red color replaces the black areas of the image. If other layers are visible below the Art3 layer, you can see the starburst as a muted orange color. If no other layers are visible, the starburst is red. Leave the starburst image selected, or reselect it with the Direct Selection tool now.

6   In the Transparency palette, select Screen blending mode and leave the Opacity value at 100%. The starburst changes colors based upon the layers that are visible beneath it.

Importing and adjusting Illustrator files that use transparency

When you import Adobe Illustrator files into your InDesign layout, InDesign CS2 recognizes and preserves any transparency interactions that were applied in Illustrator. You can also apply additional transparency settings within InDesign, adjusting the opacity, blending modes, and feathering to the entire image.

1   Make sure that the Art3 layer is the active layer in the Layers palette. Choose the Selection tool (**↖**) from the toolbox, and then choose Edit > Deselect All.

2   Choose View > Fit Page in Window.

3   Choose File > Place. Activate the Show Import Options feature at the bottom of the Place window.

4   Locate the 10_d.ai file in your Lesson_10 folder, and double-click to select it.

5   In the Place PDF dialog box, be sure that the Bounding Box option for Crop to: is selected, then click OK.

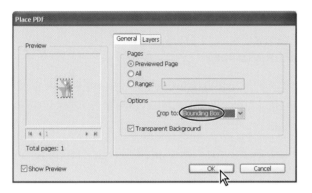

6   Position your cursor, which becomes a loaded graphics icon (🖫), over the red circle in the middle of the right side of the page. Click to place the graphic image. If necessary, drag the image so that it is approximately centered over the red circle.

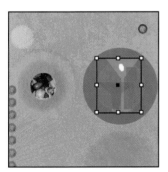

7   In the Layers palette, click to hide the Art2, Art1, and Background layers so that only the Art3 layer is visible. This allows you to see the transparency color interactions within the original image. After viewing the placed image on its own, click within the Layers palette to make the Art2, Art1, and Background layers visible. Notice that the white "olive" shape is completely opaque while the other shapes of the drinking glasses are partly transparent.

8   With the glasses graphic still selected, change the Opacity setting in the Transparency palette to **80%**. You can now see the spiral behind the white olive and that the glasses are more subdued in color. Keep the image of the glasses selected.

9   In the Transparency palette, select Color Burn as the blending mode. Now the colors and interactions of the image take on a completely different character.

10   Choose File > Save to save your work.

Applying transparency settings to text

Changing the opacity of text is as easy as applying transparency settings to graphic objects in your layout. Next, you'll change the color and opacity of some text that you will add to the layout.

1   In the Layers palette, click to lock the Art3 layer and then click to unlock and make visible the Type layer to the layout.

2   In the toolbox, select the Type tool (T). Click to place an insertion point in the text frame "I THINK, THEREFORE I DINE," and choose Edit > Select All. If necessary, zoom in so that you can read the text easily.

3   In the Swatches palette, click to select the Fill box (■) and then click to select the swatch labeled [Paper].

4   Switch to the Selection tool (↖) and click to select the same text frame.

5   In the Transparency palette, select Overlay blending mode and type **70%** as the Opacity value.

Note: You cannot specify transparency options when the Type tool is active. By switching to the Selection tool, the transparency options can be applied to the text frame and its contents.

6   Choose Edit > Deselect All and then choose File > Save to save your work.

Creating a drop shadow

You can create the impression that an object is embossed or floating above the page by adding a drop shadow. You can apply settings that soften the shadow without changing the object itself.

1   Using the Selection tool (✦), select the large "Bistro nonXista" image in the center of the page. This graphic is an imported EPS file, created in Adobe Illustrator.

2   Choose Object > Drop Shadow.

3   In the Drop Shadow dialog box, select the following settings:

• Select the Drop Shadow check box to enable the other options.

• Select the Preview check box so that you can see the results in the document as you change the settings.

• In Mode, select Multiply.

• In Opacity, type **50%**.

• In both X Offset and Y Offset, type **0.0972 in**.

• In Blur, type **0.02 in**.

• Leave [Black] selected under Color.

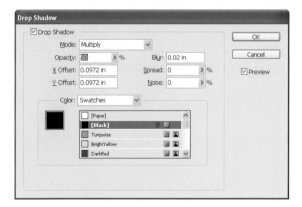

4   Click OK to close the dialog box. Then, using the Selection tool, click the text frame at the bottom of the page, with five city names. If necessary, zoom in so that you can see the text.

5   Choose Object > Drop Shadow, and confirm the following settings:

- Select the Drop Shadow check box and the Preview check box.

- In Mode, select Normal.

- In Opacity, type **50%**.

- In both X Offset and Y Offset, type **0.03 in**.

- In Blur, type **0.02 in**.

- Under Color, select Swatches in the drop-down menu and click the Navy swatch.

6   Click OK to close the dialog box.

7   In the Layers palette click to lock each layer and then choose File > Save.

When applying a drop shadow, the X Offset and Y Offset values determine the horizontal and vertical lengths of the drop shadow. Positive numbers offset the shadow below and to the right of the selected object while negative values offset the shadow above and to the left.

Note: *When you export your InDesign document as an Adobe PDF, transparency is preserved when you create a file using Adobe Acrobat 5.0 or later as the compatibility setting.*

You can download a free copy of the Adobe Reader from Adobe.com.

To see your work as it will look when printed, choose Edit > Deselect All and then select the Preview Mode button in the lower right corner of the toolbox.

Congratulations. You have completed the lesson.

Exploring on your own

Try some of the following ideas for working with InDesign transparency options:

1   Scroll to a blank area of the pasteboard and create some shapes (using the Drawing tools or by importing new copies of some of the image files used in this lesson) on a new layer. Position your shapes so that they overlap each other, at least partially. Then:

•   Select the topmost object in your arrangement of shapes and experiment with other blending modes, such as Luminosity, Hard Light, and Difference, by selecting them in the Transparency palette. Then select a different object and select the same blending modes to compare the results. When you have a sense of what the various modes do, select all your objects and select Normal as the blending mode.

•   In the Transparency palette, change the Opacity value of some of the objects but not others. Then select different objects in your arrangement and use the Object > Send Backwards and Object > Bring Forward commands to observe different results.

•   Experiment with combinations of different opacities and different blending modes applied to an object. Then do the same with other objects that partially overlap the first object to explore the enormous number of different effects you can create.

2   Double-click the Page 1 icon in the Pages palette to center it in the document window. Then try clicking the eye icons for the different Art layers one at a time, to see the differences this creates in the overall effect of the project.

3   Choose Help > InDesign Help. At the top of the left pane of the Help window, click Search. Then in the Find Pages Containing box, type **flattener**, and then click Search. After a short wait, click "To create or edit a flattener preset" in the lower area of the left pane to open that topic in the right pane. Then follow the procedure described there for creating a flattener style for exporting transparency pages to PDF.

Review

▶ **Review questions**

1   How do you change the color of the white areas of a black-and-white image? The black areas?

2   How can you change transparency effects without changing the Opacity value of an object?

3   What is the importance of the stacking order of layers and of objects within layers when you work with transparency?

4   Will the transparency effects you create in InDesign CS2 appear in a PDF that you export from InDesign?

▶ **Review answers**

1   To change the white areas, select the object with the Selection tool and then select the color in the Swatches palette. To change the black areas, select the object with the Direct Selection tool and then select the color you want to use in the Swatches palette.

2   Besides selecting the object and changing the Opacity value in the Transparency palette, you can also create transparency effects by changing the blending mode, feathering the edges of the object, or adding drop shadows that have transparency settings. Blending modes determine how the base color and the blend color will be combined to produce a resulting color.

3   The transparency of an object affects the view of objects below (behind) it in the stacking order. For example, objects below a semitransparent object can be seen behind it—like objects behind a colored plastic film. Opaque objects block the view of the area behind them in the stacking order, regardless of whether the objects behind them have reduced Opacity values, feathering, or blending modes.

4   Yes, if you export the PDF using compatibility settings of Acrobat 5.0 or later, the transparency is preserved in the resulting PDF file.

You can assemble your individual InDesign documents into multi-file books. Automatic page numbering from file to file is just the beginning. You can also create tables of contents and indexes for the entire book. Additionally, using the book features, multiple files can be printed or converted to PDF in one step.

11 | Working with Long Documents

In this lesson you'll learn how to do the following:

- Join multiple InDesign documents into a book.

- Specify page numbering across separate documents using a book.

- Create a Table of Contents for a book.

- Assign a source document for defining styles.

- Update book files after modifying documents.

- Create index references.

- Generate an index file and sort entries.

- Edit index references.

Getting started

In this project, you'll gather together a collection of several InDesign CS2 documents, each representing one chapter of a cookbook. Using InDesign CS2, you'll assemble these chapters into a book so that you can easily create common elements, such as a table of contents, index, unified page numbering, styles, and color definitions.

To ensure that the tools and palettes function exactly as described in this lesson, delete or deactivate (by renaming) the InDesign Defaults file and the InDesign SavedData file. See "Restoring default preferences" on page 2.

Note: If you have not already copied the resource files for this lesson onto your hard disk from the Lesson_11 folder from the Adobe InDesign CS2 Classroom in a Book CD, do so now. See "Copying the Classroom in a Book files" on page 4.

Defining a book

Your project will pull together six existing chapters into a book. Defining a book means that you specify the relationships among multiple existing InDesign files, including which files are included in the book and in what order they appear.

The sample files you'll use for this project are from the *Powerful Food for Powerful Minds & Bodies* cookbook.

Creating a book file

The next task is to define which InDesign files will be part of the book.

1   Start Adobe InDesign CS2.

2   Choose File > New > Book.

3   In the New Book dialog box, type **Cookbook.indb** as the filename, and save the file in the Lesson_11 folder. The Book palette opens. The palette is empty, as you have not yet specified any InDesign files to be a part of the book.

Note: An .indb file is a book file, which opens the book palette. It contains references (links) to all the InDesign documents that are a part of the book—but it does not contain copies of the actual documents.

4   In the Book palette menu, choose Add Document, to open the Add Documents dialog box.

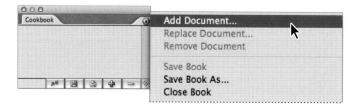

5   Open the Lesson_11 folder and select the following InDesign CS2 documents: breakfast, lunch, dinner, intro, snacks, and treats. Do not select the index and table of contents files.

💡 *To select multiple files in one step, click one of the six documents and then Ctrl+click (Windows) or Command+click (Mac OS) each of the other five files. Or, you can add documents one at a time, repeating steps 4–5 for each one of the six files.*

6   With all six files selected, click Add (Windows) or Open (Mac OS).

The six document names now appear in the Book palette. Notice that the page numbers for each chapter also appear in the palette.

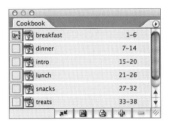

7   Examine each of the documents listed in the Cookbook book palette and notice the order of the files. The order in your Book palette may differ from the illustration above, depending on the order in which you selected and added the files.

Setting the order and pagination

The plan for the cookbook is to organize the chapters in the order they will appear in the book. The book will start with the introduction, and the meals will begin with breakfast, then lunch, dinner, snacks, and finally treats. Your next task is to organize the chapters in the order appropriate for the book, so that the sequence and page numbers flow as needed.

1   In the Book palette, click and drag the intro.indd file to the top of the list. When a black bar appears just under the tab in the palette, release the mouse. Notice that the pagination changes to reflect the new sequence of the files in the book.

2   As necessary, drag the other files into position on the list so that they appear in the following order (from top to bottom): intro, breakfast, lunch, dinner, snacks, treats.

Notice that the treats chapter starts on an even-numbered page. You want each chapter to start on an odd numbered page, keeping the start of each chapter consistent. Next you'll set the documents to always start on an odd numbered page.

3   In the Book palette menu, choose Book Page Numbering Options.

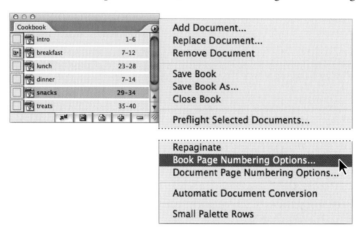

4   In the dialog box that appears, in the Page Order section, select Continue on next odd page. Also click to select the Insert Blank Page option, causing InDesign to add blank pages at the end of a document to facilitate starting each new chapter on an odd page. After choosing these two options, click OK. All chapters will now begin on an odd-numbered page.

5   In the Book palette, click once to select the intro file and then choose Document Page Numbering Options from the Book palette menu.

Note: Selecting the Document Page Numbering Options command in the Book palette menu will also automatically open the file.

6   Select the Start Page Numbering at option and type **3** so that the first page of the document appears on page 3. Then click OK.

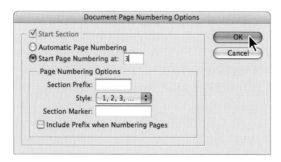

7   Choose File > Save and then choose File > Close to close the intro document, but do not close the Book palette.

Working with a table of contents

A table of contents (TOC) for a book can be a separate InDesign document, or it can be placed in an existing document that is part of the book. You can also create a table of contents inside a single document, even if you have not created a book file. Here you will create a TOC for the section titles and recipe names in the cookbook.

Adding the table of contents file

If you create a new file to be used for the book TOC, be certain to carefully select the same document-setup specifications used in the other chapters of the book, such as the page size and paper orientation. For this lesson, the TOC file has already been created for you, but it is empty and you will add the actual content.

1   In the Book palette, choose Add Document, and then locate and double-click the TOC.indd file in your Lesson_11 folder.

2   Drag the TOC.indd file to the top of the Book palette list, so it is the first file listed in the Book palette.

3   In the Book palette, double-click the TOC.indd file name to open it in the document window. At this point, this document is a single, blank page. You will now set the page numbering of the TOC to use Roman numerals.

4   From the Book palette menu, choose Document Page Numbering Options.

Note: You can also double-click the page numbers of a file in the Book palette list to open the Document Page Numbering Options for a specific file.

5   Select the Start Page Numbering at option and type **1**.

6   Under Style in the Document Page Numbering Options dialog box, select the lowercase Roman numerals option, i, ii, iii, iv..., and then click OK.

7   Choose File > Save to save the document, and then in the Book palette, choose Save Book from the Book palette menu to save the book file. Keep the TOC file open.

Generating a table of contents for the book

You will now have InDesign create the TOC listings for you.

1　In the TOC file, choose Layout > Table of Contents.

2　At the top of the dialog box, choose TOC Cookbook from the TOC Style menu. The Title changes to "Powerful Food" as the Title and other attributes of the TOC have been partially prepared for you. The Style, located to the right of the Title, changes to TOC Title. The words "Powerful Food" will appear at the top of the Table of Contents page, formatted in the TOC Title paragraph style.

3　Under the Other Styles list on the right side of the dialog box, select recipes, and then click the Add button. This places the recipe style in the Include Paragraph Styles list along the left side of the dialog box.

All paragraphs in the book that are formatted in the recipe paragraph style will be listed in the table of contents.

4　Click to select recipes in the Include Paragraph Styles list.

5　Under Style: recipes, select TOC cookbook body text for the entry style. This applies the selected paragraph style to the listings which will be created in the Table of Contents.

Because Include Book Documents is selected, all text in any of the book documents that is styled with the recipe Paragraph Style will be listed in the TOC.

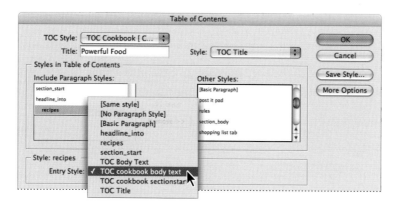

6 Click to select Create PDF Bookmarks. This automatically creates PDF bookmarks using the TOC entries. The PDF bookmarks enhance navigation of the document if you convert the book files to PDF.

7 Click OK to generate the table of contents which you will place into the document in the next step.

8 Move the loaded-text icon (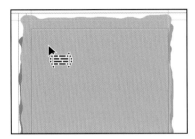) to the center of page 1, and click to place the TOC text that InDesign generated. The TOC flows into the page, showing the separate chapter names, headlines, and recipes.

9 Choose File > Save.

Note: In this file, custom paragraph styles for the table of contents were created for you. When working with your own documents, you can adjust and format the text and style definitions of the TOC entries as you would any other text frame.

If the text in the book has changed and the TOC needs revisions, open the file containing the TOC, insert the cursor in the TOC text and choose Layout > Update Table of Contents.

Maintaining consistency across book files

You can ensure that paragraph-style specifications and color definitions are consistent throughout the book, creating a unified look for your long publication. To make this easier to manage, InDesign designates one of the files as the style source document. The style and color definitions in this source document are then used in all the other documents. By default, the first file that you place in the book becomes the style source. This is not necessarily the file at the top of the list in the Book palette.

You can tell which file is the style source by looking in the Book palette. A style source icon (⬛) appears in the box to the left of the designated source file. This box is empty for all other book files.

Reassigning the style source

Designating a file as the style source is an easy, one-click process. Here you'll make the dinner file the style source file with just one click.

*   In the Book palette, click the empty box to the left of the dinner file.

The style source indicator now appears in the box next to the dinner file.

Synchronizing book documents

When you synchronize documents, InDesign automatically searches all the style and swatch definitions in the selected files and compares them to the definitions in the designated style source file. When the set of definitions in a file does not match the set in the style source file, InDesign adds, removes, and edits the definitions in the selected file so that they match those in the stylesource file. After synchronizing, all documents in the book have identical sets of styles, ensuring consistency throughout the book.

Currently, the paragraph definitions for several of the paragraph styles are defined differently in the various chapters of the book. You'll update the style and color definitions of each file using one simple process.

1   Make sure that the style source icon ( ) appears next to the dinner file in the Book palette, indicating that it is the designated style source file.

2   Holding down Shift and clicking, select these five files in the Book palette: breakfast, lunch, dinner, snacks, and treats. It is not necessary to select the TOC or intro files.

3   In the Book palette menu, select Synchronize Selected Documents.

Note: If all documents are selected, the option will be to "Synchronize Book" as opposed to "Synchronize Selected Documents."

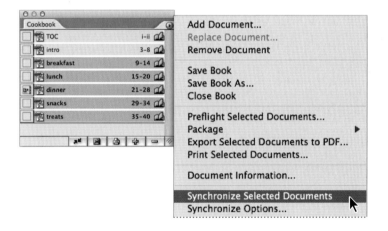

4   After a short delay, a message appears, telling you that synchronization was successful and that some documents may have changed. Click OK.

Indexing the book

Creating a good index is an art, as every reader who has tried to find a reference to a specific topic appreciates. Indexing is also a work that traditionally requires extraordinary attention to detail, with precise checking and rechecking of the entries. InDesign CS2 makes the job easier by facilitating the mechanical aspects of the process.

To create an index using InDesign CS2, you embed index references in the text. When you add or delete text, and the pagination changes, the embedded index references flow with the text. This ensures that an updated index always shows the correct page. These embedded index entries can display markers to show their location, or you can disable their visibility as you work. The index markers themselves never appear in the printed document.

You can create indexes for individual chapters, but you'll usually want to publish just one index at the end of this book, covering the entire contents of all chapters.

Creating index references

Some indexing has already been embedded in the project documents for this lesson. You'll add some index markers so you'll know how to do this yourself.

1   In the Book palette, double-click to open the breakfast document.

2   Navigate to page 10 to view the "Eggs & Fruit breakfast" recipe.

3   Choose Window > Type & Tables > Index to open the Index palette.

4   Select the Type tool (T) in the toolbox, and select the words Eggs & Fruit breakfast in the recipe title.

5   Press Ctrl+U (Windows) or Command+U (Mac OS) then click OK in the New
Page Reference dialog box that appears. The entry Eggs & Fruit breakfast is added to the
Index palette. If necessary, scroll down the list to the letter E and click the arrow to see
the new page reference.

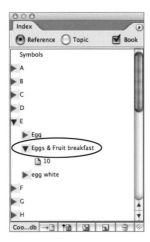

6   With the Eggs & Fruit breakfast recipe title still selected on the page, choose New
Page Reference on the Index palette menu. This adds another index reference to the
same page.

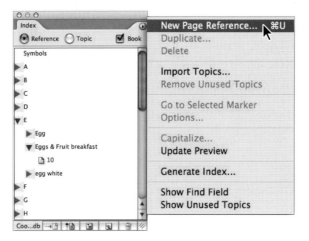

7   In the dialog box that opens, under Topic Levels, click the downward facing arrow, moving the Eggs & Fruit breakfast to Topic Level 2. Type **Breakfasts** in the box labeled "1." This creates an entry for "Breakfasts" and the specific breakfast will be listed under this heading as well. Click OK.

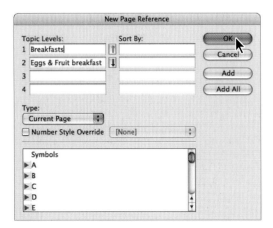

8   In the Index palette, scroll to review your new page references in the index list. If necessary, click the arrows adjacent to the letters to expand and collapse items in the index list.

Creating index cross-references

Many indexes include cross-references to other listings within the index. In this procedure, you'll add a cross-reference directing readers who are looking in the index for entries under "melon" to look under "cantaloupe" instead.

1   In the breakfast.indd file, choose Edit > Deselect All.

2   In the Index palette menu, choose New Cross-reference.

3   In Topic Level 1, type **melon**.

4   In the Type drop-down menu, select See.

5   In the Referenced text field, type **cantaloupe**.

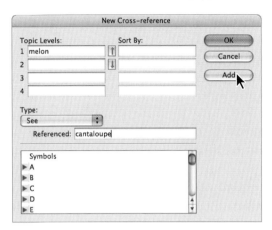

6   Click Add, then click Done.

7   Scroll down the list in the Index palette to see the new cross-reference. Choose File > Save to save your work.

Generating the index

Like the table of contents, you can place the index in a separate InDesign file or on pages of a file in the book that also contains other content. In this project, you'll put the index in a separate file.

1   In the Book palette, click an empty area to deselect all files, then in the Book palette menu, choose Add Document.

2   Locate the index.indd file in your Lesson_11 folder and double-click to add the file to the book. If the index file is not at the bottom of the list in the Book palette, drag it to that position now, so it becomes the bottom document listed in the Book palette.

3   In the Book palette, double-click the index file name to open the index document.

4   If the Index palette is not already open, choose Windows > Type & Tables > Index, and then select Generate Index from the Index palette menu.

5   In the Generate Index dialog box, if necessary, select Include Book Documents and deselect Replace Existing Index, then click OK.

Note: InDesign may require you to save the files before the index is generated.

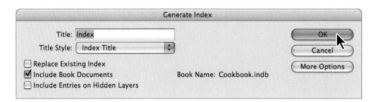

6   After a short pause, the pointer appears as a loaded text icon (📑). Move the cursor to the center of the document page. Click with the loaded cursor, and the text flows onto the page, filling all three columns.

7   Choose File > Save.

The index combines all index references embedded in the book files into one unified index.

💡 *Always use the Index palette to enter and edit index entries. Although you can edit the index directly, like any other text frame, those changes will be lost when you regenerate the index.*

Congratulations! You have completed this lesson.

For more information about creating, refining, and formatting table of contents and index files, see "Tables of Contents" and "Indexes" in the InDesign Help.

Exploring on your own

1   Open the snacks file and delete several pages. Save the file. Then update your book numbering by doing the following:

• In the Book palette menu, choose Repaginate.

• In the index file, using the Index palette menu, choose Generate Index. Make sure that the Replace Existing Index and the Include Book Documents check boxes are selected, and click OK.

• In the TOC file, select the table-of-contents text frame and choose Layout > Update Table of Contents.

In each case, notice the changes in the page numbering on the Book palette, index references, and table-of-contents references, respectively.

2   Examine the available options when you select all the files in the Book palette and then choose the following commands (one at a time) on the Book palette menu:

• Preflight Book.

• Package Book for Print.

• Export Book to PDF.

• Print Book.

3   Create an index reference for a range of pages. For example, in the breakfast file, select the word "Fruit" on page 10 and choose New Page Reference on the Index palette menu. Then, under Type, select the To End of Section option to create an index reference from pages 10 to 14.

Review

▶ Review questions

1 What are the advantages of the book feature in InDesign CS2?

2 Describe the process and the results of moving a chapter file in a book.

3 What is the best way to edit an index? Why?

▶ Review answers

1 The book feature makes it easy to coordinate related elements in a long document that consists of multiple files. By defining documents as a book, you can automate what would otherwise be time-consuming work, including the following:

- Maintaining the proper sequence of documents.

- Updating the pagination of the entire book after adding or removing pages.

- Generating a book-wide index and table of contents with accurate page references.

- Specifying options for preflight, packaging, exporting, and printing the entire book.

2 To move a file within a book, first select the file in the Book palette, then drag it to the desired location in the list of book files. After repositioning a book file, the index and table of contents entries for the book may become inaccurate. If automatic repagination has been disabled for the book, you will want to choose the repaginate command from the book palette. When you repaginate the book, update the index, and update the table of contents; all page references that involve pages that were below the moved file now change. Although the file is moved in the book, the file is not changed on your hard disk.

3   Always update index page references in the Index palette. To do this, double-click the index reference you want to edit in the Index palette (or select it and choose Topic Options on the Index palette menu), and then make your changes in the dialog box and click OK. When you finish making changes to index references, open the Index file. Then, on the Index palette menu, choose Generate Index and replace the existing index for all book documents.

It is important to do your editing in the Index palette instead of simply editing the index text directly. The reason is that any edits you make directly in the index text will be lost when you regenerate the index. If you then make changes in the book pagination, you risk having many incorrect index page references. If you edit in the Index palette, all those references are automatically updated when you generate a new index to update the existing one.

You can use Adobe InDesign's advanced printing and print preparation controls to manage your print settings, regardless of your output device. With Adobe InDesign, you can easily print to your laser printer, inkjet printer, high resolution film, or computer-to-plate imaging device.

12 | Printing and PDF Exporting

In this lesson you will learn how to do the following:

- Confirm that an InDesign file and all its elements are ready for printing.

- Generate a PDF file for others to proof your work.

- Assemble all necessary files for printing or delivery to a service provider or printer.

- Print documents containing spot colors.

- Select appropriate print settings for fonts and graphics.

- Create a Print preset to automate the printing process.

Getting started

In this lesson, you'll work on a single page product marketing sheet that contains full-color images and also uses a spot color. The document will be printed on a color inkjet or laser printer for proofing and also on a high-resolution imaging device, such as a computer-to-plate or film imagesetter. Prior to printing, the file will be sent for review as an Adobe PDF file, which you will export from Adobe InDesign CS2.

Note: Even if you don't have a printer on your computer or have access to only a black-and-white printer for proofing, you can still follow the steps for this lesson. You will use some default print settings that help you better understand the controls and capabilities InDesign CS2 offers for printing and imaging.

Before you begin, restore the default preferences for Adobe InDesign, using the procedure in "Restoring default preferences" on page 2.

Note: If you have not already copied the resource files for this lesson onto your hard disk from the Lesson_12 folder from the Adobe InDesign CS2 Classroom in a Book CD, do so now. See "Copying the Classroom in a Book files" on page 4.

1   Start Adobe InDesign CS2.

2   Choose File > Open and open the 12_a.indd file in the Lesson_12 folder, located inside the Lessons folder within the InDesignCIB folder on your hard disk.

3   An alert message informs you that the document contains missing or modified links. Click Don't Fix, as you will correct this problem later in this lesson.

When you print or generate an Adobe PDF file, InDesign CS2 must access the original artwork that was placed into the layout. If the original artwork is moved, has its name changed, or the location where the files are stored is no longer available, InDesign CS2 alerts you that the original artwork cannot be located. This alert occurs when a document is first opened, when a document is printed or exported, and when a document is checked for printing using the Preflight command. Additionally, InDesign CS2 shows the status of all files necessary for printing in the Links palette.

4   Choose File > Save As, rename the file **12_brochure.indd** and save it in the Lesson_12 folder.

Using Preflight

Adobe InDesign provides integrated controls for checking the availability of all files necessary for imaging a document. You can use these controls to preflight your file, confirming that all graphics and fonts used in the file are available for printing. You can also check the colors used in the document, including fonts and colors used in placed graphics.

1   Choose File > Preflight. The Preflight dialog box opens.

2   In the Preflight dialog box, review the summary panel that appears. InDesign alerts you to several potential concerns, noted by the yellow triangle adjacent to the information. These include:

• One image is missing.

• One image uses RGB colors.

• Duplicate spot-colors may exist.

The summary section of the Preflight dialog box provides a fast overview of possible concerns in a document. For more detailed information you can click each of the six options along the left side of the dialog box.

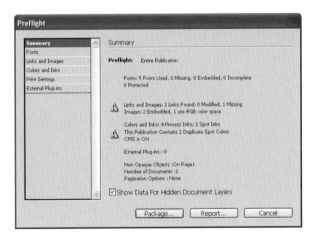

3   Click the Fonts option to see a detailed list of fonts used in the document. You can learn about the fonts used in this job and whether they are OpenType, PostScript, or TrueType. You can also obtain additional information about fonts used in this job, including:

- Whether a font is available for printing, missing, or incomplete.

- If a font is protected from embedding in a PDF by the font manufacturer.

- The first page on which the font is used.

- The location of the font file being used.

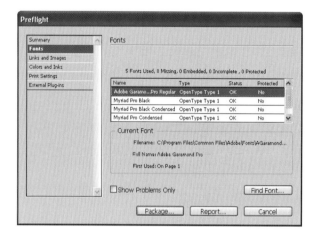

4   While continuing to examine the Fonts, click to select the Show Problems Only checkbox at the bottom of the Preflight dialog box. Notice how no fonts are listed, as all fonts are available for printing and there are no problems with them.

5   Click the Links and Images option along the left side of the Preflight dialog box.

Notice that information regarding all images used in the file is displayed. We want only to view possible problems.

6   Click to select Show Problems Only. Notice that three images are displayed as possible problems. One file, slapshot.tif, uses RGB colors. Because the document will be printed using CMYK colors, this could be a problem. The other image, blammo_logo.ai is missing and needs to be located before the document can be printed.

You will replace the Blammo logo with a revised version that includes a trademark symbol along with the logo. You will address the RGB image in the printing process.

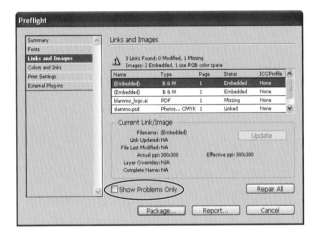

7   Click the Repair All button. Browse to the Links folder inside the Lesson_12 folder. This folder is located inside the Lessons folder within the InDesignCIB folder on your hard disk. Double-click the blammo_logo_revised.ai. The new file is now linked, in place of the original file.

8   Click to select the blammo_logo_revised.ai then click Update.

Because the file name is different, InDesign did not automatically update the image. If the selected file had not been modified since it was originally placed, InDesign would not have required you to update the link.

Note: The Repair All allows you to repair missing or modified links. It does not allow you to change the color space defined in a placed graphic. You can do this by opening the linked image in Photoshop and changing its color space or you can have InDesign convert the colors for printing.

9   Click the Colors and Inks option.

Notice that the four subtractive primary colors are listed: Cyan, Magenta, Yellow, and Black along with three variations of Pantone 2582. The C is for coated, M is for matte, and U is for uncoated. Because we will not want all three of these colors to print independently, we will want to correct this at the time we print this document.

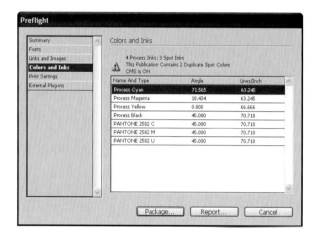

10   Click the Cancel button.

Note: You could directly package the file as the next step in preparing your file for delivery. For this lesson we have decided to create the package as a separate step.

Using Package

You can use the package command to gather a copy of your InDesign document, all linked items, including graphics. InDesign also copies all fonts needed for printing.

1   Choose File > Package.

2   Click Continue in the dialog box that warns of possible problems discovered during Preflight.

Whenever you Package a file, InDesign CS2 automatically uses the Preflight command to confirm that all elements are available and that there are no possible problems. Because you still have not corrected the RGB image, InDesign CS2 alerts you to its presence. You will convert this image to CMYK for printing using InDesign CS2 later in this lesson.

3   In the Printing Instructions window, enter the file name for the instructions file that will accompany the InDesign document and also enter your contact information, then click Continue.

Adobe InDesign uses this information to create an instructions text file that accompanies the InDesign file, links, and fonts. This can be used by the recipient of the file to better understand work you want done on the file, or how to contact you if they have questions.

4   In the Package Publication dialog box, browse to locate the Lesson_12 folder and confirm the folder being created for the package is named 12_brochure Folder. InDesign automatically names the folder based upon the document name, which you created in the Getting Started section of this lesson.

5   Confirm that the following are selected:

- Copy Fonts.

- Copy Linked Graphics.

- Update Graphic Links In Package.

6   Click the Package button.

7   Read the Font Alert message that informs you about the various licensing restrictions that may affect your ability to copy fonts, then click OK.

8   Switch to your operating system and navigate to the 12_brochure Folder in the Lesson_12 folder (located inside the Lessons folder within the InDesignCIB folder on your hard disk).

Notice that Adobe InDesign created a duplicate version of your document and also copied all fonts, graphics, and other linked files necessary for high resolution printing. Because you selected the Update Graphics Links In Package, the duplicate InDesign file now links to the copied graphic files located in the package folder instead of the original linked files. This makes the document easier for a printer or service provider to manage, and also makes the package file ideal for archiving.

Close the 12_brochure Folder when finished viewing its contents.

Creating an Adobe PDF proof

If your documents need to be reviewed by others, you can create Adobe PDF files easily and efficiently to share them. Adobe InDesign CS2 exports directly to the Adobe PDF file format.

1 Choose File > Export.

Choose Adobe PDF from the Save as type (Windows) or Format (Mac OS) drop-down menu, and for Save as (file name) enter **proof**. If necessary, navigate to the Lesson_12 folder, then click Save. The Export Adobe PDF window opens.

2 From the Adobe PDF Preset drop-down menu, choose [High Quality Print]. This setting creates PDF files suitable for output on an office laser printer.

3 From the Compatibility drop-down menu, choose Acrobat 6 (PDF 1.5). This allows you to use more advanced features in the PDF file, including layers.

4 In the Options section of the window, click to enable the following two options:

• View PDF after Exporting.

• Create Acrobat Layers.

Automatically viewing the PDF after exporting is an efficient way of checking the results of the file export process. The Create Acrobat Layers option coverts the layers from the InDesign CS2 layout into layers that can be viewed in the resulting Adobe PDF file.

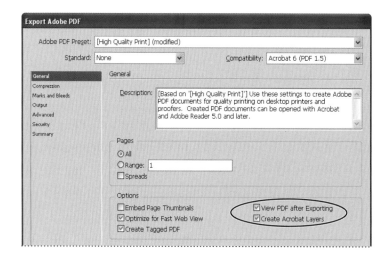

5   Click the Export button.

An warning window is displayed, informing you that some objects in the layout are on hidden layers. Click OK to close this window. An Adobe PDF file is generated and displays on your monitor.

6   Review the Adobe PDF file, then return to Adobe InDesign CS2.

Viewing a Layered Adobe PDF file using Adobe Acrobat 7

Use the following steps to view a layered PDF file created from Adobe InDesign CS2.

1 Click the Layers tab along the left side of the document window, or choose View > Navigation Tabs > Layers, to display the Layers pane.

2 Click the plus sign (+) located to the left of the document name in the Layers pane.

The layers in the document are displayed.

3 Click the eye icon (👁) to the left of the English Text layer. As the icon is hidden, so are all objects on this layer.

4 Click the empty box to the left of the Spanish text icon. An eye icon appears and all objects on this layer are displayed.

5 Choose File > Close to close the document. Return to Adobe InDesign CS2.

Separation preview

If your documents need to be color separated for commercial printing, you can use the Separations Preview palette to gain a better understanding of how each portion of the document will print.

1   Choose Window > Output > Separations Preview.

2   Click to select Separations from the View drop-down menu in the Separations Preview palette.

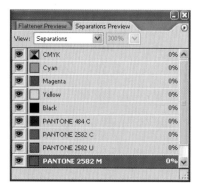

3   Click the eye icon (👁) adjacent to each of the Pantone 2582 colors to disable each color.

Notice how certain objects, images and text disappear as you click to disable viewing each color separation. Each of these objects has a different variation of the Pantone color associated with it. You will correct this later using the Ink Manager feature.

4   Choose Off from the View drop-down menu in the Separations Preview palette to enable viewing of all colors.

Transparency flattener preview

The images in this brochure have been adjusted using the transparency feature. You use the Transparency Flattener to determine how the transparency will impact the final printed version.

1   Choose Window > Output > Flattener Preview.

2   Choose Affected Graphics from the Highlight drop-down menu in the Flattener Preview palette.

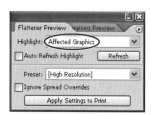

3   Choose High Resolution from the Preset drop-down menu. This is the setting you will use later in this lesson when imaging this file.

Notice how a red highlight appears over some of the objects on the page. These are the objects that will be impacted by the transparency that has been used in this document. You can use this highlight to help identify areas of your page that may be unintentionally affected by transparency and can adjust your transparency settings accordingly.

Transparency can be applied in Photoshop CS2, Illustrator CS2, or directly in the InDesign CS2 layout. The Flattener Preview can identify transparent objects, regardless of whether the transparency was created using InDesign or imported from another program.

4   Choose None from the highlight menu in the Flattener Preview palette.

About flattening transparent artwork

Whenever you print from InDesign or export to a format other than Adobe PDF 1.4 (Acrobat 5.0) or later, InDesign performs a process called flattening. Flattening cuts apart transparent art to represent overlapping areas as discrete pieces that are either vector objects or rasterized areas. As artwork becomes more complex (mixing images, vectors, type, spot colors, overprinting, and so on), so does the flattening and its results.

For your convenience, InDesign includes three predefined transparency flattener presets. The settings are designed to match the quality and speed of the flattening with the appropriate resolution for rasterized transparent areas, depending on the document's intended use. The flattening settings are used only if the artwork contains transparency or if Simulate Overprint is selected in the Output panel of the Export Adobe PDF dialog box.

Low Resolution—Use for quick proofs that will be printed on black-and-white desktop printers, and for documents that will be published on the web or exported to SVG.

Medium Resolution—Use for desktop proofs and print-on-demand documents that will be printed on PostScript color printers.

High Resolution—Use for final press output, and for high-quality proofs such as separations-based color proofs.

—From InDesign Help

Previewing the page

1   Double-click the Hand tool (✋) to fit the document to the available window size.

2   Choose Edit > Deselect All.

3   In the bottom right corner of the toolbox, click the Preview Mode button. Any guides, frame edges, or other non-printing items are hidden.

4   Click and hold the Preview Mode button and choose Bleed Mode. Additional space outside the perimeter of the final document size is displayed. This confirms that the color background will print outside the edge of the document. After the job is printed, this excess area will be trimmed, or cut off, to produce the final document size.

5   Click and hold the Bleed Mode button in the bottom right corner of the toolbox, then choose Slug Mode. The page now displays additional space beyond the edge of the bleed area. This additional area is often used to print production information about the job being printed. You can see this information below the bottom of the document in the center of the screen.

After confirming that the file looks acceptable, you are ready to print it.

Printing a laser or inkjet proof

InDesign makes it easy to print documents to a variety of output devices.

1   Choose File > Print.

2   From the Printer drop-down list, choose your inkjet or laser printer.

Notice how Adobe InDesign automatically selects the PPD (printer description) that was associated with this printer at the time you installed the printer.

Note: If you do not have a printer connected to your computer or computer network, choose PostScript File from the Printer list and choose Device Independent from the PPD list. This allows you to follow the steps in this lesson without being connected to a printer.

3 Click the Setup option on the left side of the Print window and choose the following options:

- Paper Size: Letter.

- Scale to Fit.

Note: If you selected PostScript File along with the Device Independent PPD, as opposed to an actual printer, you will not be able to apply scaling or adjust the positioning of where the file will image.

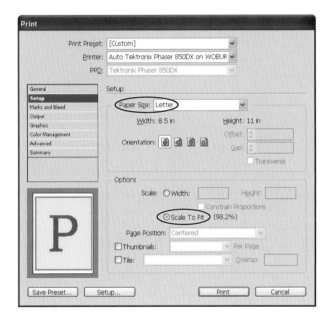

4 Click the Marks and Bleeds option on the left side of the Print window and click to enable the following options:

- Crop Marks.

- Page Information.

- Use Document Bleed Settings.

- Include Slug Area.

Enter a Marks offset value of **.1875 in**. This value determines the distance from the page where the specified marks and page information will image.

The crop marks print outside of the page area and provide guides showing where the final document will be trimmed (cut) after printing. The page information automatically adds the document name along with the date and time it was printed, to the bottom of the document.

Using the document bleed and slug settings causes InDesign to print objects that extend outside the edge of the page area. These check boxes eliminate the need for entering the amount of extra area that should be imaged.

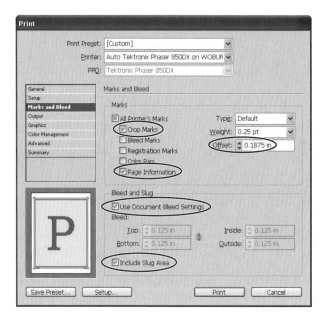

5   Click the Output option on the left side of the Print window. Confirm that Color is set to Composite CMYK in the Color drop-down menu.

This setting causes any RGB objects, including images, to be converted to CMYK at the time of printing. This setting does not change the original, placed graphic. This option is not available if you are printing to a PostScript file.

Note: You can have InDesign maintain the existing colors used in a job by choosing Composite Leave Unchanged in the Color drop-down menu. Additionally, if you are a printer or service provider and need to print color separations from Adobe InDesign, choose Separations or In-RIP separations based upon the workflow that you use.

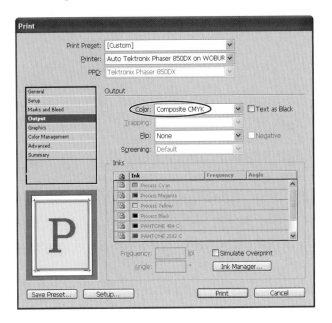

6   Click the Ink Manager button in the lower right corner of the Print Window.

You can use the Ink Manager to convert spot colors, such as Pantone colors, to process (CMYK) colors, and to manage duplicate spot colors. You will address both these issues.

7   In the Ink Manager window, click the spot icon (◉) to the left of the Pantone 484 color swatch. It changes to a CMYK icon (▣). This color will now print as a combination of CMYK colors as opposed to printing on its own, separate color plate. Keep the Ink Manager window open.

8 In the Ink Manager window, click the Pantone 2582 U color swatch and then select Pantone 2582 C from the Ink Alias drop-down menu. The Ink Alias tells Adobe InDesign to treat these two colors as if they are identical, so they will print as one color separation rather than as multiple separations.

By applying an Ink Alias, all objects with this color will now print on the same separation as its Alias color. Rather than getting two separate color separations, you will get one. Repeat this process to select Pantone 2582 M and choose Pantone 2582 C from the Ink Alias drop-down menu. Now all three duplicate Pantone colors will print on the same separation. Click OK.

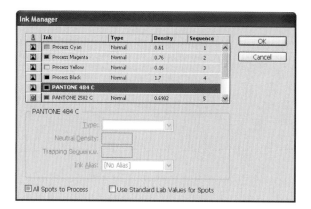

9 Click the Graphics option on the left side of the Print window. Confirm that Optimized Subsampling is selected from the Send Data drop-down menu.

When Optimized Subsampling is selected, InDesign sends only the image data necessary for the printer you have selected in the Print window. To have the entire high-resolution image information sent to the printer, which may take longer to image, select All from the Send Data drop-down menu.

Note: This option cannot be changed if you selected the Device Independent PPD.

Note: When printing to a PostScript file, this option is not available.

10 If necessary, select Complete under the Font Download drop-down menu.

This causes all fonts used in the job to be sent to the output device.

Options for printing graphics

When you are exporting or printing documents that contain complex graphics (for example, high-resolution images, EPS graphics, PDF pages, or transparent effects), it will often be necessary to change resolution and rasterization settings in order to obtain the best output results.

Choose from the following options in the Graphics section of the Print dialog box to specify how graphics are handled during output.

Send Data—Controls how much image data in placed bitmap images to send to the printer or file.

All—sends full-resolution data, which is appropriate for any high-resolution printing, or for printing grayscale or color images with high contrast, as in black-and-white text with one spot color. This option requires the most disk space.

Optimized Subsampling—Sends just enough image data to print the graphic at the best possible resolution for the output device. (A high-resolution printer will use more data than a low-resolution desktop model.) Select this option when you're working with high-resolution images but printing proofs to a desktop printer.

Note: InDesign does not subsample EPS or PDF graphics, even when Optimized Subsampling is selected.

Proxy (72 dpi)—Sends screen-resolution versions of placed bitmap images, thereby reducing printing time.

None—Temporarily removes all graphics when you print and replaces them with graphics frames with crossbars, thereby reducing printing time. The graphics frames are the same dimensions as the imported graphics, so you can still check sizes and positioning. Suppressing the printing of imported graphics is useful when you want to distribute text proofs to editors or proofreaders. Printing without graphics is also helpful when you're trying to isolate the cause of a printing problem.

—From InDesign Help

Options for downloading fonts to a printer

Printer-resident fonts are fonts stored in a printer's memory or on a hard drive connected to the printer. Type 1 and TrueType fonts can be stored either on the printer or on your computer; bitmap fonts are stored only on your computer. InDesign downloads fonts as needed, provided they are installed on your computer's hard disk.

Choose from the following options in the Graphics section of the Print dialog box to control how fonts are downloaded to the printer.

None—Includes a reference to the font in the PostScript file, which tells the RIP or a postprocessor where the font should be included. This option is appropriate if the fonts reside in the printer. TrueType fonts are named according to the PostScript name in the font; however, not all applications can interpret these names. To ensure that TrueType fonts are interpreted correctly, use one of the other font downloading options.

Complete—Downloads all fonts required for the document at the beginning of the print job. InDesign automatically subsets fonts that contain more than the maximum number of glyphs (characters) specified in the Preferences dialog box.

Subset—Downloads only the characters (glyphs) used in the document. Glyphs are downloaded once per page. This option typically results in faster and smaller PostScript files when used with single-page documents, or short documents without much text.

Download PPD Fonts—Downloads all fonts used in the document, even if those fonts reside in the printer. Use this option to ensure that InDesign uses the font outlines on your computer for printing common fonts, such as Helvetica, Times, and so on. Using this option can resolve problems with font versions, such as mismatched character sets between your computer and printer or outline variances in trapping. However, unless you commonly use extended character sets, you don't need to use this option for desktop draft printing.

—From InDesign Help

11   Click the Advanced Tab and set the Transparency Flattener Preset to High Resolution from the Preset drop-down menu.

You can choose the appropriate transparency flattener preset for your needs. The preset determines the quality of placed artwork or images that include transparency. The preset also impacts the quality of objects with transparency applied to them using InDesign's transparency feature, including objects with drop shadows or feathering.

12   Click the Save Preset button and name the preset **Proof** and click OK.

Creating a Print preset saves these settings so you do not need to individually set every option each time you print to the same device. You can create multiple presets to meet various quality needs of individual printers you may use. When you want to use these settings in the future, you can choose them from the Print Preset drop-down menu at the top of the Print dialog box.

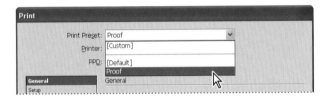

13   Click the Print button.

If you are creating a PostScript file, click Save and browse to the Lesson_12 folder, located inside the Lessons folder within the InDesignCIB folder on your hard disk. The PostScript file could be provided to your service provider, commercial printer or converted to an Adobe PDF using Adobe Acrobat Distiller. If you do not have Adobe Acrobat Distiller, you can delete the PostScript file after you have completed this lesson.

You can use absolute page numbering when working with documents that are broken into sections. For example, to print the third page of a document you can input +3 in the Page Range section of the print dialog box. You can also use section names. For more information see "Specifying pages to print" in the InDesign Help.

Exploring on your own

1 Create a new Print preset by choosing File > Print presets > Define. Use the resulting dialog boxes to create presets to use for oversize printing or for printing to various color or black-and-white printers you may use.

2 Open the 12_brochure.indd file and explore how each color separation can be enabled or disabled using the Color Separation Preview. Switch to viewing the Ink Limit preview using the same palette. See how the total ink settings used in creating CMYK colors affects how various images will print.

3 Using the 12_brochure.indd file, Choose File > Print. Then click the Output option on the left side of the Print window and examine the different choices for printing color documents.

4 Choose Ink Manager from the Swatches palette menu and experiment with using add ink alias for spot colors and with converting spot colors to process.

Review

▶ ## Review questions

1   What elements does InDesign gather when it packages a file?

2   What problems does InDesign look for when using the preflight command?

3   If you want to print the highest quality version of a scanned image on a lower resolution laser printer or proofer, what options can you select?

▶ ## Review answers

1   Adobe InDesign gathers a copy of the InDesign document along with copies of all fonts used in the document and copies of all graphics used in the original document. The original items remain undisturbed.

2   You can confirm that all items necessary for high-resolution printing are available by choosing File > Preflight. This command looks to confirm that all fonts used in the document or inside-placed graphics are available. InDesign also looks for linked graphic files and even linked text files to confirm that they have not been modified since they were initially imported.

3   InDesign sends only the image data necessary to an output device as its default setting. If you want to send the entire set of image data, even if it may take longer to print, you can choose All from the Send Data drop-down menu in the Graphics options of the Print window.

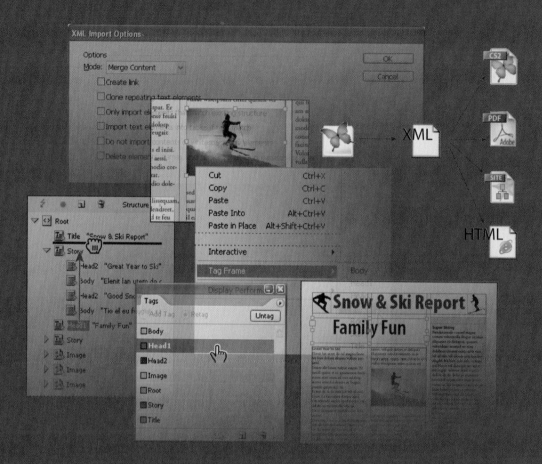

Use the powerful XML capabilities of InDesign CS2 to build and share documents for multiple destinations. InDesign CS2 supports tagging of content, including text, tables, and graphics. Tagged objects can be organized in the Structure pane and then exported as XML. InDesign CS2 lets you import XML and place it into a structure layout either automatically or manually.

13 | Using XML

In this lesson, you'll learn how to do the following:

- Import XML tags.

- Apply XML tags.

- Map styles and tags.

- Use the Structure pane.

- Import XML.

- Export XML.

Getting started

In this lesson, you'll take a completed InDesign layout and apply XML tags to the document. You'll then confirm the structure of the document, export the contents as XML, and then import the XML into another InDesign layout. Before you begin, you'll need to restore the default preferences for Adobe InDesign.

1 To ensure that the tools and palettes function exactly as described in this lesson, delete or deactivate (by renaming) the InDesign Defaults file and the InDesign SavedData file. See "Restoring default preferences" on page 2.

2 Start Adobe InDesign CS2.

To begin working, you'll open an existing InDesign document.

Note: If you have not already copied the resource files for this lesson onto your hard disk from the Lesson_13 folder from the Adobe InDesign CS2 Classroom in a Book CD, do so now. See "Copying the Classroom in a Book files" on page 4.

3 Choose File > Open, and open the 13_a.indd file in the Lesson_13 folder, on your hard disk.

4 Choose File > Save As, rename the file **ski_brochure.indd**, and save it in the Lesson_13 folder.

About XML

eXtensible Markup Language (XML) is used to distribute content, including text and images, to multiple destinations. XML separates content from its appearance on a page or in a layout. XML files use tags that identify the content in the file. Because the content of an XML file is identified with tags, it can be repurposed for distribution in print, on-line, or in some other format, such as PDF.

XML files are not dependent upon a specific layout, and can be formatted to match the needs of the viewer or viewing device. For example, an XML version of a typical brochure might be formatted to display as a traditional vertical layout when printed. The same information can be converted to a horizontal layout for on-screen viewing as a PDF. The same content can also be converted to HTML and placed onto a web page.

While XML allows for data to be presented in a variety of formats, it also has advantages for revising and customizing print layouts. When InDesign documents are converted to XML, you can easily extract some or all of the data to re-use in other InDesign layouts. For example, a single XML file can be the source for a sales brochure, a price list, and a catalog.

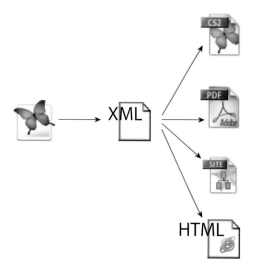

If you design web sites using Adobe GoLive or other programs, you may be familiar with Hyper Text Markup Language (HTML). While XML and HTML have similar names, and both markup languages include tags, they are actually quite different. HTML tags describe the appearance of the content in an HTML file, and how it should be formatted. Conversely, XML tags describe the content itself and do not describe formatting. With XML, formatting decisions occur when the XML is placed into a specific layout.

To use the XML features of InDesign CS2, you do not need extensive XML knowledge. To learn more about the XML capabilities of InDesign CS2, choose Help > InDesign Help. Then select XML in the InDesign Help Contents.

Viewing XML tags

InDesign CS2 uses XML tags to identify the type of content that is, or will be, placed on a page. These tags are used when XML is either imported or exported from an InDesign layout. Frames can be tagged, or specified, to contain certain types of text, such as stories or headlines. Frames can also be tagged to contain graphics. The same tags may be used multiple times within a document. For example, a document may contain multiple headlines, and each headline may contain the same tag name identifying it as a headline.

 If you regularly work with XML, you may be more familiar with XML elements. Tags applied using InDesign CS2 identify the specific occurrence of an XML element.

In this exercise you'll examine some existing XML tags that have been applied to an InDesign CS2 layout.

1   Choose Window > Tags to open the Tags palette. The Tags palette opens, displaying a list of XML tags that have previously been created with this document.

2   Choose the Selection tool (➤) and click the text frame containing the text "Snow and Ski Report" along the top of the document. Notice that the Title tag in the tags palette becomes highlighted as this frame is selected. The highlighting indicates that the Title tag is applied to this text frame.

3   Choose Edit > Deselect all.

4   Choose the Type tool (T) and click in the headline text "Great Year to Ski." In the tags palette, the tag Head2 becomes highlighted, indicating that this text also has an XML tag applied to it.

5   Choose View > Structure > Show Tagged Frames. The two text frames we've examined display a colored border and background.

The border and background color corresponds to the color of the XML tags that are applied to the frames. Notice that the Title tag is Magenta and this is the color that is displayed around the title of the publication.

6   Choose the Zoom tool (🔍) and click and drag a box around the text "Great Year to Ski" along with several lines of type beneath this text. The magnification of this area of the page increases.

7 Choose View > Structure > Hide Tag Markers. The XML tag markers at the start and end of the Great Year to Ski headline disappear. Choose View > Structure > Show Tag Markers. Markers are displayed to the left of the word Great and the right of the word Ski. The markers are purple, which corresponds to the color of the Head2 tag in the Tags palette.

> **Great Year to Ski**
> Elenit lan utem do od mag
> irit lore dolum aliquat, vull
> aessi.
> Senim alit loreet vulput au
> suscili quisci et et, quamco
> ectem nissi etum ad esto o

Tag markers are also visible in the Story Editor.

8 Double-click the Hand tool (🖐) to view the entire page.

Note: The tag indicators help identify which objects have been tagged, and these markers display only on screen, not when a document is printed.

Importing and applying XML tags

You can create XML tags within your InDesign CS2 layout, or you can import them from another InDesign CS2 document or a Document Type Definition (DTD). In this exercise, you will import several new tags, and then apply the tags to objects in the layout.

1 Select the Type tool (T) and click anywhere in the text of the sidebar titled "Super Skiing" along the right side of the document. No tags in the Tags palette are highlighted, as tags have not been applied to this text.

When the cursor is placed within tagged text, or when a tagged object is selected, the tag applied to the text or object is highlighted in the Tags palette. Because this text is not yet tagged, no tag name is highlighted. You will import several new tags, and then apply them.

2   Choose Edit > Deselect All.

3   In the Tags palette, choose Load Tags from the palette menu. Navigate to the Lesson_13 folder and choose the tags.xml file, then click Open. InDesign adds two new tags into the Tags palette: Head1 and Image. You will apply these tags to objects and text in your layout.

Note: The names of the tags must exactly match those used in your XML workflow. XML is very precise, causing head1 and Head1 to be considered different tags.

4   In the tools palette, choose the Selection tool (➤), click the text frame containing the headline text "Family Fun," and click the Head1 tag in the Tags palette. The Head1 tag is now applied to this text frame and all its contents. The frame containing the Family Fun text becomes blue, reflecting the tag that has been applied to it.

5   In the Tools palette, select the Type tool (T). Click and drag to select the headline "Good Snow" in the second column. Click the Head2 tag in the Tags palette. The tag is applied to the selected text. Brackets appear at the start and end of the selected text, identifying that the text is tagged. The color of the brackets corresponds to the color of the tag. If necessary, choose View > Structure > Show Tag Markers to display the text tags.

Note: You may need to deselect the text to clearly see the tag markers that are applied to it. Choose Edit > Deselect All to deselect the text.

6   Click and drag to select the body text that follows the "Good Snow" headline. Be sure to select the text in the final two paragraphs of this story, at the bottom of the second column. While the text is selected, click the Body tag in the Tags palette.

7 If necessary, scroll to view the sidebar in the far right column of the page. Continuing to work with the Type tool, click and drag to select the "Super Skiing" headline, and then click the Head2 tag to apply the tag to this text.

As the Head2 tag is applied, tag markers are displayed at the start and end of the tagged text. The frame also changes colors, as a tag was applied to it at the same time you applied a tag to the headline. This is because a frame must have a tag if any of the contents are also tagged. The tag applied to the frame may be different from the tag applied to the text.

8 Continuing to work in the sidebar, click and drag to select the remaining text in the third column. Be sure to select all the text that follows the "Super Skiing" headline, without selecting the headline itself. With the text selected, click the Body tag in the Tags palette.

You have completed tagging all the text in the layout.

9 Choose Edit > Deselect All.

10 Choose File > Save.

Tagging images

1   In the Tools palette, choose the Selection tool (↖).

2   Click the image of the snow volleyball players in the far left column to select it. In the Tags palette, click the Image tag so that it is applied to this graphic.

3   Click the image of the downhill skier in the second column to select it. Right-click (Windows) or Ctrl+click (Mac OS) and choose Tag Frame > Image from the contextual menu that is displayed.

You can use the contextual menus to apply tags to frames as well as text.

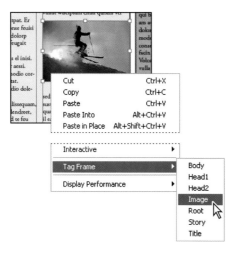

4   Repeating the process from the previous step, click to select the image of the two skiers in the third column, and then right-click (Windows) or Ctrl+click (Mac OS) and choose Tag Frame > Image from the contextual menu.

You have completed the process of tagging all the frames for content that will be exported as XML.

Viewing and organizing structure

Before exporting the document as XML, you want to confirm that the structure of the XML matches the hierarchy of your layout.

1   Choose View > Structure > Show Structure. The Structure pane is displayed.

The Structure pane displays the tags that have been applied to objects in the layout, in the sequence in which they were applied.

Note: You may need to move your Tools palette to view all the contents of the Structure pane.

2   In the Structure pane, click the triangle (▷) to the left of the Root tag. The Root tag is the highest-level tag; all other tagged objects appear beneath the Root tag. All documents must have at least one Root tag.

The Root tag can be renamed if your workflow uses a different name for its top-level tag.

3   Click the triangle to the left of the top Story tag. All the structured elements under this tag are displayed, including both Head2 tags and both Body tags.

You can see the tags that you applied, as well as tags that had been previously applied to the document. The Head2 and Body tags are children of the Story tag, which was previously applied for you. The tags are listed in the order they were applied to objects on the page, and should match the relationship of objects in the layout. For example, all related text is typically placed under the same parent tag. In this case, the Head2 and Body tags are related, so they are placed together under the Story tag. Each Head2 tag is placed before each Body tag, just as the headlines are before the body text in the layout.

4   In the Structure pane, click the menu in the upper right corner and choose Show Text Snippets. The Structure pane now shows the first portion of the text to which each tag is related.

5   In the Structure pane, click the Head1 Tag, which displays the text snippet "Family Fun." In the layout this is the highest-level headline, placed immediately beneath the title. In the Structure pane, this tag is positioned between two Story tags. As a primary headline, it should be one of the top-most items in the structure. Because InDesign adds items to the Structure pane in the order in which they are tagged, it is incorrectly positioned. Click and drag the Head1 tag up so that it is positioned under the Title tag. Release the Head1 tag when a black line appears under the Title tag. The position of the tag in the Structure pane now reflects the position of this headline in the layout.

Note: InDesign CS2 also supports using DTDs to validate the structure. For more information about using DTDs to validate structure see InDesign Help.

6   Choose File > Save.

Viewing and applying attributes

Tagged objects may also include additional information about the objects. This information which describes the tagged object is known as an attribute.

1   In the Structure pane, click the triangle to the left of the top Image tag. InDesign displays the attribute icon (●) followed by the location of the image file.

2   Continuing to work in the Structure pane, click to select the Title tag with the text snippet "Ski & Snow Report." Right-click (Windows) or Ctrl+click (Mac OS) the Title tag and choose New Attribute. The New Attribute window opens.

3   In the New Attribute window, for Name enter **Issue_Number**. Press the Tab key, and for Value enter **12**. Click OK and the attribute is added to the Title tag.

Attributes can be used to provide additional descriptive information such as the publication date or copyright status.

4   Choose File > Save to save the document.

Exporting XML

After applying XML tags to the text and graphics in the InDesign layout, you can create an XML file.

1   Choose File > Export. The Export window opens.

2   If necessary, in the Export window, navigate to the Lesson_13 folder, then choose XML from the Save as type drop-down menu (Windows) or Format drop-down menu (Mac OS). Enter the file name **snow.xml**. Click the Save button and the Export XML window opens.

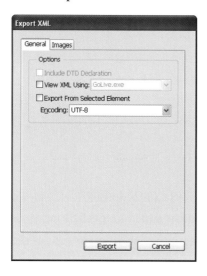

3   In the Export XML window, click the Images tab. Confirm that all the options are unchecked.

When exporting XML from InDesign CS2, you can have images from the layout copied or moved into the same folder as the XML file by selecting the options under the Copy to Images Sub-folder section of this window. This allows for images that have been tagged to be re-used in other print or web layouts. Because you will be working with the XML file using the same computer that extracted the XML, none of these options is necessary.

4   Click the Export button. The XML file is generated. Keep this document open, as you will return to work in it later in this lesson.

Importing XML

Next you will open an existing InDesign layout that already includes XML tags, and you will import XML that was created in the previous exercise.

1   Choose File > Open, and open the 13_b.indd file in the Lesson_13 folder, on your hard disk.

2   Choose File > Save As, rename the file **online_brochure.indd**, and save it in the Lesson_13 folder.

3   Choose View > Structure > Show structure. The Structure pane is displayed.

4   In the Structure pane, click the triangle to the left of the Root tag. All the tags that have been applied to objects in this document are displayed.

Note: The top-level structure of the online brochure matches the structure used in the original print layout.

5   Choose File > Import XML. The Import XML window opens.

In the Import XML window, choose Show XML Import Options and click to select the Merge Content radio button. Click to select the snow.xml file, then click the Open button. The XML Import Options window opens.

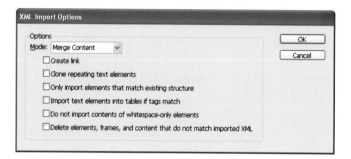

6   In the XML Import Options window, confirm the Mode drop-down menu is set to Merge content and deselect all the check boxes so that all the options are unchecked, and click OK. The XML is imported into the horizontal layout designed for on-screen viewing.

All the text and graphics which were tagged in the original document are flowed into their new layout. The text will be formatted in the next section of this lesson.

Appending vesus merging XML

When importing XML, you can either append or merge the XML content into your document. Appending adds the new XML content to your document, leaving the existing structure and content unchanged. Merging replaces existing content and, depending on the options you select, adds new content where it finds no equivalent elements. You merge XML into a document in the following situations:

- The document contains placeholder frames that you want to fill with the incoming XML file.

- The document contains XML that you want to replace with the incoming XML file.

- The document doesn't contain any XML structure, and you want InDesign to replace the default root with the root of the incoming XML file.

XML import options

When importing XML files using the Merge Content option, the XML Import Options dialog box has the following options:

Create link—InDesign creates a link to the XML file and lists the XML file in the Links palette. If the XML file changes, the modified link icon is displayed and you can update the XML file just as you would any other linked item in your layout.

Clone repeating text elements—Replicates the formatting applied to tagged placeholder text for any repeating content. The tags and structure of the XML content must match the tags and structure in the placeholder text. Use this option when importing content with multiple items that all have the same structure, such as a list of names and addresses, or products and prices.

Only import elements that match existing structure—Filters the imported XML content to include only elements that match the tags and structure in the Structure pane.

Import text elements into tables if tags match—Imports elements into a table if the tags match the tags applied to the placeholder table and its cells. Use this option to place database records into a table, for example, when generating price lists or inventory sheets.

Do not import contents of whitespace-only elements—Leaves any existing content in place if the matching XML content contains only whitespace (such as a return or tab character). Use this option if you've included text between elements that you want preserved. For example, when laying out recipes generated from a database, you might add labels, such as "Ingredients" and "Instructions." As long as the parent element that wraps each recipe contains only whitespace, InDesign leaves the label in place.

Delete elements, frames, and content that do not match imported XML—Removes elements that don't have matches in the XML file from the Structure pane and from the layout. For example, when importing names and addresses, you might have placeholder text for an element containing the company name. If one of the names doesn't include the company element, InDesign deletes the element containing the placeholder text.

Mapping tags to style

Now that you have imported XML into the document, you will format and style the text. Because the document is structured with tags, you will automate the process of formatting by establishing a relationship between the tags and styles.

1 In the Structure pane, click the menu option in the upper right corner and choose Map Tags to Styles. The Map Tags to Styles window opens.

2 In the Map Tags to Styles window, click the Map By Name button. Because this document already includes paragraph styles with names that are identical to the XML tags, InDesign CS2 can apply styles to this text. Keep the Map Tags to Styles window open.

3 Click the Preview checkbox. The tagged text becomes formatted as the Paragraph styles are applied to it. Click OK.

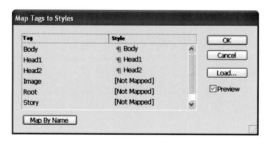

4 Choose File > Save.

Using XML snippets

A snippet is an XML file that is a full representation of InDesign content, including page items and any XML structure applied to those page items. A snippet lets you reuse the content, formatting, tags, and structure of a document. You can store snippets in an Object library, and place them in other documents. Use snippets to easily reuse objects—even those with complex formatting.

1　Choose Window > ski_brochure.indd to switch to the original document you worked on earlier in this lesson.

2　Choose the Selection tool (▶), and click anywhere on the document.

3　Choose View > Fit Page in Window.

4　Arrange your application window (Windows) or document window (Mac OS) so that you can see both your desktop and the InDesign layout.

5　Click to select the outline image of the snowboarder to the left of the headline. The outline of the skier and the arc across the top of the page all become selected, as they are part of a group.

6　Click and drag the two images and arc to the desktop of your computer. An icon appears on the desktop with a name that begins as Snippet. This XML snippet file includes all the information necessary to reproduce these images in another InDesign layout.

7　Choose Window > online_brochure.indd. If necessary, arrange your InDesign windows so that you can see both the snippet file you dragged to your desktop as well as the InDesign layout.

8   Click and drag the snippet file from your desktop onto your layout. The images and the arc are imported into the document.

Snippets retain the x and y coordinates of the original objects, making them perfect for objects that need to be reused in multiple versions of an identical document. In this case, we are using a different sized layout, so we'll move the images.

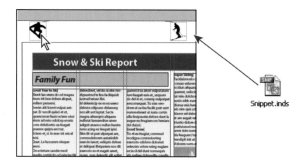

Snippet.inds

9   Click and drag the outline image of the snowboarder and position it to the left of the Snow & Ski Report headline text.

10   Choose File > Save.

Congratulations. You have completed this lesson.

Exploring on your own

1   Explore the Structure pane by right-clicking (Windows) or Ctrl+clicking (Mac OS) the various tags. Examine the options available in the Structure pane menu.

2   Apply XML tags to your own document and export the XML. Practice importing the XML into another InDesign layout.

3   Import XML into an InDesign layout and map the tags to InDesign styles used in the document, formatting the XML text.

Review

▶ **Review questions**

1   How and why are XML tags used in InDesign CS2?

2   What steps are necessary before an InDesign CS2 layout can be exported as XML?

3   What is the Structure pane, and what role does it play in exporting or importing XML?

▶ **Review answers**

1   XML tags are applied to content in an InDesign CS2 layout, including text, graphics and frames. Tags describe the content, allowing for it to be exported as XML. Additionally, tagged frames can have XML imported into them.

2   Prior to exporting an InDesign CS2 layout as XML, all objects that will be a part of the XML must be tagged. Additionally, the sequence of the XML tags must be verified in the Structure pane, and any attributes necessary must be added in the Structure pane.

3   The Structure pane provides a listing of all tagged objects used in an InDesign CS2 layout. It is used to import, manage and export XML. It is used to organize the hierarchy of tagged objects, apply attributes, and establish the relationship between tags and styles.

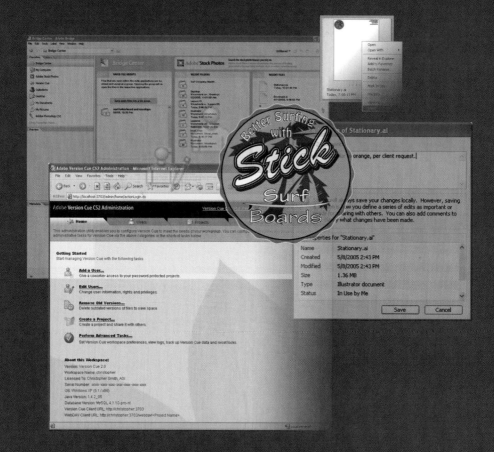

Adobe Bridge provides powerful tools for locating, previewing, and organizing your files.

If you use Adobe InDesign as a part of the Adobe Creative Suite 2, you can take advantage of Version Cue to help manage your files.

14 | Working with Adobe Bridge and Version Cue

In this lesson, you'll learn how to do the following:

- Use Adobe Bridge to access and organize files.

- Save files as groups.

- Set up a Version Cue project.

- Create and use file versions.

Note: This lesson is for users who have installed Adobe InDesign as part of Adobe Creative Suite 2. If you use Adobe Creative Suite 2, you have access to the full set of Version Cue features discussed in this lesson, including Version Cue Administration. If you use only InDesign CS2, you have access to the features of the Adobe dialog box only. You can use Bridge, rather than the Adobe dialog box, for file browsing. If you don't have Adobe Creative Suite 2, you can gain access to the full Version Cue feature set by participating in a shared project; that is, if another user on your network installs Adobe Creative Suite 2 and gives you access to a Version Cue project in a Version Cue Workspace.

Getting started

In this lesson, you'll use the Adobe Bridge to locate and access Adobe InDesign files. You will then create a Version Cue project and create multiple versions using Version Cue.

1 Start Adobe InDesign CS2.

2 Start Adobe Bridge by doing either one of the following:

- Choose File > Browse from within Adobe InDesign CS2.

- Click the Go to Bridge button (⬚) in the Control palette.

The Adobe Bridge application starts, and a new window opens.

Using Adobe Bridge

The new Adobe Bridge provides a convenient, central location for accessing and managing your files and projects. With Adobe Bridge, you can easily locate, preview, and group your project files. Adobe Bridge also provides access to Version Cue's file tracking and organization tools.

Navigating and viewing files

1 Click Bridge Center in the upper left corner of the Bridge window, located under the Favorites tab. The Bridge Center window is displayed.

Use Bridge Center to easily access the Creative Suite 2 documents you've most recently accessed, including those from InDesign, Illustrator, and Photoshop. These are saved in the Recent Folders and Recent Files sections of this window.

2 Click the Folders tab in the upper left corner of the Bridge window, and navigate to locate the Lesson_14 folder that you copied to your computer. In the Folders tab, click to select the Lesson_14 folder.

All the files in this folder are displayed.

Adobe Bridge provides previews of all Creative Suite 2 documents, including multi-page PDF files.

3 Click once to select the envelope file. Adobe Bridge displays a larger preview of the selected file beneath the Folders tab, along the left side of the Bridge window. Additional information is displayed in the lower left corner of the window.

Keep the envelope.indd file selected.

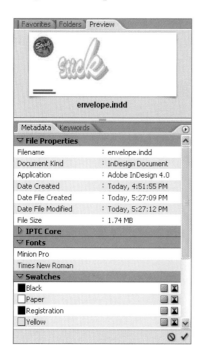

4 Press the Shift key and then click to select the stationery.indd file. Both the envelope and stationery files should remain selected.

5 Choose File > Open to open both files using Adobe InDesign CS2.

You can use Adobe Bridge to locate and open your files. Keep the two files open.

Saving file groups

1 Click Adobe Bridge in your Taskbar (Windows) or Launcher (Mac OS) to return to Adobe Bridge.

2 Click the Favorites Tab in the upper left corner, then click Bridge Center. In Bridge Center, click Save open files into a file group, located under the Saved File Groups section, in the center portion of the window.

In the Adobe Bridge window that opens, enter the name **surf letterhead and envelope** and click OK. All open files in Creative Suite 2 applications are then saved as a file group. If you were to return to InDesign, you would see that both the files you had previously opened are now closed.

3   In Bridge Center, click once to select the Surf letterhead and envelope group you created in the previous step, and click Open this file group. All the files in the file group are reopened. In this case, both InDesign files reopen.

Working with Version Cue

If you own Adobe Creative Suite Standard or Premium, you can take advantage of Adobe Version Cue, an integrated workflow feature designed to help you be more productive by saving you, and others you work with, valuable time.

With Version Cue, you can easily create, manage, and find different versions of your project files. If you collaborate with others, you and your team members can share project files in a multi-user environment that protects content from being accidentally overwritten. You can also maintain descriptive comments with each file version, search embedded file information to quickly locate files, and work with robust file-management features while working directly within each application.

Note: The Version Cue workspace is a feature of Adobe Creative Suite 2. If you purchased Adobe GoLive CS2, Adobe Illustrator CS2, Adobe InCopy CS2, Adobe InDesign CS2, or Adobe Photoshop CS2 separately, and don't own Adobe Creative Suite, you can use the Version Cue feature in your Adobe CS2 application only if an owner of Adobe Creative Suite gives you network access to their Version Cue workspace.

If you previously installed Version Cue, it must be turned on. Open the Adobe Version Cue preferences from the Control Panel (Windows) or System Preferences (Mac OS), and choose On from the Version Cue drop-down menu. Click Apply Now.

Creating a new project and adding files

1 In Adobe InDesign CS2, click the Go to Bridge button () in the Control palette. In Adobe Bridge, choose Tools > Version Cue > New Project.

• For Project Location, choose the default workspace on your computer.

• For Project Name, enter **Surf Company Identity**.

• For Project Info, enter **Create new logo and supporting materials for surf company**.

Click OK.

New Project creates a location where you can store and track all the documents for a particular project. You can drag items into the project from your operating system folders, or you can save directly to the project from within your Creative Suite 2 applications.

2 Return to Adobe InDesign and choose File > Save As. In the Save As dialog box, click the Use Adobe Dialog button in the lower left corner.

3 In the Save As dialog box, click Version Cue along the left side and double-click to open the Surf Company identity in the right side of the dialog box. Click the Save button.

A version of the file is now saved in Version Cue in the Surf Company Identity project.

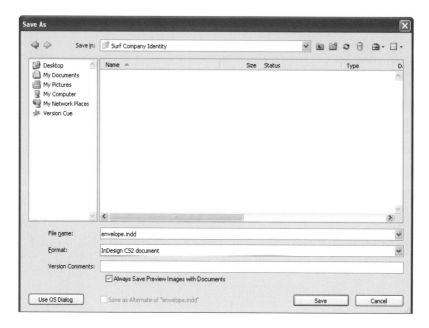

Note: If Version Cue is not available in your Save As dialog box, you may need to enable the Version Cue preference in Adobe InDesign CS2. In InDesign CS2, choose Edit > Preferences > File Handling (Windows) or InDesign > Preferences > File Handling (Mac OS). Select Enable Version Cue, and click OK.

4 Close the envelope file by choosing File > Close. Keep Adobe InDesign CS2 open.

You can also add files into a Version Cue project by dragging them into the Version Cue window directly from the operating system.

5 In the stationery.indd file, repeat the process used in the previous step, using the Save As command to save a copy of this file into the Surf Company Identity project in Version Cue.

6 In the stationery.indd file, choose the Direct Selection tool (↖). Click to select the background of the logo, positioned in the upper left corner of the stationery.

7   In the Swatches palette, click the Fill box and choose the color orange, replacing the brown gradient in the logo.

8   Choose File > Save a Version. The Save a Version dialog box opens. In the dialog box, enter **Changed logo color to orange, per client request**. Click the Save button. An alternate version of the original file is saved.

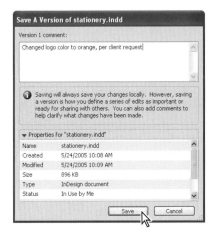

Working with file versions

File versioning with Version Cue ensures that no one overwrites the work of anyone else in a Version Cue project, but also prevents users from locking out others who need to work on the same file. You can use versioning to seamlessly retain multiple states of a single file as you work on it, in case you need to restore the file to a previous version. You can also use versioning to quickly compare file versions with team members or with a client before selecting a final version.

1   Click the Go to Bridge button (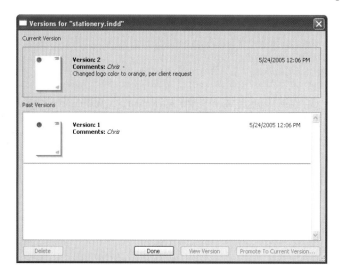) in the Control palette, then click the Version Cue icon in the Favorites tab on the left side of the window.

2   Double-click to open the Surf Company Identity project folder. Move your cursor over the stationery file and pause, waiting for the Tool Tip to appear. Note that the Tool Tip indicates that the file has two versions.

3   Right-click (Windows) or Ctrl+click (Mac OS) on the stationery icon, and choose Versions from the context menu. The Versions window opens.

4   Click the icon for Version 1 and click Promote to Current Version. In the dialog box that opens, click OK to confirm your decision. The Save a Version window opens. In the Save a Version window, enter **Client liked original design better** in the comment section, then click Save.

Bridge now displays the current version. Other versions can be viewed at any time by choosing the Versions command.

💡 *You can also view versions of a document by clicking the Versions and alternates view icon in the lower right corner of the document window.*

Version Cue Workspace Administration

By default, you can easily share your Version Cue projects with your peers by choosing the Share this project with others option when creating the project. If your environment requires a more secure workflow, you can set up a controlled environment in which users have to log in before accessing your Version Cue projects. Using the Version Cue Workgroup Administration utility, you can set up user IDs and define their project privileges, remove file locks, edit Version Cue Workspace preferences, and perform other project and workspace maintenance.

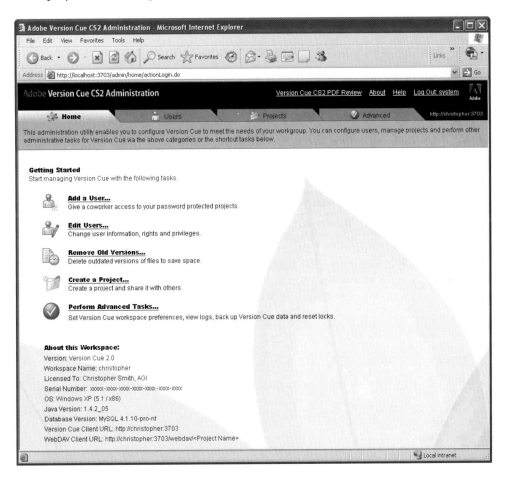

To display the Version Cue Workspace Administration utility log-in page, open the Adobe Version Cue preferences from the Control Panel (Windows) or System Preferences (Mac OS) on the computer where the Version Cue workspace is located, and click Advanced Administration.

For a more complete look at Bridge, Version Cue, and all the Creative Suite 2 features, choose Help > Version Cue Help. *Adobe Creative Suite 2 Classroom in a Book* also provides a step-by-step guide to using the Creative Suite 2 tools and resources that enhance your ability to collaborate and manage your files and projects.

Organizing and locating files

Adobe Creative Suite 2 applications let you enter a wide variety of information about your documents in the File Info dialog box and in Adobe Bridge. Information added in the File Info dialog box gets embedded into a document as XMP metadata. For example, the metadata might contain a document's title, copyright, keywords, description, properties, author, and origin. Also, any comments you add to each file version when using Version Cue, which is discussed later in this lesson, are included in the file's metadata.

1   Open Adobe Bridge, and click Version Cue under the Favorites tab in the upper left corner of the window.

2   Double-click to open the Surf Company Identity project folder. All the items that are a part of this project are displayed.

3   Locate the stationery.indd file and right-click (Windows) or Ctrl+click (Mac OS) and from the context menu, choose Label > Red. An Adobe Bridge warning message may appear, indicating that the label information is stored as part of the document metadata. Click OK to close the dialog box. A red label band appears along the bottom of the document. Keep the stationery.indd file selected.

Note: If the stationery file is still open, you will not be able to change the label. If the context menu for the stationery file does not display the Label option, you can perform this and the next step using the envelope file instead.

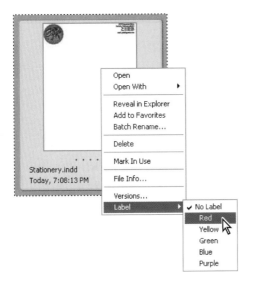

4   Choose Label > ✱✱✱. An Adobe Bridge warning message may appear, indicating that the label information is stored as part of the document metadata. Click OK to close the dialog box. Three stars appear inside of the red label band along the bottom of the document.

You can use color and star labels to help identify and locate your files.

Note: The Label menu provides additional choices not available under the context menu.

5   Click the Unfiltered drop-down menu in the upper right corner of the Adobe
Bridge window. Choose Show Red Label. Only the item labeled as red is displayed.
The drop-down menu in the upper right corner now indicates that the view is being
filtered—it is showing only selected items. Click the Filtered drop-down menu and
choose Show All Items.

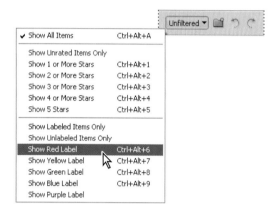

You can also use the Find command available in Adobe Bridge to locate files based
upon their name, label, or other metadata. In Adobe Bridge, choose Edit > Find and
enter the search criteria you wish to use.

Congratulations. You have finished the lesson.

Exploring on your own

Create your own Version Cue project. Add files to the project, create multiple versions
and alternates of the files in the project.

Open Adobe Bridge, then add files to the Favorites section. Label additional files using
colors and stars.

Review

▶ **Review questions**

1 What type of files can be accessed using Adobe Bridge?

2 What are the advantages of using Version Cue?

3 Do all participants in a Version Cue workflow need to have Adobe Creative Suite 2?

▶ **Review answers**

1 Adobe Bridge allows you to access all the files that you can normally access through your computer, including files stored on other computers or servers. Additionally, you can use Adobe Bridge to access files that are part of Version Cue projects that are either on your computer or on other computers if the project has been shared.

2 Version Cue provides immediate access to multiple variations of files. When files are part of a Version Cue project, the original design remains safe, as each subsequent revision does not overwrite the original file. Version Cue projects can easily be set up for sharing among other users of Adobe Creative Suite 2 applications.

3 Users of individual Adobe Creative Suite 2 applications can still participate in Version Cue projects, provided that the project has been set up for sharing. This applies to users of Photoshop, Illustrator, InDesign, GoLive, and Acrobat.

Index

A

Adobe Acrobat
    exporting to PDF 398
Adobe Bridge 8, 15, 240, 295,
    325, 432-437, 442-445
Adobe GoLive1, 415, 437, 460
Adobe Illustrator
    on-screen display of 304
Adobe Photoshop
    color management 214, 239
    paths, 295
Adobe Training and Certification
    Programs 6
Align to Baseline Grid button,
    188, 190
aligning
    text 19, 155, 188
alpha channels 305, 308-314, 327
arranging objects 95, 107, 125

B

background, removing 305
baseline grid 83, 185-190, 192,
    210
bleeds 129, 403
blending modes 353, 356, 358-
    359, 364, 369-370
Book Page Numbering Options
    376
Book palette 374-377, 380-382,
    385, 387-388
bounding boxes 113, 117, 125
bringing objects forward
    See arranging objects

C

cell options (tables) 336-337
cell strokes (tables) 332, 336
center point 108, 115-117, 124,
    126, 133, 137, 139, 177
Center-Justified tab button 204
chapters 373-377, 381-382
Character palette 33, 86, 110,
    174, 181, 209
character styles 34-35, 263, 269-
    270, 272-274, 277-278, 284,
    345-346, 351
Character Styles palette 270, 272-
    273, 277, 345-346
Clipping Path command 305, 310
clipping paths 295, 305, 308, 312
Color box 49-50
Color Dodge blending mode 361
color management
    Adobe Illustrator 214, 239,
    253
    Adobe Photoshop 214, 239
    color-lookup tables 247
    imported graphics 245
    profiles. See ICC profiles
    rendering intents 238
    separations profile 242, 248
color management engine 213,
    236-240, 244, 260
color matching module 238
color space 236-237, 239, 243,
    246-247, 251-252, 260-261,
    395
colorizing 355-356

colors

    adding to Swatches palette
    216
    applying to objects 217
    applying to text 228
    device-independent 236-237
    out-of-gamut 236, 238
    Paper 259, 335, 366
    process 28, 212, 216, 236, 259-
    260, 358, 391, 395, 405-406,
    410
    spot 212-213, 227-228, 260,
    391, 405, 410
    unnamed 216
columns, changing 158
columns (tables)
    deleting 339
    dimensions 338
composing text 201
context menus 28, 45, 68, 122,
    130
continuation notes 162-163
Control palette 29, 191
copying
    frames 114, 143
    lesson files 4
    objects 353
Create Guides command 80
creating
    book files 75, 214, 380, 386
    character styles 34, 269-270,
    274, 277-278
    index references 382, 386
    object libraries 324
    tables 207, 270, 280, 329, 382,
    386
cropping images 37, 41, 303
crossed-out pencil icon, 67-68
cross-references (indexes) 384

Production Notes

The *Adobe InDesign CS2 Classroom in a Book* was created electronically using Adobe InDesign. Additional art was produced using Adobe Illustrator and Adobe Photoshop.

A special thank you to Dr. Rene Thomas for the use of her recipes from her *Natures Mighty Bites Cookbook* for use in Lesson 11. Also, thanks to istockphoto.com for supplying photographic images in many of the lessons. Other references to company names in the lessons are for demonstration purposes only.

Team credits

The following individuals contributed to the development of new and updated lessons for this edition of the *Adobe InDesign CS2 Classroom in a Book*:

Project coordinator, technical writer: Christopher G. Smith

Additional technical writing: Greg Heald, Jeremy Osborn, Jennifer M. Smith, Greg Urbaniak

Production: AGI Training: Elizabeth Chambers

Artwork production: Lisa Fridsma

Proofreading: Jay Donahue

Technical Editors: Joda Alian, Cathy Auclair, Eric Rowse, Patti Scully-Lane

Typefaces used

Set in the Adobe Minion Pro and Adobe Myriad Pro OpenType families of typefaces. These along with Adobe Chaparral Pro and Adobe Garamond Pro are used throughout the lessons. More information about OpenType and Adobe fonts is located inside the Studio folder on the *Adobe InDesign CS2 Classroom in a Book* CD.

Images

Photographic images and illustrations are intended for use with the tutorials only.

Images provided by Claudia Murray Photography: Lesson 11 (cookbook). Illustrations for Lesson 11 provided by Jennifer M. Smith.

Images provided by iStockphoto.com:

Lesson 4: Mira Janacek, Eric Limon, Juergen Sack, Melissa King, Bill Grove, Paige Falk, Matt Feyerabend, Bruce M. Baillie, Robert Miller, Steffen Foerster

Lesson 5: Norman Reid, Jeffrey Waibel, Janusz Doboszynski

Lesson 7: Edyta Pawlowska, Jim Jurica, Sergey Kashkin, Suzannah Skelton, Roberto Adrian, Lance Bellers